CARIBBEAN DEMOGRAPHY

CARIBBEAN PALEODEMOGRAPHY

Population, Culture History, and Sociopolitical Processes in Ancient Puerto Rico

L. ANTONIO CURET

THE UNIVERSITY OF ALABAMA PRESS
Tuscaloosa

Copyright © 2005
The University of Alabama Press
Tuscaloosa, Alabama 35487-0380
All rights reserved
Manufactured in the United States of America

Typeface: AGaramond

∞

The paper on which this book is printed meets the minimum requirements of American National Standard for Information Science—Permanence of Paper for Printed Library Materials, ANSI Z39.48-1984.

Library of Congress Cataloging-in-Publication Data

Curet, L. Antonio, 1960–
Caribbean paleodemography : population, culture history, and sociopolitical processes in ancient Puerto Rico / L. Antonio Curet.
p. cm.
Includes bibliographical references and index.
ISBN 0-8173-1461-X (cloth : alk. paper) — ISBN 0-8173-5185-X (pbk. : alk. paper)
1. Indians of the West Indies—Puerto Rico—Antiquities. 2. Indians of the West Indies—Puerto Rico—Population. 3. Indians of the West Indies—Puerto Rico—Migrations.
4. Excavations (Archaeology)—Puerto Rico. 5. Island archaeology—Puerto Rico.
6. Demographic archaeology—Puerto Rico. 7. Puerto Rico—Antiquities. I. Title.
F1969.C87 2005
304.8′097295—dc22

2004023853

To my parents, Salim and Edith, who gave me
the motivation to follow my dreams.
To my beloved wife, Elena, who gave me the inspiration to follow my dreams.
And to my children, Miguel and Daniel,
for whom I dream everything good in life.

Contents

Figures and Tables ix
Acknowledgments xiii
1. Demography and Ancient Populations in the Caribbean 1
2. Cultural and Social History of Ancient Puerto Rico 11
3. Migration, Colonization, and Cultural Change: An Anthropological Approach 27
4. Ancient Migrations in Puerto Rico: Issues and Possible Explanations 62
5. Intraisland Population Trends: Regional Analysis 95
6. Population, Carrying Capacity, and Population Pressure: Ancient Demography of the Valley of Maunabo 144
7. Paleodemography at the Local Level 185
8. Conclusions: Paleodemography and Caribbean Archaeology 220
References Cited 235
Index 269

Figures and Tables

FIGURES

1.1 Map of the Caribbean Basin.   2

2.1 Taxonomic system developed by Rouse (1986, 1992).   12

2.2 Chronological chart for Puerto Rico according to Rouse (adopted from Rouse 1992).   14

5.1 Map of Puerto Rico showing the four regions included in the intraisland study.   98

5.2 Map of the Loíza River Basin showing the location of sites belonging to the Hacienda Grande style (adopted from Rodríguez 1992).   101

5.3 Map of the Loíza River Basin showing the location of sites belonging to the Cuevas style (adopted from Rodríguez 1992).   102

5.4 Map of the Loíza River Basin showing the location of sites belonging to the Monserrate style (adopted from Rodríguez 1992).   103

5.5 Map of the Loíza River Basin showing the location of sites belonging to the Santa Elena style (adopted from Rodríguez 1992).   104

5.6 Map of the Loíza River Basin showing the location of sites belonging to the Esperanza style (adopted from Rodríguez 1992).   105

5.7 Distribution of number of sites through time in the Loíza River Basin and Vieques Island.   106

5.8 Distribution of sites across physiographic regions in the Loíza River Basin.   106 x / Figures and Tables

5.9 Distribution of site types through time in the Loíza River Basin.   107
5.10 Map of Vieques showing the location of sites belonging to the Hacienda Grande style.   109
5.11 Map of Vieques showing the location of sites belonging to the Cuevas style.   109
5.12 Map of Vieques showing the location of sites belonging to the Monserrate style.   110
5.13 Map of Vieques showing the location of sites belonging to the Santa Elena style.   110
5.14 Map of Vieques showing the location of sites belonging to the Esperanza style.   111
5.15 Distribution of sites across physiographic regions in the Island of Vieques.   112
5.16 Distribution of site types through time in the Island of Vieques.   113
5.17 Map of the Salinas River Basin showing location of sites belonging to the Saladoid series.   116
5.18 Map of the Salinas River Basin showing location of sites belonging to Elenan Ostionoid subseries.   117
5.19 Map of the Salinas River Basin showing locations of sites belonging to Chican Ostionoid subseries.   118
5.20 Distribution of number of sites through time in the Salinas and Yauco River Basins.   119
5.21 Distribution of sites across physiographic regions in the Salinas River Basin.   119
5.22 Distribution of site types through time in the Salinas River Basin.   120
5.23 Map of the Yauco River Basin showing locations of sites belonging to Saladoid series.   124
5.24 Map of the Yauco River Basin showing locations of sites belonging to Ostionan Ostionoid subseries.   125
5.25 Map of the Yauco River Basin showing locations of sites belonging to Chican Ostionoid subseries.   126
5.26 Distribution of site types through time in the Yauco River Basin.   127
5.27 Distribution of number of sites through time in all regions.   130
6.1 Map of the Valley of Maunabo.   146
6.2 Map of the Valley of Maunabo showing the surveyed area (transects and blocks) and location of sites.   161

Figures and Tables / xi

 6.3 Population and carrying capacity estimates through time for the Valley of Maunabo. 177

 7.1 Map of Puerto Rico showing the three sites included in the paleodemographic study. 187

 7.2 Distribution of age-at-death for the site of Punta Candelero. 201

 7.3 Distribution of age-at-death for the site of Tibes, adjusted proportionally. 206

 7.4 Distribution of age-at-death for the site of Tibes, adjusted equally. 207

 7.5 Distribution of age-at-death for the site of Paso del Indio. 210

TABLES

 5.1 Diachronic Comparison of Regional Information for the Four Regions. 135

 6.1 Contents of 100 g Edible Portion of Raw Manioc Roots and Dry Whole Kernel Yellow Maize (From Roosevelt 1980, Tables 1, 2, and 5). 165

 6.2 Estimates Used for Calculating the Carrying Capacity. 167

 6.3 Estimates of Maximum Number of People That Could Have Been Supported in the Two Areas under Cultivation Based on Manioc Production in the Valley of Maunabo, Assuming a 10 Percent Loss of the Annual Crop. 169

 6.4 Estimates of Maximum Number of People That Could Have Been Supported in the Valley of Maunabo on Maize, Assuming a 20 Percent Loss of the Annual Crop. 172

 6.5 Surface Area and Estimated Population for all Sites and Strata from the Valley of Maunabo. 175

 7.1 Abridged Life-Table for the Punta Candelero Population (Both Sexes). 200

 7.2 Fertility Values for the Skeletal Samples from All Sites. 203

 7.3 Abridged Life-Table for the Tibes Population Adjusting Age-at-Death Distribution by Distributing Indeterminate Adults Proportionally among All Adult Age Categories (Both Sexes). 205

 7.4 Abridged Life-Table for the Tibes Population Adjusting Age-at-Death Distribution by Distributing Indeterminate Adults Equally among All Adult Age Categories under 50 Years Old (Both Sexes). 206

 7.5 Abridged Life-Table for the Paso del Indio Population (Both Sexes). 209

Acknowledgments

The idea for this book developed during the process of revising my dissertation for publication. Realizing that my dissertation was limited in scope and that it dealt with only one of the many issues and problems of how population and demography are used in archaeology, I decided to expand it by including multiple levels of analysis and several additional topics and questions. My interest in paleodemography, however, goes beyond my dissertation work, having grown from a course on demography I took in graduate school with George Cowgill. George's insights and knowledge on the topic motivated me to pursue further my research on paleodemography. I was able to put the chapters that follow together under the rubric of demography in great part thanks to my training with him.

Many people deserve to be acknowledged and thanked for their help with different aspects of this book. I want to thank Daniel Corkill for providing several key references used in the preparation of Chapter 3. My long conversations with Reniel Rodríguez on the interaction between the Saladoid, La Hueca people, and foraging groups were very influential in the preparation of Chapter 4. These discussions were so intense and lengthy that at the end it was difficult for us to remember whose idea was whose. So, it should not be surprising to the readers that some of Reniel's publications overlap with some arguments presented in this book. Reniel and Scott Fitzpatrick also commented on the final versions of Chapters 3 and 4. Joshua Torres very generously shared some of his data and provided helpful insights for Chapter 5. He was also responsible for the preparation of the original versions of maps in

Figures 5.17–5.19 and 5.23–5.25. The regional study he conducted in southern Puerto Rico for his master's thesis was also influential in some of the ideas I presented in that chapter. Discussions with Miguel Rodríguez were also instrumental in the preparation of the chapter.

With some additions, updates, and improvements, Chapter 6 is an offshoot of my dissertation. I have to thank my dissertation committee, Barbara Stark, Sylvia Gaines, Keith Kintigh, Geoffrey Clark, Kate Spielmann, and Diana López, for their comments, encouragement, and support during the long and tedious preparation of the thesis. George Cowgill also provided helpful comments on some aspects of my dissertation work. Edwin Crespo Torres and William Pestle reviewed and provided useful comments on Chapter 7. The comments contributed by these two physical anthropologists on this very technical chapter are greatly appreciated. Jill Seagard deserves credit for the final versions of all maps and Figures 2.1–2.2, 5.17, 5.23–5.25, and 6.1–6.2. I want to thank Marjorie Pannell for her help in making the editorial corrections of the text and for providing helpful suggestions in the organization of the work.

I also would like to thank William Keegan and Samuel Wilson for taking the time and energy to review the book for The University of Alabama Press. They provided excellent critical comments that did nothing but strengthen many aspects of the book. I want to express my gratitude to the staff of The University of Alabama Press, who from the beginning gave their support to this project, and for their patience during its preparation. I began working on this book in January 2001, but health-related problems in my family delayed it several times. The press staff was always very supportive and never lost their faith in my ability to finish this monograph.

Last, but most importantly, I want to thank my wife, my parents, my children, and my brothers and sisters, who one way or another have always unconditionally supported me in all my endeavors. My wife and children, especially, have to be commended for tolerating me and for their love and patience with all the emotional, physical, and psychological traumas involved in the preparation of a book. To them goes all my love and for them I give thanks to God every day.

CARIBBEAN PALEODEMOGRAPHY

1 / Demography and Ancient Populations in the Caribbean

The Caribbean archipelago extends from the Florida peninsula to the mouth of the Orinoco River in Venezuela. Trending in a leisurely arc east-southeastward, this bulge of islands, channels, lesser archipelagos, and continental edges forms the eastern front of Central America. The climate is tropical to subtropical, and the land and sea area although loosely circumscribed is large (Figure 1.1).

The Caribbean archipelago has long been of interest to archaeological anthropologists interested in reconstructing the culture history and population movements of ancient peoples. From these reconstructions we now know that the Caribbean has been populated at least since 5000 B.C., with the first migrations probably coming from the Orinoco delta and possibly from somewhere in Central America. As more people migrated over time, the physiogeography of the island chain began to exercise its influence in both permissive and restrictive ways in regard to the movement of goods and people. The arrangement of the islands in a stepping-stone pattern connecting two continents facilitated interisland movement, while the water passages between the islands imposed at least temporary barriers to movement. Thus, both linear diffusion of cultures and the differential development of groups that settled on the same island came to characterize the early history of the Caribbean. The result was a rich mosaic of cultures and intercultural interactions between and among island groups, with the cultural fabric constantly renewed by new arrivals (or the departure of earlier settlers in back-migrations) and by ongoing changes among older, more settled groups. Social developments showed a

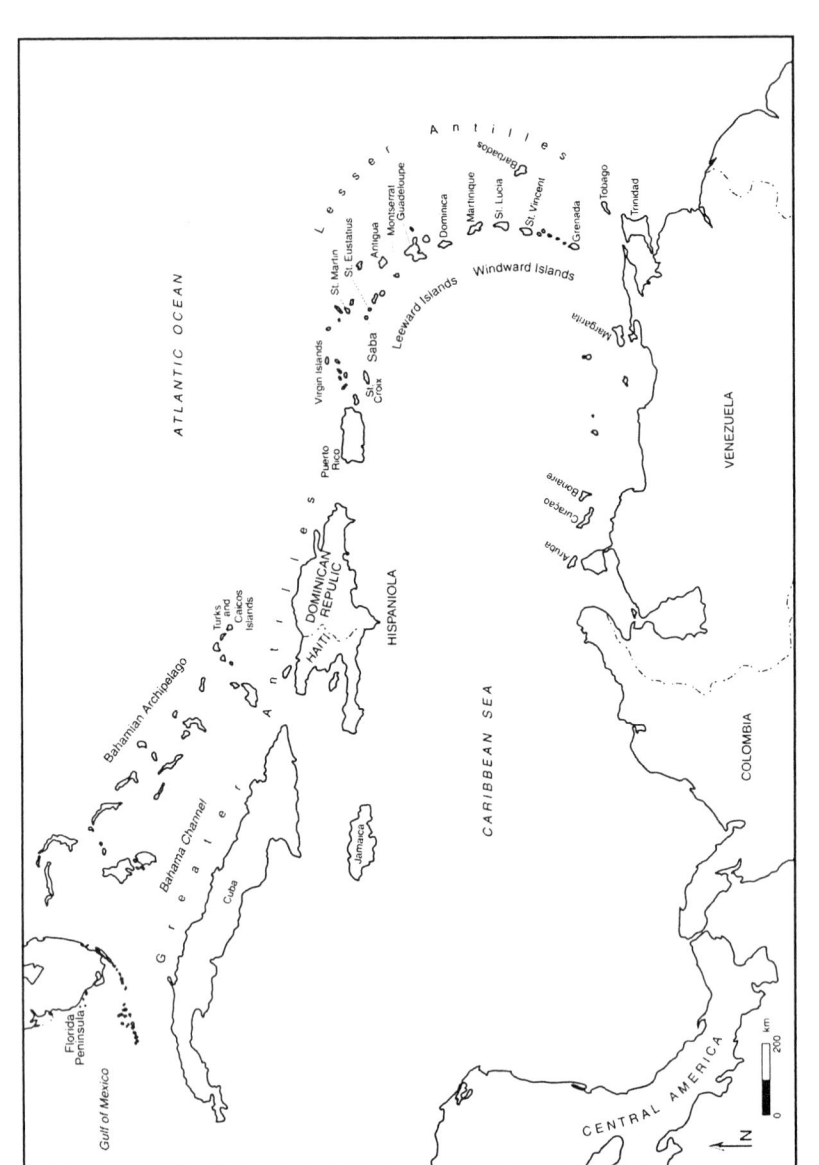

Figure 1.1. Map of the Caribbean Basin.

similar complexity, with the emergence of a variety of stratified societies in different areas of the Caribbean.

In this book I investigate the relationship between population dynamics and demographic factors, on the one hand, and cultural and social change on the other. Each of these elements should be understood as having multiple factors and dimensions—for population, those factors are population size and density, increases and decreases, movements (migrations), and distribution over the landscape; for demography, age and sex distribution, fertility and mortality rates, life expectancy, site size, and aggregation of population; and for sociocultural changes, the variables of different kinds of social organization, changes in settlement patterns, and cultural markers—any of which may influence and in turn be influenced by the others. In splicing together population and demographic variables as a basis for exploring cultural change, my aim is to reconstruct a more faithful picture of ancient human behavior in the Caribbean than has been available thus far. By "human behavior" I mean the full range of possible behavior, from personal or household-level behavior such as reproductive decisions and the treatment of the dead to society-wide behavior such as economic strategies and political alliances. The reconstruction cannot, at this time, be complete, in part because of the paucity of data from some of the regions I compare, and in part because not all behaviors leave their mark in the archaeological record. However, because demography can look at very small social units and consider behavior at small, local levels, the picture I put together should be denser and richer than one in which demographic factors are subordinated to a grand theory. Simply put, detecting reasons for cultural change is much more difficult if the scale is too large, the brush too broad. If demography teaches us one thing, it is that scale matters.

In working toward this reconstruction, I will be departing from several established avenues of work. In the past, "population" as a dependent or independent variable was commonly introduced in arguments concerning migration, changes in subsistence patterns, and sociocultural change. Particularly prevalent were models that sought in population-resource imbalance an explanation for changes in the archaeological record. In most such cases, population was treated somewhat simplistically as a factor with only two dimensions, size and density. An excess in either size or density was then taken as *the* driver of social and cultural change. Today the pendulum has swung back to the opposite extreme, so that population factors are now considered of little importance. A more nuanced understanding of population dynamics and their integration with demographic factors would be expected to reveal different, more complex drivers of behavior, and thus to result in very different modeling of prehistoric human behavior in the Caribbean.

DEMOGRAPHY AND THE STATE OF CARIBBEAN ARCHAEOLOGY

Fortunately for my endeavor, Caribbean archaeology, after a long period in the backwater of New World studies, is experiencing a renaissance. In earlier eras, Caribbean archaeology concentrated almost exclusively on the important but limited issues of migration and cultural histories. Fairly simple methods of excavation and data analysis were used, and issues relating to social and cultural practices—human behavior—were ignored, or the behavior was assumed. Since the early 1980s, however, Caribbean archaeologists have begun expanding their investigative horizons by adding a wide variety of research topics, including interaction between human communities (e.g., Crock 2000; Hofman 1995; Hoogland and Hofman 1999), social and cultural processes (Curet 1992a, 1992b, 1996; Curet and Oliver 1998; Oliver 1998; Siegel 1989, 1991b, 1996a, 1999; Valcárcel Rojas 1999, 2002; Veloz Maggiolo 1991, 1993), subsistence systems (e.g., deFrance 1989; deFrance et al. 1996; Newsom 1993; Newsom and Deagan 1994; Wing 2001a, 2001b, 2001c), and social organization (e.g., Curet 2002, 2003; Keegan and Maclachlan 1989; Keegan et al. 1998; Tavares María 1996). Furthermore, new field, laboratory, and data-processing methods have been developed to ensure the collection of appropriate data to address these topics. One consequence of this renewed attention to multidisciplinary studies and research design has been the appearance of faunal, botanical, geologic, and soil specialists as standard staff members on many archaeological projects. This revival of archaeological interest in the region and the increased professionalism of the fieldworkers have resulted in an enormous amount of new and reliable information becoming available. Needless to say, many of the new avenues of research have forced a reevaluation of accepted understandings of the past inhabitants of the region. Data previously collected await reinterpretation within critical frameworks that enjoy strong theoretical and statistical support. With these tools in hand, researchers should be in better position to generate hypotheses concerning the archaeological samples and human populations of the ancient Caribbean.

The discussions presented in the following chapters, then, concentrate on evaluating old and new assumptions about the groups that populated the ancient Caribbean by looking at available information from different perspectives and at different scales of analysis. The topic of demography runs as a thread through Caribbean archaeology almost from the beginning, and through most of New World neotropical archaeology as well. Demographic issues simply have not been very well understood or articulated. At times they have been occluded by researchers' intense focus on a particular method or line of historical reasoning that has since been superseded. It is axiomatic that the trajectory of a discipline becomes self-evident only in the rearview mirror. By calling the attention of Caribbean studies to demography, I hope to assemble a picture of ancient Caribbean society that answers questions raised by more strictly cultural accounts. If at the same time the work provides a corrective to certain misunderstandings that have been repeated in the literature or helps researchers understand how to use basic demographic data, that would be an additional benefit.

PLAN OF THE BOOK

In this book I use basic demographic data as the analytic materials for investigating the social construction of culture at four levels or scales: most broadly, the whole-archipelago or *interisland* level, followed by the *intraisland* (regional comparative) level, then the *regional* (single-region) level, and finally the *local* (single-site) level. It should be recognized that a great number of issues could be discussed for any of these levels. However, for each horizon I decided to choose a single topic to serve as the focal point for organizing the discussion. Various minor issues arc through the discussion of each major topic, providing new vantage points and suggesting different ways of connecting data.

Geographically, I concentrate on Puerto Rico and neighboring islands, with occasional reference to the rest of the Greater Antilles, the Lesser Antilles, and the Bahamas. The period of my study is the Ceramic Age, which in Puerto Rico lasted for about 1800 years (ca. 300 B.C. to A.D. 1500), although I will also refer to the Archaic groups that preceded the later horticultural groups and co-inhabited the islands with them for some time. There are a couple of reasons for limiting the scope of the analysis in this way. First, more of the information and data necessary for making the detailed reconstruction that I attempt are available for the Ceramic Age than for other ages, and particularly for Puerto Rico. Second, Puerto Rico effectively serves as a natural laboratory for investigating demographic and population issues at a variety of levels: as an island, it participated in island-hopping and progressive dispersal of culture at an interisland level; because it is a relatively large island, it became home to several groups that settled and embarked on different lines of development in the east and in the west simultaneously, thus allowing regional or intraisland comparisons; and, finally, good site and regional data are available in Puerto Rico, thus allowing fairly intimate scrutiny of local practices. I should also mention that Puerto Rico is the focus of my personal research, and I am interested in identifying and understanding demographic trends in this part of the Caribbean that could be used in comparative studies of populations on other islands or during other eras. Even more interesting, from a research perspective, would be the finding that the conclusions I present for Puerto Rico are not applicable to other islands or other regions of the Caribbean. Such a finding would suggest that different processes and different demographic trends were at work in those areas.

Interisland Populations

Migration is an alluring topic for students of island cultures, and the Caribbean archipelago has proved to be a particularly rich ground for developing theories about population movements. At least since the beginning of the twentieth century, archaeologists and historians have been working to identify the origins and the routes of migration of the early inhabitants of the Caribbean (e.g., Fewkes 1907; Rainey 1940; Rouse 1952). Migration has become the explanation par excellence for a number of phenomena, including social and cultural change. The standard template of migration has been a monochromatic one: migration of relatively large populations as a unitary, one-way *event* with a termination and an endpoint, to be followed some time later by another unitary, one-way event, in each case involving the resumption of the migration (hence the wave theory of migration). Push-pull models are quite common in this setting: either a strong attractor, such as a better food supply, pulls the population toward a new settlement site, or a strong detractor, such as warfare or exhausted resources, pushes the population into migrating. But cross-cultural studies on the anthropology of migration would seem to refute this depiction of migration being just an event. We might instead think of hesitations, reversals, decisions made and unmade at the level of household or communities, a return to a previous settlement site three generations later—in short, migration as an ongoing, multilayered process proceeding in multiple directions at once and in different population densities, from few to many persons. The difference between the view of migration as event and position of migration as process would again seem to be one of scale: the event approach entails population behavior in the aggregate and is analyzed at the macrolevel, whereas a process entails multiple individual and small-group movements and is analyzed at the microlevel. Chapter 3 draws together work by a number of researchers to show how modern anthropological theory models migration. The theory treats migration as a multidimensional process and somewhat favors microlevel processes, but it attempts to harmonize macrolevel and microlevel factors in a structural conception of migration. One interesting result of this work is the finding that, while migrations can vary in multiple ways, once they have begun, patterns do emerge: the process is not entirely haphazard but proceeds in a somewhat predictable order. Thus, multidimensional modeling favoring microscaled behavior does indeed bring us back to regularities, but of a different kind from those espoused by traditional archaeologists, for the regularities are processual rather than involving the wholesale displacement of a population or culture in one event.

This view of migration as a complex process with microlevel dimensions is further developed in Chapter 4 by way of two examples for Puerto Rico, the Saladoid–La Hueca migration (ca. 300 B.C.) and the Ostionoid expansion (ca. A.D. 600). Archaeological reconstructions indicate that the process of the early Saladoid migration involved information gathering, decision making, and prior social interactions with the Archaic groups into whose territory the Saladoids moved and with whom they thereafter cohabited. Available information now suggests alternative hypotheses of population movement to replace the traditional unidirectional, replacement hypotheses. In the case of the Ostionoid migration, or, as I prefer, the Ostionoid expansion, which chronologically followed the Saladoid migration, the archaeological data are open to conflicting interpretations. A tentative conclusion offered here is that the Ostionoid expansion may have involved one or more complex processes of interaction and transculturation between the Archaic and Saladoid societies normally not considered by the traditional view. In exploring this and alternative hypotheses, anthropologists have had to confront directly social questions, such as whether language, culture, and people must migrate simultaneously or whether some factors, such as diet (as part of culture) or language, may experience faster rates of change. At the microscalar level, uncertainties over the relations of different populations have also led anthropologists to look more closely at the possibility of smaller communities within larger populations or cultures acting autonomously and independently from the larger population, with the independent interactions accumulating over time to produce mixed populations interacting with other mixed populations. These two major Puerto Rican migration issues, which still await complete understanding, highlight the inadequacy of conventional population-replacement theories to explain social developments during and after contact and suggest that researchers might do better to locate an account of population movements in social factors.

Intraisland Populations: Population Distribution and Settlement Patterns

The issue of different processes co-occurring differentially in Puerto Rico, such as during the major island migrations, moves our analytic focus to the level of comparative regional or intraisland developments. Chapter 5 examines trends in population dynamics—population increases and decreases, site sizes and distributions—in four regions of Puerto Rico as foundational data for arguing against homogeneous demographic, social, and political development across cultural areas. According to the cultural-chronological model most commonly applied to the islands, that of Irving Rouse, similarity in culture equates with similarity in other realms. In other words, this view tends to assume homogeneity over large areas implying similarity in behavior over the whole expanse. However, analysis of population dynamics shows differences among the four areas in respect to population distribution and dynamics suggesting the presence of variability in resource use, political strategies, and social decisions occurring during the same cultural epoch. Perhaps most interesting, data on architectural differences, when combined with data on population dynamics and site distribution, can be used to reconstruct the features of the ancient political economies of these areas. In particular, the emergence of abundant ceremonial architecture in some regions may be a manifestation of the rise of some form of hierarchical society. Other regions do not show this florescence of monumental architecture suggesting that in these cases the political and social process followed different paths. These reconstructions show substantial comparative differences in social and political organization among the sites, differences that slice across a shared culture for Puerto Rico.

Regional Populations

One of the factors long considered to motivate population trends has been an imbalance between the carrying capacity of the environment and the size of the population in that environment, or in some cases how the population used the environment. This important and misunderstood topic is isolated and examined in Chapter 6 as part of a continuing discussion of regional population dynamics that was begun in Chapter 5. In particular, we would want to know whether management (or exhaustion) of natural resources could be linked to the rise of social stratification. For Puerto Rico and other parts of the Caribbean, archaeologists have proposed that agricultural techniques that shaped the landscape, such as the construction of irrigation ditches, led to excess agricultural product, which led to the need to distribute the product, which led to the rise of the elite to control all of the various aspects of agricultural production and distribution. The logical bridges in this multistep process, however, can be disrupted at any point. For example, the construction of *montones* and terraces does not necessarily imply a need for intensive communal labor. Thus, changes in the population did not necessarily trigger social change, although the two kinds of change may have co-occurred. Indeed, demographic reconstructions of indigenous populations and the availability of resources suggest that prehistoric groups were well able to produce food, in surplus, without the need for large communal works requiring organized labor. Against this observation, however, we must place the explosion of stratified societies sometime between A.D. 600 and 1200.

Personal research in the Valley of Maunabo was designed to test whether population-resource imbalance could be related to the emergence of social stratification through the use of demographic factors. An exhaustive investigation of the availability of calories and proteins to ancient groups in the valley indicates ample resources to support all identified population increases, a finding that undoes the presumed link between population-resource imbalance and the rise of stratified societies. Once this link is severed, we can begin to consider resource availability, population dynamics, and social change (that is, the emergence of stratification) as independent variables that do not necessarily have causal effects on each other. Instead, it suggests that they are related in more complex ways, where they are continuously interacting with each other. This position represents a critical advance in understanding the behavior of prehistoric people.

Local Populations

The last study in the book opens the question, what are the attributes of a population? Whereas investigations at higher scales find it all too easy to treat "populations" as equivalent in composition and relatively static in their internal makeup over time, single-site studies show that the structure of local populations can vary markedly in factors such as sex ratios, age ratios, crude birth and death rates, and "productivity"—the availability of individuals of appropriate age and sex to carry out the tasks necessary for the continuation of the population. Small changes in the internal structure of a population can result in meaningful social group changes within the span of a generation. Unfortunately, the raw archaeological materials for drawing inferences about prehistoric populations are mortuary assemblages, which cannot be assumed to correctly represent the population as it was in life. Chapter 7 reviews the skeletal collections obtained from three different sites in Puerto Rico and analyzed by the same osteologist, Edwin Crespo Torres (1994, 1998, 2000). A variety of analytical techniques are introduced, and their use demonstrated, to show how under- and over-representation in a mortuary sample can be detected and adjusted for in later analyses. Although the results of this chapter are still equivocal, they demonstrate that various local populations can have different internal structures and demographic dynamics that can affect social and cultural processes at higher levels. Using this type of thorough methodology and analysis can also help evaluate the representativeness of the skeletal samples for demographic and pathological studies. Thus, the data that are beginning to accrue over time are expected to help researchers detect demographic trends in the structure of archaeological populations and so help us understand past social and cultural processes.

The studies in this book, then, are supposed to be a contribution to the process of reconstructing the narrative that is the ancient history of the Caribbean. Each chapter can be read as a complete study in its own right, but all should be understood as part of a developing picture whose unifying frame is demography. Throughout, a variety of demographic factors are used as probes to a past of not only cultures, but also of social groups, communities, and individuals. It is also hoped that the book presents several examples of how demographic methods used at multiple levels can provide some useful hints about this intricate history.

I am building a parallel picture, from the ground up, that is complementary to but often diverging from established accounts in the literature on Puerto Rico. One such account is the important cultural chronology of Irving Rouse, to whose work we turn in the next chapter. Instead of emphasizing the generalizations, norms, and large cultural units (culture or supracultural units), I argue that we should also focus more often on the particulars, the variability, and smaller units of analysis. It is this approach, I believe, that will bring us closer to completing the picture of the history of the ancient inhabitants of the Caribbean.

2 / Cultural and Social History of Ancient Puerto Rico

The figure of Irving Rouse looms large in studies on the ancient history of Puerto Rico and the greater Caribbean. Since the 1930s, Rouse has focused on developing a regional sequence for the entire Caribbean, using information gleaned from a number of islands and from Venezuela, the prospective origin of several of the island groups. He has revised this sequence time after time as new information has become available through fresh investigations. In reconstructing a cultural sequence for the Caribbean, Rouse has worked out his own classificatory methods and concepts, which are uniquely applicable to the Caribbean and parts of lowland South America. Others have challenged portions of this chronology and have proposed alternatives, especially sequences at the regional and local levels. In the main, however, Rouse's work stands as an unparalleled achievement in Caribbean cultural history, offering subsequent researchers a broad organizational framework for further studies. Because his chronological model provides a reference for all later Caribbean archaeological research, I will spend some time reviewing his methods and chronology here. In addition to reviewing the ancient history of Puerto Rico and the cultural traits as defined by Rouse, I will also be investigating aspects of social organization relevant to demographic studies.

THE CONCEPTUAL STRUCTURE OF ROUSE'S CHRONOLOGY

Rouse's first work in the Caribbean consisted of his dissertation research in Haiti (Rouse 1939, 1964b). It was during the analysis of the materials from

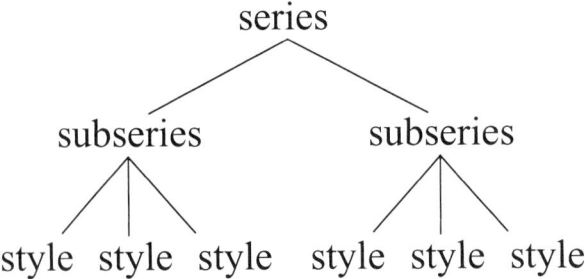

series: the most inclusive category that consists of a set of styles or complexes that have developed one from another.

subseries: smaller geographical, chronological, and cultural units, intermediary between series and styles.

styles: all the pottery found within each people's spatial and temporal lines; in practice, styles represent both the ceramic assemblages and the people that created them.

Figure 2.1. Taxonomic model developed by Rouse (1992).

these excavations that he discovered the insurmountable difficulties of using standard typologies based on artifact types and varieties, and turned his attention to developing an alternative system. The system he eventually worked out is based on cultural norms (abstract concepts whose physical representations exist in the archaeological record in a form he calls modes) rather than on the traditional type-variety analysis used in many archaeological field studies. This modal analysis became the foundation for Rouse's naming and defining ceramic categories for most areas of the Caribbean. At the same time, these category names are also used to designate the archaeological cultures, peoples, and communities (Rouse 1992), as well as the migratory routes followed in the peopling of the Caribbean.

Rouse's system is hierarchical and has three main levels: the series, the subseries, and the various styles (also called complexes) associated with each subseries (Figure 2.1). Rouse intended these categories to be used in tracing cultural traditions through space and time (Rouse 1986; Siegel 1996b), and his system has been successful at the level of the archipelago when used for this purpose. Time is tracked on the vertical axis and space on the horizontal axis of a table or chart, producing, in Rouse's words, categories that are made "culturally as homogeneous as possible," such that each spatiotemporal combination "ought to contain a different people and culture" (Rouse 1986:7). *Series* is the most inclusive of these categories. According to Rouse (1992:1), a series consists of a set of related styles or complexes. Series are divided into *subseries,* which in practice refer to smaller cultural units localized in a smaller geographic area or to shorter periods of time (or both). Finally, subseries are divided into one to many *styles* or complexes, the lowest classificatory level. Initially, Rouse considered styles to be a term for the totality of a ceramic assemblage found within each people's spatial and temporal sequence; later on, he fleshed out the idea of style by adding other elements of a people's culture (Rouse 1992:33). Thus, in practice, styles refer both to the ceramic assemblage and to the group that created it.

Methodologically, styles are defined first according to archaeological materials, then they are grouped into subseries by comparison, synchronically and diachronically, with other styles. Finally, subseries are grouped with other, related subseries from different regions or time periods to form series. This method allows Rouse to represent regional sequences as charts or matrices, with the horizontal axis representing geographical distribution and the vertical axis representing time. An example—Rouse's chronology for Puerto Rico—is shown in Figure 2.2, where the "homogeneous" categories of styles, subseries, and series fill out the matrix. An interesting feature of this hierarchical system is that styles assigned to one series (or subseries) cannot be connected archaeologically or culturally to styles assigned to another series (or subseries). Instead, styles can be related only if they belong to the same series or subseries. This creates problems if a new and unrelated style is identified in the archaeological record but there is no preexisting series to which it could be assigned.

With some exceptions, Rouse's system has generally been successfully applied to delineating obvious cultural traditions through time and space for the Caribbean culture area as a whole, and even for some of the islands individually. Perhaps for this reason, and because Caribbean archaeology has traditionally been oriented toward cultural history (Curet 2003), Rouse's model and its embedded concepts have been extensively adopted by many researchers in the region. However, few of the resulting studies have acknowledged the limitations of Rouse's system for purposes other than migration and culture history studies. Specifically, the sequence works well at the level of the archipelago but less well at island and intraisland levels, and is considerably challenged by observations of greater diversity at the local level than is accounted for in the model. We should also note the homogeneity imposed by Rouse

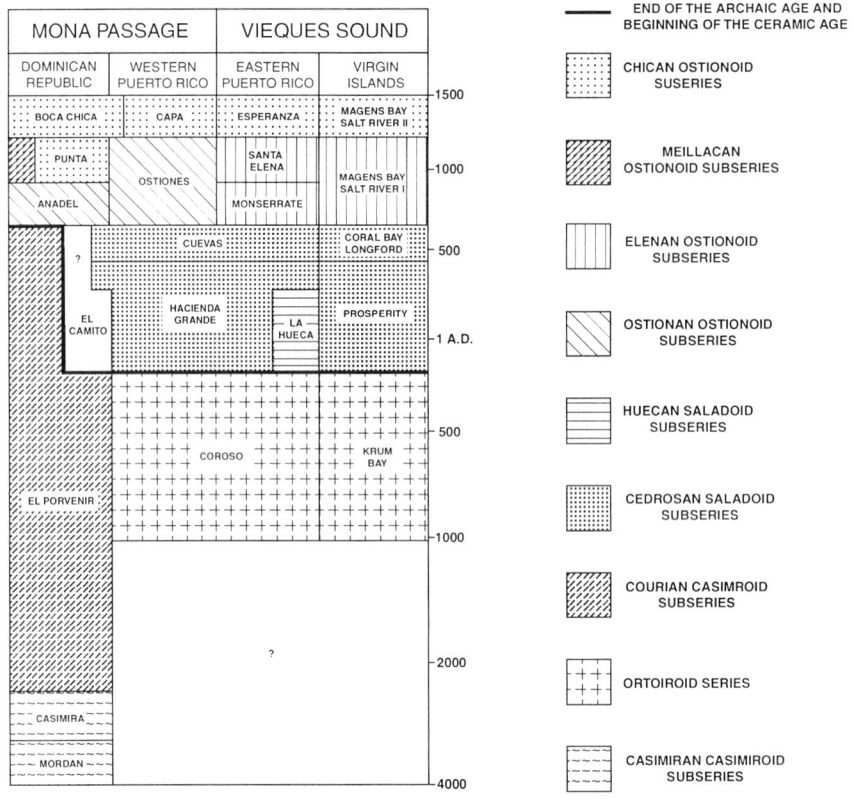

Figure 2.2. Chronological chart for Puerto Rico according to Rouse (adopted from Rouse 1992).

with his spatiotemporal groupings cannot help us understand many social aspects of culture: the categories of series, subseries, and style do not operate at the same scale and level as many social processes do (e.g., Keegan 2001; Wilson 2001a, 2001b; see also Curet 2003 for a review of these issues).

Rouse's model is used in this book mostly as a cultural-chronological referential background for the various analyses already presented. I have decided to maintain Rouse's categories because most if not all of the information available and used here is organized following his model. However, when possible I use the lowest and smallest unit, style, because it is most appropriate for social analysis. That is, I try to use styles as the fundamental unit of analysis since the style is the smallest category in scale and duration that is closer to any social unit relevant to most of my analysis. Unfortunately, in some instances the information available is organized at the level of series or subseries, forcing the discussion to be conducted at that level. The level at which abundant, good information is available usually reflects the differential intensity of archaeological studies in different parts of the island, with some regions/sites receiving far more scrutiny than others. On other occasions, extremely detailed data are available for specific settlements, and in these cases the analysis is conducted at the immediate *local* level, a unit not included in Rouse's model. This is not a trivial issue since, as shown in the following chapters, many sociodemographic processes tend to be determined by smaller social units than those identified by Rouse, such as households, communities, or regional populations.

THE CULTURAL CHRONOLOGY FOR PUERTO RICO

The ancient history of Puerto Rico extends back more than 4,000 years prior to the arrival of Europeans. The rest of this chapter summarizes this cultural history by describing the material culture and social organization of the archaeological cultures. Although my concern is with the Ceramic Age, I have decided to discuss as well the early peopling of the island by preceramic groups. The early Archaic groups left only modest indications of their cultures, but they do appear to have interacted with the ceramic groups in many areas and to have contributed to the various demographic processes discussed in this book.

The Coroso Period (4000 B.C.–A.D. 100)

The first period of human occupation in Puerto Rico is called the Coroso or Archaic period. Archaic cultures have traditionally been interpreted as small mobile bands of hunter-gatherers and fishermen, but recent evidence of large groupings (Ayes Suárez 1989) and more sedentary settlements (Rodríguez 1997, 1999) at least points to the possibility of larger or more permanent social units. Rouse discovered several Archaic sites during his early work in Puerto Rico but never excavated them (Rouse 1952).

Archaeologically, Archaic groups are characterized by the absence of ceramics and the predominance of stone and shell artifacts. Most sites are small and typically located in coastal or estuarine environments (Alegría et al. 1955; Ayes Suárez 1989; Moscoso 1999; Rodríguez 1997, 1999; Rouse and Alegría 1990; Veloz Maggiolo et al. 1975), although larger, inland sites have been located recently (Ayes Suárez 1989; Moscoso 1999). The origin of the Corosan (Archaic) people is unknown, but it has been argued there were multiple migrations coming from multiple areas, the Yucatán Peninsula and Venezuela being the most accepted regions of origin. Dates for this period range from 4000 B.C. in Angostura (Ayes 1989) to 3000 B.C. in Maruca (Rodríguez 1997, 1999), 325–295 B.C. in Cayo Cofresí (Veloz Maggiolo et al. 1975), and 30–40 B.C. in Cueva María de la Cruz (Rouse and Alegría 1990).

The Saladoid Series (300 B.C.–A.D. 600)

The second major cultural period embraces the first horticultural and ceramic groups that migrated to Puerto Rico from the South American continent, particularly from the mouth of the Orinoco River, and is known as the Saladoid series. The Saladoid series is characterized by high-quality ceramics and the use of paint as the main technique of decoration. In general, Saladoid ceramics are hard, relatively thin, well-fired, and of fine paste. Decoration usually consists of one or more colors of paint applied to the vessels, with white-on-red, white-on-orange, and red-on-buff being the most common combinations. Other decorative techniques include false negative, cross-hatched incisions and engraving, excisions, and modeled zoomorphic and anthropomorphic handles known as *adornos.*

The particular ceramic tradition has undergone some changes in characterization over the years and today is known as the Cedrosan subseries of the Saladoid series, which in Puerto Rico consists of at least two styles, the Hacienda Grande and the Cuevas styles. More recently, Rouse has added a new subseries and style in response to questions raised by the investigations of Chanlatte Baik and Narganes Storde (Chanlatte Baik 1981, 1995; Chanlatte Baik and Narganes Storde 1983, 1985, 1986) at the site of La Hueca, where a ceramic style contemporaneous with the Hacienda Grande style but differing from it in many significant respects was discovered. The importance of this discovery is that it suggests that more than one cultural group migrated from the South American continent to the islands. The new subseries is called Huecan, and the style is called La Hueca. Not everyone accepts the creation of a new style and subseries, and debate continues over the nature of the ceramic assemblages found at La Hueca. I believe the materials are sufficiently different to support the classification of at least separate styles and have so treated them in the following discussion. An unresolved issue, however, is whether the differences are strong enough to justify the creation of a new subseries or even a new series. Until more light is shed on this issue, and for the purposes of the present discussion, I have decided to describe La Hueca along with the Cedrosan Saladoid subseries. This does not mean that I agree with Rouse's and others' assignment of La Hueca to the Saladoid series, and to maintain a distinction here, I have decided to use the synonymous term of La Hueca complex instead of Rouse's term, La Hueca style.

Hacienda Grande Style

Ceramically, the Hacienda Grande style (dated between 300 B.C. and A.D. 400) is characterized by monochrome, bichrome (in particular white-on-red), and polychrome designs, and to some degree by the use of incisions, especially zone-incised crosshatched designs, which seem to have been made during the leather-hard stage of prefired ceramics. The most diagnostic characteristic of this style is the designs in painted pottery, in particular white-on-red painting, which most frequently depicts curvilinear, naturalistic, and anthropomorphic designs.

This style also contains the earliest evidence in Puerto Rico of cassava griddles made of clay used to bake manioc bread and other foods, and which many consider the first direct evidence for horticulture in Puerto Rico (e.g., Rodríguez 1983; Rouse 1952). For this reason, the Hacienda Grande has traditionally been considered the first farming group in the Caribbean islands.

Hacienda Grande sites tend to be relatively large and are usually located close to streams near the coast. However, material culture belonging to this style has also been found in the bottom layers of assemblages at inland sites (Curet et al. 2003; Curet and Rodríguez Gracia 1999; Curet et al. 2004; González Colón 1984; Maíz López 2002). This may indicate the spread of settlements to the interior hills and mountains of Puerto Rico at a much earlier date than has previously been appreciated. The little information available about community patterns indicates that most of the domestic structures were large enough to house several families (Curet 1992b), and they seem to have been arranged in circular or semicircular patterns around a central clearing lacking deposits. At some sites this central clearing evidently functioned as a burial ground for the community (Curet et al. 2003; Curet and Oliver 1998; Siegel 1999).

La Hueca Complex

The new La Hueca style that Rouse has added to his chronology as contemporaneous with the Hacienda Grande style has important ramifications for migration theory. Previously, Rouse thought that the Greater Antilles were colonized by only one horticultural-ceramic group. However, this has been challenged recently by Luis Chanlatte Baik and Yvonne Narganes Storde

(Chanlatte Baik 1981, 1986; Chanlatte Baik and Narganes Storde 1983, 1985, 1986; Oliver 1999). During his excavation of the site of La Hueca–Sorcé on the island of Vieques, Chanlatte Baik found two different types of deposits from early ceramic times. In one type of deposit, ceramics typical of the Hacienda Grande style were unearthed: white-on-red vessels, polychromes, effigy vessels, and so on. The second type of deposit consisted almost entirely of the modeled-incised component of the Hacienda Grande style, with painted designs almost completely absent. Included in these deposits were large amounts of certain types of decoration that in the Hacienda Grande style would normally be present only in small quantities, such as crosshatched incisions, some of them filled with red or white paint; bowls with tubes for sniffing *cohoba* (snuffing vessels); and modeled zoomorphic handles (rare in the Hacienda Grande assemblages). The differences between these two ceramic assemblages go beyond the specific decorative techniques as La Hueca material presents considerably different designs, motifs, representations, and vessel forms from the Hacienda Grande pottery with crosshatched incisions. In addition, a large number of high-quality lapidary pieces made of foreign materials (probably obtained from as far as Brazil or the Guyanas) were discovered, including figures representing birds (which Chanlatte Baik has interpreted as Andean condors) holding in their claws what may be human head trophies, which have not previously been reported for the Caribbean.

Based on these discoveries, Chanlatte Baik has argued that, contrary to Rouse's scheme, there were two, almost simultaneous migrations from South America, which he calls Agro-I (or Huecoid) and Agro-II (the Hacienda Grande style people or Saladoid). In addition, he stresses that the different lines of ceramic development for later times in Puerto Rico arose from differences between these two groups and in their interactions with the Archaic population. In short, Chanlatte Baik (1986; Chanlatte Baik and Narganes Storde 1986) is suggesting a whole new chronological and cultural scheme for Puerto Rico, even though some of the series and styles are shared with Rouse's chronology.

Chanlatte Baik's and Narganes Storde's suggestions sparked a heated debate among Caribbeanists that has gone on for more than two decades. The issue of which cultural sequence better represents the historical reality has not been satisfactorily resolved, and the debate appears to have reached an impasse (Oliver 1999). A reductionist view would hold that the difference is merely one of ceramic practice. However, I believe that in addition to ample ceramic evidence (Chanlatte Baik 1981, 1995; Chanlatte Baik and Narganes Storde

1983; Rodríguez 1989a, 1991), there is also solid faunal (Chanlatte Baik and Narganes Storde 1983; Narganes Storde 1985), lithic, (Narganes Storde 1995; Rodríguez Ramos 2001a, 2001b), and intrasite evidence to conclude that the two assemblages represent groups with different cultural identities, not merely different ceramic practices. Thus, it is assumed here that, at least for Puerto Rico and Vieques, the Saladoid series and the La Hueca complex represent two different cultural groups that migrated more or less at the same time, either together or separately.

Cuevas Style

The second ceramic style of the Saladoid series is the Cuevas style (A.D. 400–600). In this time span we see changes not only in ceramic attributes but also in settlement pattern and in subsistence strategies. In terms of ceramics, the Cuevas style is characterized by a gradual decrease in the use of polychrome painting, modeling, and incisions for decoration (Rouse 1964a, 1982). White-on-red painting, one of the best markers of the Saladoid series, is retained, but in smaller proportions and appearing mostly in geometric designs. Throughout this period a gradual disappearance of the use of paints is registered in the archaeological record, leaving only monochrome painting and simple modeled face lugs by the end of the period, around A.D. 600.

The settlement pattern still includes settlements on riverbanks not far from the coast, but more settlements were founded farther inland. In fact, the type site of Cuevas is located along the bank of the largest river in Puerto Rico, but several kilometers inland, not far from the central mountain ranges of the island. In addition, people belonging to this style seem to have settled a small area in eastern Hispaniola (Veloz Maggiolo 1972, 1991, 1993). Although the evidence is scant, it seems that Cuevas sites were still relatively large and that the people lived in multifamily or communal houses arranged around a central clearing. Mortuary practices seem to have been similar to those of the Hacienda Grande style.

Saladoid Social Organization

Evidence on the Saladoid cultures that has accumulated in the past three decades has allowed the reconstruction of several aspects of the Saladoid social organization. Based on the lack of evidence of social stratification in burials and household deposits, most Caribbean researchers agree that Saladoid groups were egalitarian or tribal in nature (e.g., Boomert 2001; Curet 1996; Curet and Oliver 1998; López Sotomayor 1975:103; Moscoso 1986:307; Rouse

1992:33; Siegel 1996a, 1999; Veloz Maggiolo 1991:147–167, 1993). As an example, Veloz Maggiolo (1977–1978:58) has related the social system of this time to that defined by Steward (1948) as "Tribes of the Tropical Forest." Curet and Oliver (1998) have also argued that the presence of clusters of burials in the central clearing of sites is a reflection of the presence of linear descent groups that operated as economic corporate groups characteristic of egalitarian societies. Furthermore, they argue that the centralized location of the dead ancestors symbolically emphasizes the community as the basic unit of the social structure. Similar mortuary patterns, however, have not been found in Saladoid sites of the Lesser Antilles, indicating that the social organization and dynamics of these groups may have varied throughout the region.

The Ostionan and Elenan Ostionoid Subseries (A.D. 600–1200)

The third major period in Rouse's chronology, the Ostionoid series (A.D. 600–1200), represents the first series resulting from local development in Puerto Rico rather than from in-migration. Interestingly, by this time Puerto Rico seems to have developed two distinct cultural divisions, the Elenan and Ostionan subseries (of the Ostionoid series), each with its own styles. The Elenan subseries of the Ostionoid is associated with the Monserrate and Santa Elena styles and is more prevalent in eastern Puerto Rico. The Ostionan subseries is divided into the Pure and Modified Ostiones styles (Rouse 1982) and is concentrated on the western side of the island. In Chanlatte Baik's chronology, all these groups are classified as Agro-III and are considered to have evolved from the interaction of the Saladoid and La Huecan groups with the Archaic groups that inhabited the island.

Monserrate and Pure Ostiones Styles

During the early styles of these subseries (that is, the Monserrate style of the Elenan subseries and the Pure Ostiones style of the Ostionan subseries, both ca. A.D. 600–900) some of the technology and vessel forms of the final Saladoid pottery were retained, including the tabular lugs, strap handles, and red-painted and slipped ceramics, while a limited number of other kinds of decoration were added. The persistence of a few Saladoid traits into the early part of the Ostionoid period makes the assignment of this pottery to one or the other series very difficult, since there is no clear break in the ceramic trend. The distinction between the series becomes clearer at a later date, when both the Pure Ostiones and the Monserrate style are characterized by large amounts of plain and red-slipped pottery, in contrast to the more varied and prevalent decoration of the previous Saladoid series.

Although the Pure Ostiones and Monserrate styles share many ceramic attributes reminiscent of their Saladoid past, they also exhibit some distinctions, which are distributed unevenly throughout Puerto Rico (Rouse 1964a, 1982, 1986). In general, the Monserrate ceramics are thicker, coarser, and rougher, and the shapes are simple. Vessels tend to have outcurving sides, although upcurving shapes start to increase in number. In addition, incised designs become less common, and red-painted designs are still present. Black, negative resist, and smudging designs can also be found. Ceramics belonging to this style are mainly concentrated on the eastern side of Puerto Rico and in the Leeward Islands.

In contrast, the Pure Ostiones ceramic presents a more conservative style than the Monserrate style. In this style, pottery continues to be thin, fine, and smooth-surfaced, similar to Saladoid ceramics. Red-painted designs, red and lilac slips, and polished surfaces are also more abundant than in the Monserrate style. The Pure Ostiones style is found mostly on the western side of Puerto Rico and on eastern Hispaniola.

It is interesting to note that whereas Puerto Rico was roughly divided in two cultural areas, east and west, the influence of each subseries (Elenan and Ostionoid) extended beyond the coasts. Indeed, Rouse (1951) noted that at this point in his chronology, the boundaries between ceramic styles in the Greater Antilles occurred between islands rather than across islands. More precisely, ceramic subseries seemed to have been distributed on both sides of passages between islands, suggesting connections across bodies of water, while dissimilarity in ceramics increased between opposite ends of the same island. For example, the Ostionan Ostionoid of western Puerto Rico is more similar to materials found in eastern Hispaniola on the other side of the Mona Passage than to the assemblages from the Vieques Sound area, which includes eastern Puerto Rico and the Virgin Islands (Rouse 1964, 1986, 1992). This division into cultural-geographical areas, defined by the distribution of Elenan and Ostionan Ostionoid subseries, continues to hold into the later Chican Ostionoid subseries (A.D. 1200–1500).

Modified Ostiones and Santa Elena Styles

The similarities between the Ostionan and the Elenan subseries become more marked during the second half of the Ostionoid series (the Modified Ostiones and Santa Elena styles, ca. A.D. 900–1200) when more drastic changes in ceramic decoration and technological attributes occurred. Although both subseries show a return to the practices of modeling and incision, particularly in the creation of zoomorphic and anthropomorphic handles, other changes differentiate the two subseries in terms of ceramic styles. The Santa Elena style of the eastern part of Puerto Rico, the Vieques Sound area, shows a gradual increase in the number of thicker, coarser, and rougher ceramics, less use of red paint and slip, and simple shapes. Most of the decoration is restricted to crude, vertical, rectilinear incisions close to the rims of bowls, frequently accompanied by appliqué strips. The Modified Ostiones style, found on the western side of Puerto Rico, the Mona Passage area, continued on a more conservative path characterized by the production of relatively thin, fine, and smooth pottery. Red paint and lilac slip are still present, and most of the Pure Ostiones shapes are retained. Strap handles remain common, while incurving rather than upcurving walls are emphasized. In addition, incised designs become more common, many times resembling designs found at this time in eastern Hispaniola or later, in the Chican Ostionoid series of Puerto Rico.

Cultural Changes in the Early Ostionoid Series

During the Elenan and Ostionan subseries, Puerto Rico saw a relatively dramatic increase in number of sites, while on the islands of Vieques and the Virgin Islands the number of sites appear to have remained relatively stable (Curet 1987; Lundberg et al. 1992; Morse 1992). Also during this time, new habitats began to be occupied and new settlement patterns appeared that included the development of multiple site types such as dispersed households or small groups of households and linear arrangements along the coast. Centralized settlement patterns with a site hierarchy have been observed for at least the eastern side of the island (Curet 1992a; Rodríguez 1992; Torres 2001). In some parts of Puerto Rico, sometime during this period, houses began to decrease in size compared to the Saladoid series, possibly to house nuclear families (Curet 1992b).

Another feature of these subseries that can be identified in the archaeological record is an increase in communal ceremonialism. Monumental architecture in the form of ball courts and plazas was built in great quantity sometime during this period, mostly in the Vieques Sound area. Some sites with multiple structures that have been identified as ceremonial centers, and which may possibly have been political centers as well, date to the Elenan period. Of these, the site of Tibes, which includes at least nine ball courts and plazas, is the best example (Alegría 1983; Alvarado Zayas 1981; Curet et al. 2003; Curet and Rodríguez Gracia 1999; González Colón 1984). In addition, religious objects connected to the worship of *zemis,* or idols, seem to have increased in number and size during the second half of the Elenan and Ostionan subseries (Rouse 1982:50, 1992; Walker 1993).

With respect to subsistence strategies, intensive farming practices seem to have been developed and used for the first time in the second half of the subseries (that is, during the Modified Ostiones and Santa Elena styles). These practices included the use of *montones,* a kind of raised field, and terracing (Veloz Maggiolo 1977–1978:64, 1987:80; Oliver 1998; Ortiz Aguilú et al. 1993), which increased the production of root crops.

Early Ostionoid Social Organization

The early Ostionoid, the first epoch of local development recoverable from the archaeological record, saw marked changes in the culture, economy, and society of precontact Puerto Rico and the Greater Antilles in general. The intensity and nature of these changes have led Moscoso (1986:301) and Veloz Maggiolo (1977–1978:59, 1987:80) to argue that they are strongly related to sociopolitical changes, from which emerged institutionalized social stratification. Thus, it has been suggested that during the early Ostionoid, and most probably during the second half of that era (i.e., during the Santa Elena and Modified Ostiones styles), some form of institutionalized social hierarchy appeared for the first time in Puerto Rico. Since the earliest signs of social complexity, such as the use of intensive agricultural techniques and the construction of ball courts and ceremonial centers, are present in southern Puerto Rico, Moscoso (1986:298) and Veloz Maggiolo (1977–1978:64, 1987:80, 1991:170–172) have gone so far as to suggest that this island is the cradle of Caribbean chiefdoms. Rouse (1992:33) seems to concur by describing this period as a Formative age that may have started in eastern Puerto Rico during the Elenan Ostionoid series (Rouse 1992:Figure 8). Although chiefdoms are certainly impressive forms of social organization, the arguments presented by these various researchers omit the possibility that other forms of social organization existed and did not necessarily lead to chiefdoms (Curet 2003).

The Chican Ostionoid Subseries (A.D. 1200–1500)

The next period (A.D. 1200–1500) in Rouse's cultural chronology consists of the Chican subseries of the Ostionoid series. As in the case of the early Ostionoid, this subseries presents regional ceramic variations, in this case at the level of styles and not at the level of the subseries. In the Mona Passage the Capá style predominates, while in the eastern area of the Vieques Sound the Esperanza style is dominant. Although both styles are characterized by the use of incisions and combinations of incised lines and punctuation, the Capá style tends to have more complex or elaborate designs than the Esperanza style. Most of the designs occur above the shoulders of *cazuela*-type (incurving) bowls. The use of paint is almost absent, although vessels slipped with red paint may be still present in some areas of western Puerto Rico. Strap handles are absent, but modeled-incised head lugs are still common.

According to Rouse (1964a, 1986, 1992), the Chican subseries originated in the Dominican Republic sometime during the latter half of the Ostionan Ostionoid series and expanded eastward through the Mona Passage and Vieques Sound areas to the Virgin Islands, possibly reaching as far as the island of Saba, about 300 km southeast of Puerto Rico (Hofman 1993; Hofman and Hoogland 1991). It also spread westward, stopping in eastern Cuba, and perhaps in some of the Bahamian islands (Rouse 1986, 1992). However, some incised designs similar to the ones present in the Chican Ostionoid have been observed for the late Ostionan Ostionoid of western Puerto Rico contemporaneous with the appearance of the former in Dominican Republic. If confirmed by future studies, this suggests that the development of this subseries was not a localized but a more generalized phenomenon.

Other archaeological materials that characterized the Chican Ostionoid are the stone artifacts, which include personal ornaments, *zemis,* or idols, of different sizes, masks, *duhos,* or stools, and enigmatic artifacts such as the elbow stones and stone collars. In addition, the Chican Ostionoid groups seem to have mastered woodcrafts, judging from the number of wooden vessels, musical instruments, *zemis,* and *duhos,* found mostly in Hispaniola (Beeker et al. 2002; Caro Alvarez 1977a, 1977b; Conrad et al. 2001; Ortega and Atiles 2003), where the chronicles mention centers of production, and to a lesser degree in Puerto Rico, Jamaica (Saunders and Gray 1996), and Cuba (Graham et al. 2000; Jardines Macías and Calvera Roses 1999; Pendergast 1997, 1998).

Based on linguistic and chronological evidence, Alegría (1955) and Rouse (1986:119–120, 1992:37–42) have argued that the Chican people are the historic Taíno Indians who occupied most of the Greater Antilles at the time of contact. Both Alegría and Rouse use some of the early Spanish chronicles to stress that all groups (with few exceptions) from these islands shared the same culture and seem to have belonged to the same ethnic and linguistic group.

However, Veloz Maggiolo (1989) maintains that the documentary evidence of the chronicles is contradicted by strong archaeological evidence indicating great cultural variability within and between the islands. Veloz Maggiolo suggests that this less-than-homogeneous picture may have resulted from differential development, in which some Ostionan groups survived the development of the Chican subseries and conserved the Ostionan culture. More arguments for high diversity between and within islands have been presented by a number of scholars in recent years (e.g., Curet 2002, 2003; McGinnis 1997, 2001; Tavares María 1996; Wilson 1990, 2001a, 2001b). In the case of Puerto Rico, I agree with Rouse's interpretation of the linguistic evidence, in the sense that the Taínos are a linguistic group that shares the same linguistic roots throughout Puerto Rico and Hispaniola. Nevertheless, I also recognize that cultural diversity exists within this linguistic group, which can be manifested in differences in the material culture, social organization, economy, and political structure. This issue is discussed in more detail from a population perspective in Chapter 5.

In terms of settlement pattern, the Chican subseries in Puerto Rico seems to include ceremonial (and probably political) centers, nucleated villages, and isolated houses, although there is some evidence that the number of sites decreased (Curet 1992a; Rodríguez 1985, 1992; see also Chapters 5 and 6). More and bigger ball courts (Oliver 1998) were also built during this period than during the previous Ostionan/Elenan Ostionoid subseries, and the use of intensive farming techniques continued as well. Evidence for centralized settlement patterns and site hierarchies suggests a nonegalitarian social and political organization during this series, as confirmed by the chronicles. Houses continued to be relatively small, possibly to house nuclear families (Curet 1992b). In many instances, deceased ancestors seem to have been buried within the domestic unit (Curet and Oliver 1998), but other mortuary practices are also evident. Burial caves, for example, have been reported for this period since the late 1800s. This last practice may have been reserved for the elite or for members of some privileged group (Walker 1993; Wilson 1990).

Thus, in general, artifactual and settlement pattern data suggest that the Taíno Indians or the Chican Ostionoid subseries had a more elaborate social and religious system than the groups from the Ostionan and Elenan subseries of the Ostionoid. But not all of the Taíno groups from different islands or even from the same island developed the same degree of social differentiation (Curet 2003; Tavares Maria 1996; Wilson 1990:14, 25). This could explain both the similarity in cultures as observed by the Spaniards throughout the Greater Antilles and noted in the chronicles and the variability registered in the archaeological record.

CONCLUSIONS

For decades now, the seminal work of Rouse has provided Caribbean archaeologists with a basic cultural and chronological framework to support a variety of research efforts on indigenous groups. Nevertheless, it has to be admitted that Rouse's cultural and chronological categories were developed with a goal in mind—the reconstruction of culture history and migration events—and they may not be appropriate as units of analysis for other purposes. To a certain point this approach works well at the level of the archipelago or islands, but it does not help at smaller geographic and time scales. The broad brush-strokes of Rouse's organizational scheme, while exceedingly helpful to understanding the chronology of the Caribbean, obliterate a finer characterization of human society. The great diversity that we know exists at local levels disappears into the background.

The discrepancy between the high level of Rouse's units and the low level of much of human behavior is of vital importance for the studies presented in this book because many demographic and population processes do operate at levels lower than style, subseries, and subseries. This means that applying demographic analyses for understanding ancient peoples requires information at local scales. Furthermore, demographic factors do not operate in a vacuum, but within a social context, many times independently from other cultural factors. Here again, local variability is needed in order to reconstruct and understand the social context of the different demographic processes.

Rouse's categories are used here not as the basic units of analysis but as a cultural and chronological referential background against which the various demographic analyses are conducted. These cultural and chronological concepts are mostly used throughout the book for placing certain discussions chronologically and for comparative purposes. So, the result of this is building a social and demographic history that roughly parallels Rouse's cultural history but that diverges from it in significant ways. One of these ways is that the apparent cultural diversity present in most chronological periods, but normally absent from Rouse cultural model, is added to ensure a more precise picture of the cultural panorama of ancient Puerto Rico.

3 / Migration, Colonization, and Cultural Change

An Anthropological Approach

The first type of demographic analysis discussed is the interisland movement of people or long-distance migration. The migration of the early groups that inhabited the islands has intrigued anthropologists almost since the inception of Caribbean archaeology (e.g., Lovén 1935; Rainey 1940), although the topic has been dealt with in a very loose manner. While many Caribbeanists have discussed this issue, no one has done so in such a systematic and extensive way as Irving Rouse (1986). His approach and method have been greatly influential in Caribbean archaeology, to the point that they are still being used and his conclusions widely accepted. However, many of the premises, assumptions, and epistemological principles of Rouse's strategy are based on outdated perspectives from the first half of the 1900s. The issue of migration and how it has been treated in the Caribbean is reviewed and discussed in this and the next chapter. The present chapter briefly evaluates Rouse's approach to migrations and presents an alternative perspective on migrations, in which migration is held to be a process, not a single unitary event as viewed by many Caribbean archaeologists (e.g., Alegría 1955; Berman and Gnivecki 1993, 1995; Chanlatte Baik 1981, 1995; Chanlatte Baik and Narganes Storde 1983, 1985, 1986; Keegan 1985, 1992, 1995; Rainey 1940; Rouse 1986, 1992). Special attention is paid to the multiple social dimensions and dynamics involved in the process of migration. Chapter 4 applies many of the ideas presented in this chapter to two cases from the Ceramic Age of the Caribbean.

APPROACHES TO MIGRATION IN THE CARIBBEAN

Since the 1930s, Rouse has excavated many areas of the Caribbean, along with sites in Venezuela, the presumed origin of many Caribbean groups, in an attempt to reconstruct the culture history of early groups that populated the islands and their migration routes. To this end, he developed the classificatory method described in Chapter 2, which produces a cultural-chronological table that, according to Rouse, can be used to track migrations across both space and time. The emphasis in Rouse's work is not on the actual cultural or social unit that migrates (e.g., households, kin groups, etc.), but on the archaeological assemblage, which at the same time is used to define archaeological cultures. However, Rouse clearly warns us about two things: (1) this method is only suitable for delineating the movement of populations (i.e., large groups), and not smaller cultural units such as households or communities; and (2) before concluding that a particular pattern of distribution of material culture was produced by migration, diffusion must be ruled out. Using this method, which he developed over the years, Rouse claims to have traced back migration routes and movements of cultural groups throughout the Caribbean region across time. In general, Rouse's approach appears to have been relatively successful in defining the spread of cultural practices (or modes) and cultures in the Caribbean. This migratory model of the peopling and repeopling of the Caribbean has been used by almost every scholar working in the region, often with inadequate understanding of Rouse's premises.

Rouse's approach to migration has several problems, and here I point out three:

1. Rouse's model is merely a classificatory device and has no explanatory potential. Rouse assumes that once the data are organized into cultural units that are both chronological and spatial, anyone looking at the table should be able to infer migration. In other words, the data are seen as providing the conclusions without any need of a theoretical framework (i.e., a positivistic perspective).

2. A more serious issue has to do with a basic premise Rouse adopted in setting up his system. Rouse deals only with migration at the level of "cultures or peoples" (Rouse 1986; see also Siegel 1996), while smaller cultural or social units are not considered. In fact, using his own categories, for Rouse it is the series or subseries (two supracultural units) that migrate.

3. In practice, Rouse's methodology defines the movement of material modes that are used to define cultures and does not consider the actual social groups that move and all the social processes and aspects related to them (see below).

Thus, Rouse's approach cannot be considered a true theory of migration, but more a methodology to track the dispersal of modes through time and space.

In addition to determining places of origin and migration routes, several Caribbean researchers (including Rouse) have attempted to go further by discerning the reasons for the migration. Based on the ceramic sequence that he and Cruxent (Rouse and Cruxent 1963) obtained in Venezuela, Rouse suggested that the Saladoid people were pressured by later groups to move from the central Orinoco River Basin to the delta and eventually to the Lesser Antilles and Puerto Rico. Other scholars have suggested different reasons based on economic/materialist premises, particularly using push-pull models. Goodwin (1979, 1980), for example, has suggested that the early Saladoid migration was produced by population pressure that forced or pushed them out of the South American continent to the islands. On the one hand, Keegan (1985, 1992), in what is probably the most thorough attempt to explain migration in the Caribbean, argues that the colonization of the Bahamian archipelago took place due to the abundance of resources available in these islands compared to the Greater Antilles. Migrant populations were not forced but attracted (pulled) to the Bahamian archipelago from Hispaniola. On the other hand, Berman and Gnivecki (1995) use a pull-push model to explain this colonization. Particularly, they argue that a relatively dry period registered in paleoclimatic data combined with the abundance of resources in the Bahamian archipelago motivated people to migrate to these smaller islands from Cuba.

Summarizing, even though an interest in migration has been present in Caribbean archaeology almost since its inception, this topic has been treated in an informal and inconsequential manner (see Siegel 1991 for an exception to this). Other than Keegan's dispersal model for the Bahamian archipelago (Keegan 1992, 1995) there has been no serious attempt to develop a comprehensive theoretical framework of migration. Furthermore, most of the studies have concentrated mainly on general aspects of migration without taking into consideration a number of important variables at lower levels such as migrant group size, migration type, and the structure of the migrant population. An alternative perspective to migration as a social phenomenon is presented in this chapter where several concepts, processes, and variables of modern anthropological migration theory are discussed. The implications of this perspective for the Saladoid migration and the Ostionoid expansion are discussed in the next chapter.

THE ANTHROPOLOGY OF MIGRATIONS AND COLONIZATIONS

The study of migration has a long history within anthropology. During the early part of the 1900s, migration was widely used in diffusionist arguments to explain similarities in materials and cultural practices between regions. With the appearance in the 1940s of Cultural Ecology and the revival of the concept of cultural evolution, both diffusion and migration began to be rejected as principal sources of cultural change. Since then and until recently, most anthropologists underestimated the role of migration in cultural and social processes in ancient history. However, it was the studies and publications by people like Rouse (e.g., Willey et al. 1956) that kept these issues alive within the discipline. In fact, Rouse's methodology was one of the few efforts made in anthropology to develop a theory of migration at that time. Thanks to these efforts, anthropologists acknowledge now that migration is a critical factor in the history of many social and cultural groups in ancient and modern times. However, it should be recognized that Rouse's and others' (e.g., Haury 1958; Willey et al. 1956) approach was of their time, and that time was the 1940s and 1950s, when a somewhat uncomplicated view of migration as a simple event was obtained. Many of the assumptions from these early attempts (e.g., Haury 1958; Willey et al. 1956) have been put into question recently in several studies of migration (e.g., see Anthony 1990; Clark 2001; Duff 1998 for reviews on this issue). At the same time, recent research has been developing a general anthropological theory on population movement by combining information obtained from other disciplines such as demography, geography, and history, approaches that early migration scholars within anthropology criticized and discarded as irrelevant (Haury 1958; Willey et al. 1956).

Recent work on this topic has opened up migration from another perspective and suggests many promising avenues that can be applied to the Caribbean. While this new approach views migration as a very complex process in which specific migrational behavior is difficult to predict, recent studies utilizing principles from demography, history, sociology, and geography have been able to identify some general patterns and decision-making sequences involved in migrations. In this section I discuss some of the most important issues involved with population movements. The main point to be made is that population movements are complex phenomena and cannot be considered as simple events. On the contrary, migration is a process involving multiple factors, dimensions, and levels of decision making. I must confess that certain of the issues I address cannot be fully analyzed with the sometime limited data available for the Caribbean. However, I wish to present a relatively complete alternative to Rouse's approach to migrations. Rouse's views, methods, and theoretical perspectives have been extremely influential in the Caribbean and have led to the indiscriminate use of the concepts of population movement and the abuse of migration to explain almost any visible change in the archaeological record. Thus, there are two purposes for discussing these issues in more detail than required: the first one is to demonstrate that any type of population movement is much more complex and multidimensional than the approach presented by Rouse. It is my position that this approach presents us with more and better opportunities to model and explain past population movements more accurately. The second one is to demonstrate that the use of the concepts and terms developed by Rouse without a complete understanding of their meaning has major implications and ramifications for contemporaneous accounts of past population movements. Most of the discussion that follows is based on reviews published by Anthony (1990), Clark (2001), and Duff (1998).

A Processual Definition of the Concept of Migration

A fundamental problem with past studies on migration is that they considered migration as an event rather than as a process with multiple dimensions, a view prevalent in academic circles in the mid-twentieth century. It is important to recognize, however, that the difference between an event and a process is not merely one of temporal duration. In other words, an event is not just something that occurs in a relatively short time, and a process is something that occurs over a longer period of time. A more complete understanding is that an event is something that occurs in one or very few steps and involves very few factors (or dimensions), whereas a process is a more complex phenomenon that has multiple steps and factors (or dimensions). This limited view of migration as an event is amply evident in Caribbean studies and has been exacerbated somewhat by the enthusiasts of island biogeography, who place more emphasis on distances, geographic position, island size and shape, and so on, in the quest to understanding island migrations than they give to other cultural, social, and individual factors (Rainbird 1999; Terrell 1999). While I do not deny the usefulness of many of the biogeographical principles in understanding human migrations, their indiscriminate use, especially when many social and cultural factors are ignored, tends to result in overtly simplistic models and perpetuates the view of migration as an event such as is usually envisioned for animal and plant populations.

A second problem related to the definition of migration as an event has to do with the units of analysis used in the study of the migration process. In the Caribbean, migration is normally seen as occurring at the level of cultures or supracultures (i.e., series and subseries). In Rouse's system, for example, the movement of series and subseries reflects the movement of more than cultures, since these terms are used to identify levels of cultural organization higher than culture. Units at lower levels, such as styles or complexes, in Rouse's model by definition do not migrate in an archaeologically meaningful manner. This position, in which culture or any other category at a higher cultural level is given emphasis over the actual social unit that migrates, is clear in the following passage from Rouse (1986:10):

> We should not expect to be able to trace population movements in terms of single cultural complexes. As a people migrates from area to area, it will encounter different natural and cultural conditions and will modify its complex accordingly. Moreover, replacement of an entire population takes time, and culture changes of its own accord with the passage of time. In addition, migrants may be atypical of their parent population, in which case they will not carry their entire cultural complex with them. [This phenomenon was first recognized by population biologists, who call it the founders' principle; MacArthur and Wilson 1967.]

This passage also suggests a troubling contradiction in Rouse's work on migrations. While he admits that small groups of people and perhaps a "complex" or style migrate, he also clearly argues that style (or complex) is not the appropriate unit from which to infer migration. Instead, he recommends using the series as the unit to identify migration in the archaeological record. This perspective is a direct conclusion of the culture-historical and normative approach used by Rouse (and many others), in which the cultural units worth studying are homogeneous ones, and any diversity is referred to as "atypical." However, as Anthony (1990:908) has pointed out, "'Cultures' do not migrate.

It is often only a very narrowly defined, goal-oriented subgroup that migrates." The difference between a Rousian perspective and Anthony's is not trivial for understanding migration processes, and, in fact, is the source of many unresolved issues in Caribbean archaeology. In reality, cross-cultural and demographic studies have demonstrated that in the majority of cases, the decision to migrate is made at a level lower than culture, such as at the individual, household, community, or descent-group level (Anthony 1990; Clark 1986; Duff 1998).

By this point it should be clear that in order to study migration objectively, we must first have an adequate definition of the term. Once it is recognized that migration is a process and that migration does not occur at the level of culture, a more useful and analytically powerful definition for migration can be developed. Several definitions have been proposed recently. Here I use the one suggested by Clark (2001:2). A migration is "a long-term residential relocation beyond community boundaries by one or more discrete social units as the result of a perceived decrease in the benefits of remaining residentially stable or a perceived increase in the benefits of relocating to prospective destinations."

To this definition I would add various temporary population movements, such as hunting or fishing trips, seasonal rounds, and ritual peregrination. These movements cannot be ignored, because in certain circumstances they can form part of the process of migration. For example, hunters or fishermen away from home may act as scouts to gather information about potential migratory destinations. Thus, although temporary absences from a main residence are not in themselves migrations, they can be taken into account as part of the migratory process.

As a final comment, I have avoided using size of the migrant population as a criterion to distinguish between different types of migrations as suggested by Rouse (1986:9) (i.e., immigration vs. population movement), for two reasons: first, the movement of small groups can be the beginning of a larger migration trend; and second, it is difficult to define how small is small and how large is large. The only criterion implied in Rouse's publication is that "[if] the invading social group are numerous enough and large enough, they may drive out the local population or else absorb it." In general, this criterion has four problems. First, it limits studies of migration to a very narrow range of possible population movements. Second, it is a post hoc definition, where the process is defined and studied based on the final conditions. The only migrations to be studied are the successful ones, while unsuccessful ones are ignored (an example of survivorship bias). Third, it does not consider that many major migrations are the result of multiple sequential smaller population movements. And fourth, it ignores situations in which the migrant group does not drive out or absorb the local population, such as in extreme examples of urban migrations.

To simplify the discussion, many researchers have opted instead to divide the different types of migrations into two categories based on the scale of the migration: short-distance (also called local or internal migration) and long-distance (also called interareal or external migration). Short-distance migration consists of population movements within a local area, while long-distance migration refers to movements across ecological, geographic, or cultural boundaries. Cross-culturally, short-distance migrations are more common, simpler, tend to happen in larger numbers, and occur more frequently than long-distance migrations. Also, short-distance migrations require less planning than long-distance ones. Archaeologically, however, long-distance migrations tend to leave clearer archaeological evidence than short-distance migrations. Chapter 4 deals primarily with long-distance migration in the Caribbean, while examples of shorter migrations will be discussed in Chapter 5 in the context of regional populations.

ASPECTS OF MIGRATIONS

Based on the definition presented above it is clear that migration is a complex process that involves multiple dimensions and levels of analysis. This section considers a number of aspects and factors characteristic of the process of migrations. Much of what follows originates in recent attempts by several scholars to develop a general anthropological theory of migration (e.g., Anthony 1990; Clark 2001; Duff 1998).

Reasons for Migrations

The causes and reasons of moving are among the most debated issues in migration studies. Independently of how migration is considered (i.e., as process or event), the issue of causation has been on the front page of most studies on population movements. This is true not only in anthropology or archaeology but also in other disciplines such as demography, geography, and social history. After decades of studies on population movements, one thing is clear: the causes of migration can be extremely diverse and complex, much more so than can be accounted for by most of the models used to explain migration. Indeed, Anthony (1992:898) has argued that the complexity of migration is so extreme "that in many prehistoric cases it is likely that proximate causes can no longer be identified." Although thoughtful consideration of the archaeological evidence can dispel some of the darkness veiling ancient migrations, Anthony does bring us face to face with the difficulty of developing a complete picture of past human behavior.

Most explanations for migration can be classified under the umbrella of push-pull models. Push models emphasize the role of negative factors in forcing a population to do something that under normal circumstances it would not do, namely, to abandon the settlement and move to another locality. Pull models emphasize positive factors that might attract populations toward another residential locality. Most of the push-pull models suggested for explaining migrations are confined to economic causes such as supply-demand models. In archaeology, the supply-demand models have usually focused on population-resource imbalance, in which either populations increase or resources decrease to a point that migration is perceived as a viable option over other possibilities. This materialistic approach is limited, however, and recent studies on ancient migrations have argued that ideological, social, and political factors could, at times, have been equally or more important. Anthropologists also recognize that the decision to migrate can be made out of the *perception* that life would be better elsewhere. Although this perception may be informed by some hard data, it does not require a perfect knowledge of the environment, as is assumed by many economic models. Perception is difficult to measure among modern populations and virtually impossible to measure in ancient populations.

Many of the economic models, especially of the demand-supply principles variety, also tend to overlook the social and cultural factors involved in even the most insignificant and mundane subsistence strategies. One of those factors is the social value of resources, where one particular resource can be highly valued for reasons other than economy, such as religious beliefs or family or cultural traditions. Many economic models emphasize exclusively the nutritive value of resources, and based on this and on the costs involved in acquiring them, they ranked them according to optimization. Migration will occur, then, when "the marginal return rate in the new territory (including transportation costs and long-term capital investments) is equal to or exceeds the overall mean return rate from continued production in the occupied territory" (Keegan 1985:43). In cases like this, no reference is made in terms of the social values of these resources and even idiosyncrasies such as a person's or social unit's unwillingness to move even if return rates are low.

Moreover, optimization assumes that a certain kind of rational behavior will prevail over other perceptions and values, and we know this does not always happen. From this perspective, it is assumed that all humans are rational and will try to maximize and optimize production at all times. However, these terms are normally defined from a Western, market perspective, in which the maximization of yields and rational behavior are almost always expressed in material or energetic terms. Although I agree that all people, and to that effect cultures, behave rationally, I do not agree that there is only one standard of rationality. Moreover, the concept is not a natural one but a culturally and socially constructed one.

Another problem with most purely economic models of migrations is that other social relations, such as kinship relations and political alliances, are excluded. In other words, social support groups are not considered a major factor in the decision-making process. In studies of modern migrations, however, the distance from friends and families is one of many variables that people take into consideration before making the decision to migrate (Clark 1986). There is no reason to believe that the behavior of people in ancient times would have differed markedly in these respects.

Here I do not imply that economic, subsistence, demographic, and environmental factors are neither important nor critical in explaining human migrations. Human history offers many examples of people moving because of lack of material resources, and factors related to cost-benefit considerations (such as those related to transportation and initial capital investments) are always important. Perhaps there is no better example for this than the American Southwest, where during the Pueblo IV period massive migrations from one area to another have been ascribed to a long-lasting and extensive drought in the region (Clark 2001; see also various papers in Spielmann [1998]). Rather, I argue that causes of migrations are many and varied, and in any given migration, economic factors may be less important than social, cultural, or political factors. Even when economic factors seem to rank high as a reason to migrate, a population may choose other avenues of survival. For example, a group under nutritional stress may choose to stay in a location by intensifying or broadening the breadth of food production and sacrificing optimization in order to maintain some social or cultural benefits. Similarly, a faction of a group may decide to leave a region with abundant resources due to internal conflict or to develop their own political agenda.

Thus, I am not advocating for the discard of the push-pull models. As a quick review of the definition of migration that is being used here will show, I agree that people migrate because of a perception that they will be better off (socially, economically, demographically, spiritually, emotionally) somewhere else. However, any push-pull model that attempts to explain migrations has to consider culture-specific values and belief systems, factors that can complicate any attempt (simple or sophisticated) at an objective cost-benefit analysis.

We can further our understanding of the causes of migration by considering population movement at two levels of migrations (Duff 1998:32): macro- and microlevels. Most traditional studies (including Rouse's) have concentrated on the macrolevel, where migration is considered an aggregate behavior related to the causal variables. Many push-pull models can be considered as operating at this level, especially those that focus on population-resource imbalance. Microlevel analyses, meanwhile, concentrate on the decision-making process (see next section) at a lower level, such as the individual or a household. While these approaches seem opposite to each other, they rather complement each other. Each approach informs different aspects of migration, and therefore both are important in its study. For example, Duff (1998:32) has argued that "While the initial decision to migrate is often related to macrolevel processes, these conditions are filtered through community and family dynamics." These differences between macro- and microlevel are important for understanding in a holistic manner the internal structure and dynamics of migration. Following Duff's argument, it can be argued that while a community as a whole may face a compelling reason to migrate, certain individuals or groups within the community may decide to move early, while others may choose to delay migration or not migrate at all. In human populations the early movers are often young men, and the late movers are elders with more established responsibilities and favorable social roles. Factors inhibiting migration of the community as a whole can include access to economically or socially determined critical subsistence resources, land tenure arrangements, and factional splits, and different community members can be affected in different ways by any of these factors.

Because of the difficulties of modeling and determining a complex issue such as the causes of migration, some researchers (e.g., Anthony 1990:899) have questioned whether the reasons for population movements can be realistically ascertained. Arguing that even studies on historical migrations (which have richer data sets) find problems with the definition of causes, Anthony and others suggest that the emphasis should not be on the reasons but on the "structure of migration." As Anthony (1990:909) states, "In the study of cultural evolution it is the fact of migration and its consequences that are most important; the study of causes is in more ways less significant."

Although I agree that in many cases the structure and consequences of migration may be more important than the causes, it is still worthwhile trying to establish the causes, to the degree that they can be known. Ultimately, social scientists are interested in understanding human behavior, including the motivations for that behavior. Admittedly, it is often impossible to determine the causes of migration from archaeological data. In fact, migration can be produced not by a cause or a combination of causes (in a cause-effect fashion), but by processes similar to the premises of dialectics and agency, where even the actors in the migration may be a factor, too. Once migrations are under way, of course, their consequences are more important to cultural evolution and change than are the original reason for migrating. This is a significant point that should not be underestimated. These aspects of migrations have been ignored and underrated by traditional anthropological studies (e.g., Rouse 1986; Willey et al. 1956) that have overemphasized the causes without considering other aspects of equal or more importance to the understanding and explanation of past human behavior. As Anthony (1990:896) has so eloquently pointed out: "If archaeological approaches to migration have been slowed by a failure to ask the right questions, then one of the greatest culprits must be the question of causes."

The Decision to Migrate

Even when reasons to migrate are in place and are recognized as such by a population, the decision to migrate is still not an easy one. People tend to become attached to locations in emotional, psychological, mental, and even spiritual ways. Often, the decision to migrate is in fact strongly driven by the causes of migrations, but this does not mean that it is fully determined by them. Even though ample causes for migration may exist, the decision to migrate may be delayed or possibly never made for social, ideological, or cultural reasons. Thus, the decision-making process is also a complex and multidimensional one that involves several factors that have to be considered, such as the conditions favoring migration, and, if the decision to move is taken, when and where to move.

Needless to say, the feasibility of migration and the conditions favoring migration are very influential in deciding when and where to migrate. The conditions of migration include a series of elements such as the cause(s) of migration, cost of transportation, cost of initial investment (social and economic) in establishing a new community, and the flow of information. The issue of the cause(s) of migration has been discussed already, so here the discussion concentrates on the other factors.

Compared to intercontinental migrations, insular migration presents more complex economic and survival issues, especially in terms of transportation. To be able to migrate to an island, a migrant population has to have the technology and the body of knowledge necessary for seafaring. The availability of these two elements, technology and knowledge, is in turn a major factor in determining the cost of transportation, which also determines feasibility. Technologically, people will need to know how to move, and how much can be transported by this means of conveyance. For a migrating population, large boats are good. Larger vessels are safer than smaller boats, and can carry more people—workers who will establish the new settlement—and more goods and supplies. Finally, larger vessels can be outfitted for longer voyages. Shape is another important factor since stable vessels are needed for open-ocean voyages, but long boats like canoes would be just fine for interisland hops.

There is strong ethnohistoric evidence in the Caribbean for the availability of the appropriate technology for island migration. For example, the chronicles document the existence of relatively large dugout canoes that could hold between 50 and 100 people and that were used for daily trips between islands. Although most of this information is for the Contact period, and little of the material has been preserved, it is usually assumed that the original migrant populations had access to similar technologies (Callaghan 1993, 1995, 1999, 2001, 2003; Keegan 1985, 1992).

Technology is not the only thing that is needed to move long distances across the ocean from one island to another. Knowledge about aspects such as prevailing winds and currents, weather patterns, steering and maintaining a course, the use of celestial features for guidance, location of certain landmarks, and how to read "natural" signs to determine the location of islands before they are visible is needed as well. Irwin (1992) has extensively reviewed many of these issues for the Pacific Islands, and concluded that we should not underestimate the ability of prehistoric people to explore vast regions of the oceans. He has shown that with the appropriate technology and knowledge, ancient people were able to travel extremely long distances with a high probability of surviving. Despite some differences between Pacific migrations and those in and around the Caribbean, such as interisland visibility in the latter case, Irwin supplies a good ethnographic analogy that can be applied to the Caribbean. So, the comparative data from the Pacific, where migrations were if anything more arduous and more complex, strongly suggest that Caribbean groups had appropriate seafaring knowledge to be able to transport themselves from the South American continent or from one island to another. This conclusion is especially relevant for some suggestions to be discussed in Chapter 4, of direct migration from the coasts of South America to the Greater Antilles without passing through the Lesser Antilles and that are supported by several computer simulation studies conducted by Callaghan (1993, 1995, 1999, 2001, 2003).

All of this suggests that ancient people of the Caribbean were well adapted to a seafaring life and had both the means and the knowledge to move populations on ocean voyages. Once this technological knowledge is acquired, the most critical aspects related to the costs of transportation are the construction of the vessels and physically putting them in motion through the use of paddles. However, if enough resources and enough people are available, these issues should be neither a major factor involved in the costs of transportation nor a major roadblock in making the decision to migrate. Judging from several of the chronicles that report almost daily trade trips between islands, in some cases crossing passages several tens of kilometers wide, it can be assumed that indigenous Caribbean groups had the manpower and the materials to produce the appropriate vessels and to put them in motion.

The cost of the initial investment of building up a new social unit is another issue that has to be considered by potential migrants to make a decision. These costs comprise more than just the labor and materials involved in the construction of the settlement or house. Some additional aspects that can increase these costs are the creation of new cultivation fields, the transportation of new species of plants and animals to recreate some subsistence aspects of the place of origin, the maintenance of relations with communities in the place of origin until the new community is demographically and economically independent, the development of new relations or new types of relations with people, if any, in the place of destination, and the energy and time involved in the process of mapping cognitively the distribution of social and subsistence related resources in the new areas (see various papers in Rockman and Steele 2003). Obviously, the actual cost of initial investment is going to vary from case to case depending on the particulars of the places of origin and destination, the reasons for migrating, and the cultural and social traditions of the migrant group.

The final condition for migration to be discussed here is the flow of information. The flow of information, however, is intimately related to the other two factors involved in making the decision to migrate and when and where to migrate. With few extraordinary exceptions (e.g., refugees), people simply do not migrate to a place of which they possess no information (Duff 1998:33). For this reason, an adequate flow of information about potential locations of destination is another condition favoring migration. Although physical distances may constrain movement and the flow and evaluation of information, in general, the process of collecting information is culturally and socially circumscribed. In cases where a long-distance network does not exist providing information about adequate places to migrate, long-distance migration will be considered an option of last resort. Thus, in the great majority of the cases evidence for migration implies the presence of some kind of interaction between the area of origin and of destination prior to population movement.

Cross-culturally there are many kinds of interaction that potential migrant populations can use to gather information. In cases where the potential place of destination is unoccupied, ways of gathering information include exploring expeditions (Irwin 1992), the use of special activity groups (fishing, hunting, gathering groups), and initial colonization (see below). In many occasions, these activities can be considered as some form of scouting. It is important to note that these ways of gathering information can also be used when another social or cultural group already occupies the potential place of destination. However, in these cases personal interaction in the form of kinship (especially if previous migrant relatives are present in the destination), alliances, and trade relationship can also be used in a more efficient way, and in fact are the ones most used cross-culturally to gather information (Anthony 1990; Duff 1998:33). All this information is used (1) to create a cognitive map of potential destinations, and (2) to reevaluate the conditions at the existing location to determine if migration is the best option.

The decision to move, and when and where to migrate are going to be influenced by several critical variables such as identified sources of information, personal linkages, the structure of the decision-making group, and group size. It is at this point that all of the previous factors (i.e., causes, costs of transportation and initial investment, and the information of potential destinations) are brought together to make a final decision. As Duff has pointed out: "The selection of a destination is the nexus of the interplay between macro- and micro-level processes" (Duff 1998:33). After taking all these factors into consideration (consciously or not), the final decision by the particular social unit (e.g., individual, household, descent group, or community) is taken based on the *perception* of the situation (real or not). The key word in this statement, as in the definition of migration presented above, is *perception,* as decision and information sources reflect these subjective thoughts. Therefore, the decision-making process may not always operate as models of economic rationality or physical principles may predict, even when the group in question is under extreme nutritional or demographic stress. In some cases, for example, one area is selected over another better suited one because more information was available for the former than the latter. Or, one particular destination region or island is selected because it is easier to return to the donor area in case of failure than another more resourceful region.

Colonization

Colonization is a special form of migration in which migrant groups settled in previously uninhabited areas. As is the case of migration, in the past colonization has been considered an event. However, some studies have suggested that instead it should be considered a complex process with a multiplicity of events and phases (Dewar 1995; Graves and Addison 1995; Moore 2001; Rockman and Steele 2003; Smith 1995) which includes aspects such as exploration, gathering of information (scouting) and knowledge of the availability of resources, and movement of people to a previously unoccupied territory. Graves and Addison (1995:386–387) have argued for the complexity of this process and have suggested making a distinction between colonization and establishment of human populations. In this context establishment "represents the occupation of an island or archipelago for some period of time by a population of sufficient [reproductive] size" (Graves and Addison 1995:387; brackets are mine). These authors developed this distinction from the need to explain at least two types of phenomena present in the archaeological record of the South Pacific. First, Hawaiian chronology includes few but consistent and reliable dates in good archaeological contexts that are relatively old, and which, due to a lack of a better explanation, traditionally have been considered outliers or sampling errors. Second, there is evidence from Polynesia that some islands were discovered and colonized, but that long-term establishment was never achieved (Graves and Addison 1995:387). Considering this evidence, these researchers argued that we should make a distinction between three related but not necessarily concomitant processes: discovery, colonization, and establishment. In some instances it is possible that islands or groups of islands were discovered, colonized, and established relatively simultaneous, as traditional views of migration predicated, while in others the three stages represent distinct components of a settlement process that potentially can be separated by significant periods of time. Yet, in other cases only discovery or discovery and colonization may have occurred, but full establishment was never achieved. To these three components, however, we can also add an intermediate process between discovery and colonization, the exploitation of resources in an unpopulated island by special task groups.

Some parts of this argument are supported indirectly by the results of simulation studies conducted by Moore (2001) on island colonization. Considering different types of colonization and several aspects of the structure of migrant populations, Moore was able to show that the success of colonization can be measured not only in terms of length of time but also in terms of population size and how autonomous and durable is the colonizing population in terms of reproductive capability (similar to the concept of establishment suggested by Graves and Addison). Thus, while some colonizing communities can be "reproductively" established fairly quickly, others may never be established even after hundreds of years of colonizing a location.

Taking into consideration many of these arguments, here I use a definition of colonization slightly modified from the one provided by Graves and Addison (1995:386): Colonization represents the process of the placement of human populations on discovered islands or regions; these populations eventually may or may not lead to the establishment of human populations. This definition includes the concept of colonization as a process and its relationship to other factors such as the discovery, exploration, and exploitation of unoccupied islands, but it makes it independent of the definite establishment of a human reproductive community.

As mentioned above, colonies can have an important role in further migratory processes since migrants who have relocated constitute sources of detailed information about circumscribed areas, introducing new information and reducing the impact that long distances have on information flow. Once present and established, newly founded or existing communities offer information and an attractive destination for additional migrants, often resulting in what demographers know as migration streams.

Size and Structure of the Migrant Population

The size and composition of a migrant group can create marked demographic changes in both the populations of origin and destination. On the receiving end, migration can produce population growth well beyond the biological reproductive capability of human populations. On the donor end, however, migrations of great magnitudes can produce null or negative growth rates, or in the worst of the cases, total abandonment of regions (Cameron 1995; Nelson and Schachner 2002; see also various papers in Cameron and Tomka 1993). Depending on its size, emigration on the one hand can relieve groups living under some nutritional stress produced by resource-population imbalances, or it can deprive some societies of a most-needed labor force to establish a stable economic system. On the other hand, small populations of migrants colonizing a previously unpopulated area (also called beachheads) can be extremely susceptible to random catastrophic events or can run into major reproductive problems due to poor genetic statistics.

However, the size of the migrant population is not the only aspect that has an effect on the demography of the donor or receiving populations. The composition and nature of the migrant groups can also have an impact on several population and social dynamics. Migrant populations cannot necessarily be considered a representative sample of the original population. Generally, migrant groups represent a narrow segment of the original social group, sometimes including a larger representation of a subgroup defined by age, sex, and/or social position (Anthony 1990; Clark 1986). Cross-cultural studies have shown that in the great majority of cases (not including refugees), migrant populations tend to have a proportionally larger number of young adult males, coming primarily from the ranks of disadvantaged people (Anthony 1990; Clark 1986).

The age and sex structure of the population can produce either negative or positive conditions to populations. The addition or removal of a large number of young or older people, for example, can make the difference between a beneficial or detrimental addition to a community. Young people that are in or about to enter their biologically reproductive and economically productive years can produce a positive impact similar to increased fertility in the receiving population, eventually leading to higher population growth rates (Paine 1997b; see also Chapter 7). Losing a large number of young individuals can have the opposite effect. In contrast, addition of too many older people or infants will tend to reduce population growth rates and in some instances create a heavier economic and social load on the productive individuals of society. The addition of more women in their reproductive years than men can produce eventually an increase in growth rate, regardless of the total size of the migrant population. The addition of more men, however, may have no effect on the reproductive capacity of the receiving population or it may reduce the overall population growth rate.

The size and structure of a migrant population can have effects on other social aspects of both the donor and receiving groups. Large numbers of individuals of one sex, for example, can create problems related with mate availability and selection, disturbing some fundamental aspects of the internal social relations such as marital patterns. This is true for the migration of a large number of either women or men, even though the impact of men in the total population growth rate is minimal. The addition of a large number of men, also, can create more competition for status, women, and/or wealth and increase internal conflict, but it also can dramatically increase the military ranks of an expanding polity, making it more competitive or successful.

In the case of migrant groups that are physically or socially isolated from other groups, size and structure of the population become critical issues for their survival. The classic example for the effect of these variables given by many scholars is the establishment of a colony by a relatively small group of people who due to the genetic circumstances is incapable of reproducing successfully, much less developing into an established settlement (see Anthony 1990; Clark 2001; Moore 2001). Structure can also be critical for the reproductive success of a migrant population. Groups with either too many men or women, or too many youngsters or elderly people may not be able to biologically reproduce enough to produce a genetically sustainable population. Furthermore, smaller populations are more vulnerable to random processes such as sudden environmental changes or catastrophes than larger ones (Keegan and Diamond 1987).

However, it is important to emphasize that having the appropriate size and structure for reproduction may not be enough to ensure the reproductive success or sustainability of a migrant population. Demographic variables such as population size and structure do not operate in a vacuum but in cultural and social contexts that can influence success or failure against all demographic odds. To these we can add stochastic conditions of different kinds (catastrophes, birth of more men than women, etc.) that can have a major impact. The results of the recent stochastic simulation program used by Moore (2001) to test different colonization models illustrate some of the possible effects of social and cultural variables. In the simulation several demographic variables were taken into consideration including initial population size, sex ratio at birth, distribution of sibships, maternal risk of giving birth, and risk of death. In addition he considered three cultural variables: marriage choice, polygyny, and marriage pool. This study has several conclusions that are pertinent for all research on colonization. The first one is, as expected, that small initial populations are more variable and less predictable than at larger sizes. However, "[t]he overall principle for band simulations is that if a small initial population survives these early stochastic events to reach a size where individual events are buffered, it achieves some stability and develops in a more predictable manner. I call this initial, risky period in band growth its period of 'Stochastic Crisis'" (Moore 2001:403). The bands that survived this crisis increased their total population exponentially in what he calls Malthusian Take-Off (Moore 2001:404). Nonetheless, more important, is that there is no threshold of time between the beginning of the Stochastic Crisis and the Malthusian Take-Off. In other words, "a group can endure for a long time without either becoming extinct or being very healthy" (Moore 2001:404). Or phrased in another way, a colonizing group can last for a long time without being reproductively established.

Another aspect studied by Moore was the effects of the interaction between the colonizing community and other communities (local or parental) on the migrant population. After considering interactions with different numbers of communities, he concluded that "[u]nder the vital rates used here, and with the marriage practices defined in the simulation program, a band of 100 persons only needs to exchange spouses with *one other band of the same size* to achieve a stable condition" (Moore 2001:405; emphasis in original). Moreover, "[w]hile the difference between viability in isolation and viability in contact with another band of equal size was significant, it is important to note that the viability of [the colonizing band] did *not* improve much, if at all, when the marriage system was extended to comprise a total of 3, 4, 5, and 6 bands" (Moore 2001:404; emphasis in original, brackets are my addition). Thus, the chances of success of a colonizing population increase dramatically when they interbreed with at least one other population.

Interestingly, after considering all these variables combined with stochastic factors that tend to affect smaller populations, Moore concluded that "*every* population, no matter how disadvantageous its demographic conditions might be, has *some* chance of survival, even for hundreds or thousands of years" (Moore 2001:404; emphasis in original). This suggests that even smaller, isolated groups of peoples as the ones expected in the so-called beachhead populations, against all odds and due to random, positive events, can be reproductively successful (see, for example, the case of the mutineers of the Bounty in Pitcairn Island [Terrell 1986:188–195]). Still, the chances of survival are considerably smaller in isolated small groups than in larger populations or populations interacting with at least one other group.

Thus, the reproductive success of a migrant group and turning into an established population depends on multiple factors from multiple dimensions. While the obvious demographic and biological factors that can affect a population positively or negatively have received much attention, cultural and social practices such as marital patterns and interaction with other groups are less obvious and in many instances ignored or taken as given by traditional studies (e.g., Keegan 1992, 1995, 2000; Rouse 1986, 1992). For instance, other examples of possible cultural and social factors that can affect migrant populations and that are not discussed here include differences in religion or ethnic background that may inhibit the rate of integration and reproduction of both groups. Many of these factors can be studied archaeologically as some studies from other parts of the world have demonstrated (e.g., Clark 2001; for the American Southwest see various papers in Spielmann 1998, and for studies on the Oaxacan Barrio in Teotihuacan see Paddock 1983, Rattray 1987, and Spence 1976).

Models on Migration and Colonization

Behaviorally, the patterns of migration on the landscape can take different shapes. The shape or type of migration to a certain point is going to depend on the specifics of all the aspects already discussed in this chapter (i.e., causes of migration, size and structure of the migrant group, process of colonization, etc.). Several patterns have been identified in the literature, and they are discussed here in a brief manner. However, it has to be recognized right at the onset of this discussion that the following patterns are models developed for ideal situations taking into consideration few of the many factors involved, and, in some cases, combined with untested "common sense." Reality, nevertheless, can be radically different since a multiplicity of processes could have been acting at the same time. Moreover, one pattern could have been created during the process of colonization, while other different patterns could have developed during the process of population and territorial expansion. Thus, these patterns are presented as guidance for studies on migration and for hypothesis development, and they are not meant to be perfect reflections of reality.

Long- and Short-Distance Migrations

Long- and short-distance migrations have previously been defined briefly in this chapter, but they deserve to be discussed in more detail. First of all, the definition of what is long and short distance is not universal, but culturally determined. What is far and what is close is going to be determined ultimately by several factors, including means and costs of transportation, the actual geographic distance, extension of cultural "territories," and culturally determined aspects of proxemics. For example, a settled group may perceive as far what is considered as relatively close for a nomad group. On another topic, it is important to recognize that most of the aspects of migrations discussed above are applicable to both long- and short-distance migration, but at different scales. Thus, they both can be studied in similar fashions, although, archaeologically, long-distance migrations will be easier to identify and obtain information.

Short-distance migrations are more common than long-distance migrations. Many of these local moves are related to changes of residence at marriage, or to younger families trying to improve their social and economic status. Short-distance population movements have the advantage that migrants can retain many of the social ties (including kinship and alliances) that they enjoyed in their place of origin, even though they are moving to improve their situation. Although seemingly short-distance migrations are not necessarily relevant for this chapter, they are important since many long-distance migrations may have been composed of several short movements over a relatively long period of time, but that in archaeological scale they instead look like an event. Anthony (1990:901) has argued that groups that depended on "a broad array of diversified, less localized resources" (diffuse subsistence strategies) tend to migrate in a short-distance fashion, where more frequently, but often not very far. Many hunter-gatherers, pastoralists, and some nonspecialized farmers, possibly including tropical horticulturalists, fall under this pattern. The latter type of group is of interest here because many lowland South American groups have been categorized as nonspecialized farmers that practice slash-and-burn agriculture combined with gathering, hunting, and fishing. Due to the shallowness and the low quality of South American tropical soils, traditionally it has been assumed that households, descent groups, or whole villages have to move periodically (every one or two generations) to be closer to suitable soils, reduce the transportation costs involved with the practice of food production, and allow for the forest to regenerate in the already used fields. Moving a short distance has the benefit that old, abandoned farming fields and house gardens can still be somewhat productive and exploited until the new fields are in a productive stage. In the long run, and taking into consideration the chronological resolution of archaeology, as this pattern continues, the whole process may give the impression of a migratory wave or expansion of a culture throughout the landscape. Fissioning due to any of a variety of reasons can also produce short-distance migration, where the migrant group wants to settle near some neighbors to ensure social reproduction.

Conversely, long-distance migrations are less common, take much more preparation and planning, and involve relatively high costs of transportation limiting the amount of materials that can be brought from the place of origin. Because of the long distance, the acquisition of information about potential places may depend more on the information provided by third parties such as traders, relatives that live in the potential destinations, and migrants that live in the place of origin. The processes of assessing the pro's and con's of migrating and making the final decision to migrate are made more difficult due to the fussiness of the information compared to the case of short-distance migration. While many people tend to visualize this type of migration as a one-step process, as mentioned above, several short-distance migrations can produce similar effects in the long run. Anthony (1990:901) has argued that this type of migration is more common among societies that depended on a narrow range of highly productive but relatively inelastic and localized resources (i.e., groups with more specialized subsistence strategies). The relatively long distance of these movements also affects the relationship of the migrant groups with the group of origin and the groups already inhabiting the destination area, if any exist. Obviously, the relations with the group of origin will be weaker than in short-distance migration, although, at least initially, they are not completely severed. In fact, in many cases, the long-distance relationship with the parent community can last for very long periods of time, as many modern cases testify (e.g., Mexican communities in the United States). At the same time and for reproductive, subsistence, and social reasons, long-distance migration may generate a stronger relationship between the migrant groups and local groups of other cultural or social background.

Wave-of-Advance Model

The wave-of-advance model is probably one of the most sophisticated mathematical models used by archaeologists to explain migration. Metaphorically, this model sees the expansion and migration of groups the same way that waves disperse in water as a rock hits its surface. As proposed by Ammerman and Cavalli-Sforza (1973, 1979, 1984), the model begins with the assumption that pioneer agriculturists or frontier populations will have locally high birth rates in comparison to the core of the wave. This frontier or pioneer population will be considered the wave front that eventually will develop high population densities, resulting in their movement toward less densely populated areas in an outward advance. The model assumes that population movements will be over short distances, and in the aggregate might approach a random distribution with respect to direction.

There are three major problems with this model (Anthony 1990:900). The first is that it tends to idealize and homogenize the results of diverse population movements over great periods of time, but it does not describe the dynamics of the actual population movements at smaller scales of time. Among other things, it assumes that the only reason for migration over a millennium or longer periods of time is population density. The second problem is that it assumes that each migratory move is statistically independent, when, in fact, migratory movements are highly dependent on previous moves. Third, it combines short- and long-distance movements into a single measure of "migratory activity." It assumes that the only way populations can migrate long distances is through a series of short-distance migrations. This tendency does not consider a distinction between local and interregional migration that can be critical when the latter accounts for much of the movement with very little contribution of the former.

Leapfrogging

This pattern, named after the children's game of leapfrog, basically states that "great distances may be jumped and large areas bypassed through the agency of advance 'scouts' who collect information on social conditions and resource potentials and relay it back to the potential migrants" (Anthony 1990:902). Although originally applied to continental groups, this model is probably one of the most applicable for islands, since a population cannot move homogeneously over the landscape but is forced to leap to the next available territory. In this model the role of "scouts" is critical, and they can be in the form of traders, trappers, mercenaries, craft specialists, hunters, explorers, or any other information-relaying scouting groups. Thus, archaeological information for a long-scale interregional migration should include evidence for an earlier penetration by some of these smaller groups (Anthony 1990:903; Graves and Addison 1995). Unfortunately, due to the nature of some of these groups (i.e., small size and short lasting), the archaeological evidence tends to be ephemeral at best. Graves and Addison (1995), however, have used the few, but consistent early dates registered in Hawaii to argue that they represent either early explorations or colonization attempts of the island. Other evidence can include the presence of campsites, evidence of trade, or evidence of resource exploitation in the target area prior to the large-scale migration. In the interpretation of these data, however, it is important to recognize that this information gathering can take place for reasons (i.e., trading, hunting, trapping, quarrying, exploring for status) different from those that caused the migration.

Stream Migration

In many cases, migrations may look more like a stream than a wave. Migrants tend to proceed along already known and defined routes toward specific destinations, especially places with a focus of previous migrant populations. As Anthony puts it: "the route is therefore often just as finely targeted as the destination" (1990:903). Normally, these routes follow the flow of information that is produced when earlier migrants create pathways by overcoming obstacles and, once settled, providing routing information for later migrations. Later migrations, however, may be different in goal orientation and composition from the initial migrant group. These diachronic changes in the patterns of the reasons for moving and in the structure, composition, and organization of the new migrant population can be responsible for major transformations in both the local and the migrant communities. For this reason it is important to consider these possibilities when studying ancient migrations. Some of these changes should be visible archaeologically by observing the sudden appearance of materials or designs from the original population that were not present at first in the migrant population.

Return Migration

Migration is a two-way street, and in the majority of the cases most migratory processes tend to develop a counter-stream of people moving back to the place of origin. Return migrations are difficult to assess archaeologically since the migrant (counter-migrant) group is of similar cultural background as the new destination. Studying this phenomenon requires the examination of the proposed place of origin as detailed as the proposed destination. In some cases, return migrants will carry goods from the foreign place to the place of origin, but they can be confused with long-distance trade. However, since migrant communities can be conservative, the "re-appearance" of some "old" cultural traits in a community may be an indication of return migration. In this case, migrants coming back home bring some of the old traditions back to the systemic level. Although apparently trivial, the study of return migration is important because return migrations can produce a number of social and cultural changes that can have a major impact in the community. Return migrant populations, for example, can produce major changes in the distribution of wealth and prestige in a society. They can also control some wealth, esoteric knowledge, and exotic artifacts that by their foreign nature impart some status and aura to the owners. Thus, the study of return migration can provide us with critical information to understand the "articulation between return migrants and home communities" (Anthony 1990:904), and possible explanation for sudden changes in community patterns.

CULTURAL AND SOCIAL CONSEQUENCES OF MIGRATION

Up to now the discussion has emphasized aspects of migration present before and during the movement of people. However, the process of migration can produce many social and cultural consequences that can last for long periods of time after the actual migration, and that can change markedly the nature of societies. Traditionally, the consequences of migration have been viewed as depending only on the nature of the new settlement (either colonization or settling in an area already occupied) and the size of the migrant group (e.g., Rouse 1986; Willey et al. 1956). When colonization is the case, no social or cultural consequence other than founder effect and divergence evolution is argued for. However, when two cultures come in contact as a result of migration, the most common type of expectation in traditional studies of migration is that a relationship of dominance or conflict must develop (e.g., Rouse 1986; Willey et al. 1956). If the migrant population is relatively small, it will be acculturated into the dominant and larger culture quite rapidly, leaving little archaeological evidence behind. If the newcomers are a relatively large population, however, they will eventually either acculturate the local communities, eradicate them, or push them out (Rouse 1986:12). In retrospect, it is now known that these views are overtly simplistic and overtly reliant on outdated theoretical premises or untested "common sense." Social scientists now know that human behavior, especially in situations of contact among cultural groups, is less predictable and more complex than these outdated views suggest.

Generally speaking, migration can have a major impact on the social and cultural structures of at least the three communities involved. The first one is the parent community. As mentioned before, emigration can cause great demographic changes in a community having an impact on aspects such as availability of labor and mating partners, and in the fertility, mortality, and growth rates of the population. In cases of social stratification, the emigration of a large group of people can effectively take away the demographic support needed by the elite to maintain power, leading eventually to the collapse of the polity. In other words, people can vote with their feet. Migration can also relieve some "population" pressure due to internal conflict or a reduction in the availability of resources.

The second population is the migrant population composed of those who leave the parent community. In many cases these communities can begin their own settlement, although in others they can be established in settlements of the local population. In both cases the migrant population cannot necessarily be considered a representative sample of the original population. Instead, migrant groups most often represent a narrow segment of the original social group, whose composition may be defined by age, sex, or social position (Anthony 1990; Clark 1986). Archaeologically, migrant groups may carry only a restricted range of artifact types leading to an artifactual "founder effect." In the case of colonization, these "founding" cultural traits can be combined with innovations to create relatively quickly a cultural tradition that archaeologically looks markedly different from that of the original group. The rate of change, nevertheless, depends on a number factors, one of which is the strength of the relationship between the migrant population and the parent community. Larger-scale colonizing groups that are broadly representative of the parent community may maintain their original cultural traditions for much longer periods of time, because the impact of innovation is reduced by the large number of original cultural traditions present.

The picture can be very different if the migrant group settles with or near an already established community. Migrant group size and its relationship with the surrounding community influence the extent to which it will maintain its original identity. If small families or extended family groups join existing communities, they are unlikely to express their identity in language, or in overt material culture beyond the threshold of the home. Some degree of assimilation or acculturation is likely to occur. Larger migrant groups may still experience limited acculturation and may maintain their own identity or ethnicity on several cultural or social institutions such as language, rituals, and technological style (Clark 2001). The degree to which a migrant group maintains its ethnic or any other cultural identity depends on the relationship between the migrant group and the local population. If the group identity is critical for the survival or benefit of the social group, the migrant population will tend to be culturally conservative. This stands in contrast to other situations in which the material culture of the migrant community, which is likely to endure substantial changes, depending on the particular conditions of migration, settlement, and acculturation.

Among migrant groups, changes can occur also at the level of social organization. Specifically, migration provides a context and dynamics for the development of status differences within the migrant community. For example, some of the earliest migrant kin groups typically emerge as "apex families." Their position is established as they provide housing, supplies, advice, and referrals to more recent migrants from the parent community; they become important integrators of new migrants. As the community becomes more established, the status acquired by these families may become more permanent, developing a form of status differentiation.

Interestingly, migrant families or populations might enjoy increased prestige or status in their community of origin by acquiring esoteric knowledge, exotic artifacts, and/or simply living in geographically far-away places. Helms (1979, 1988, 1993) has argued that geographic distance in many societies is considered similar to cosmological distance, and access to materials and knowledge from far-away distances can be equaled to access to the numen. The effect is intensified if migrants learn some technology or craft not available in their place of origin or if they accumulate great wealth. This aspect becomes particularly significant in the case of return migration. Through the gathering of detailed data, this aspect should be identifiable archaeologically, especially in the case of return migration.

A third community affected by migration is the local population already established in the region. Large-scale immigration is expected to have a considerable impact on the local population. Besides the obvious effects on the reproductive capacity of the population, the influx of a large number of people can provide a wider and stronger demographic and economic (in the form of labor) base of support to the community. New relations have to be established between the migrant and the receiving populations, including marital patterns and the organization of space. In some cases, fictive kinship relations can develop. Furthermore, new migrants can promote the establishment of a new or more pronounced social stratification where the local population might see them as socially inferior. In these cases, migrants are seen as a source of cheap labor or possibly as mercenaries. Yet migrants may also be considered as the carriers of esoteric supernatural, or exotic technological knowledge, in which case they may assume a prestigious rank.

An interesting situation arises when two or more cultures that practice significantly different economic strategies, such as agriculture and forager groups, come into contact. The traditional view (e.g., Rouse 1986; Willey et al. 1956) is that the more technologically "advanced" culture, in this case the agriculturists, will assume a dominant role and either acculturate, eradicate, or drive away the less developed culture, in this case the hunter-gatherers. This view grew from outdated "colonialist" theoretical perspectives according to which the more "developed" culture (i.e., Western nation) dominated the "simpler" and more "primitive" society. Unfortunately, the use of this perspective implies that migrations of cultures in ancient times almost resemble an expanding empire, with the dominant culture absorbing or physically eliminating the less developed culture. This perspective also has been extended in a post hoc manner to explain the instances in which both cultures practiced similar economic strategies, but came to be one seen as more "advanced" because of a stratified social organization or a centralized political structure.

However, several ethnographic and ethnohistoric studies have demonstrated that these situations are more complex than expected. While the specific type of relationship between migrant and local communities is going to depend on many factors such as the social organization and land ownership of both groups and the existence of some relationship prior to migration, many of the registered cases show that the expected conflictive or confrontational relations were not present. In many instances when hunter-gatherers and agriculturists came in contact, they developed some type of "symbiotic" relationship. For example, the Mbuti from Central Africa, despite disliking the recently migrated agriculturist groups, established and maintained a relationship with them (Turnbull 1962). The Mbuti provided labor and products from the forest, while the farmers provided cultivation and trade products. A similar type of relationship has been reported for Gran Quivira in the Southwest by Spielmann (1991a, 1991b; see also papers in Spielmann 1991). In this case, Pueblo people (farmers) exchanged agricultural products with Plains Indians (hunter-gatherers) for hunting products, especially buffalo meat and skin. Cornejo B. and Sanhueza R. (2003) have also reported an archaeological case for foragers' and cultivators' interaction in central Chile. In fact, as was mentioned before, if the migrant group normally has had some previous interaction with local groups (e.g., trade) prior to the movement, then, at least initially, the relationship must have been somewhat friendly. This is especially true if the migrant group needs the assistance of the local group to survive. Ironically, this is true, also, for colonial enterprises, where the early outposts established by empires are highly dependent on local products of the more "primitive" groups (e.g., see Deagan 1998). I am not trying to say that conflictive or confrontational interactions between migrant and local groups never happened. It possibly happened in many instances, as well as acculturation and transculturation. However, my argument is that we should not assume any type of relationship; instead, it should be determined empirically by considering all the evidence.

DETECTING MIGRATIONS ARCHAEOLOGICALLY

The archaeological identification of migrations can be difficult, requiring the kind of data that are not easily obtained. We have noted that different kinds of evidence can be used as sources of information on particular aspects of migrations such as migrant group size and composition, colonization, return migration, and the decision to migrate. This section concentrates particularly on the archaeological identification of migrations and migrant groups. While most of the methods included in this section are not applied in the discussion of Caribbean migrations in the next chapter, some methodological procedures are discussed here in detail to (1) provide a methodological framework to evaluate and assess the identification of migrations in the Caribbean, (2) to provide perspectives other than Rouse's on how to detect migrations, and (3) to show the complexity of the process of identification and the usefulness of fine-grained studies on material culture.

Once a group migrates to a new region their material culture can change relatively fast, even in cases of primary colonization. In others, migrant communities can be extremely conservative, retaining strongly only some aspects of the culture of their homeland. The relationship between migration and culture change is very complex and is influenced by a number of factors. Processes of acculturation, transculturation, founder effect, innovation, and divergence evolution are only a few of the factors involved in the rate and nature of culture change. To this we can add cultural and social processes such as the development of social stratification, ethnogenesis or any other new social or cultural identity, and changes in marital and kinship rules due to demographic issues. Population size and structure, fertility, and mortality are also factors that can influence the rate of culture change.

In some cases, migrant groups may conserve material culture traits from their original culture for extended periods of time. When this happens the most obvious traits and artifact types that allow the migration route to be traced from the spatial and temporal distribution of these archaeological materials are retained. This is the case of the Saladoid migration, discussed in the

Migration, Colonization, and Cultural Change / 57

next chapter. However, in most cases, tracing archaeologically the migrant populations, their place of origin, and their migration route is not an easy task. For many of the reasons presented in this chapter—founder effect, assimilation, acculturation, transculturation, and innovation—the material culture of migrant groups can change in less than a generation. Thus, in order to define and trace migration waves, it is necessary for archaeologists to develop a methodological approach that can ensure the identification of migrants versus local populations in a variety of situations, and ideally determine their place of origin. This task can be very difficult even with the methods available currently for archaeologists. In this discussion I contrast two approaches that have been developed for detecting prehistoric migrations. The first is the one developed by Rouse (1986), which I use as an example of a traditional approach. The second one is the approach developed mainly by Clark (2001), although I may add some points or suggestions raised by Duff (1998) and Anthony (1990).

A problem that keeps arising in using Rouse has to do with the homogeneity of the cultural units that migrate. In Rouse's system, we recall, the basic temporal and spatial divisions that make up the chart of cultural chronology have to be "made culturally as homogeneous as possible . . . " with " . . . each combination of the two of them [space and time], in the form of local period, [containing] a different people and culture" (Rouse 1986:7; the brackets are mine). The implication of Rouse's model is that only one culture or people can be present in one region at a time; thus, no two contemporary cultures or complexes can coexist in the same location. The problem arises when the migrant group encounters an already established group in the place of destination. Following Rouse's methodology, one of the groups either has to be eradicated or acculturated, a premise that, as we have seen, is not necessarily true. This may also explain the difficulties he had attempting to explain some phenomena such the discoveries of La Hueca complex during the early Ceramic Age in the Caribbean. This case raises the possibility of two culturally different groups migrating more or less at the same time and settling next to each other.

A second issue is that for Rouse, the basic unit of migration is culture or other supracultural units, and not actual social units or groups of people. This, combined with the issue of homogeneity, points toward an assumption that cultures are "pure" and can be easily identified in the archaeological record unless they are influenced by diffusion from other groups. When diffusion reaches an extreme, then acculturation and transculturation take place, in the course of which "one people adopts the culture of another people, thereby losing its separate identity" (Rouse 1986:13). It seems that Rouse considers these two processes, migration and acculturation, to be unrelated to each other, and approaches them as an either/or situation. He seems not to consider the possibility of both of them acting together and complicating in significant ways the empirical process of identifying and defining human migrations.

A third issue is Rouse's decision to omit what he calls social norms and to consider solely cultural norms. The main reason for him doing this is that "social structures leave fewer material traces in the ground than do cultures" (Rouse 1986:4). But, by ignoring these aspects Rouse leaves out of his methodological approach important social and individual factors. If it is agreed that most aspects of migration can be considered social actions, then methodologically Rouse's approach omits critical aspects, making his procedures questionable.

In general, the methodology proposed by Rouse is particularly designed to deal with very broad issues of migration and colonization but not with many of the smaller-scale issues presented so far in this chapter, especially the social dynamics of the process of migration. Particularly, this methodology is designed to detect only a few types of migration, specifically ones in which the migrant community retains many of the cultural norms of their place of origin. Migration is a very complex process, not simply an event where people A just moved from point 1, colonized point 2, and X number of years later, they or their descendants decided to move to point 3, where they eradicated people B. In order to study migration as a process and consider many of the issues, aspects, and factors, archaeologists have to develop a specific methodology based on strong theoretical grounds to collect the detailed data that will enable us to create realistic working hypotheses and test them.

Recent archaeological studies on migration have been developing new methods to study the multiple dimensions of the migration process. In many of these cases they have concentrated on migrant groups that move to areas already settled by other peoples, particularly in the American Southwest (e.g., Clark 2001; Duff 1998; see also other papers in Spielmann 1998). However, some examples of primary colonization can be found in the literature, as well (e.g., Dewar 1995; Graves and Addison 1995; Moore 2001; Smith 1995). In general, the newer studies indicate that migrations can be detected through the appearance of new artifact forms or series of attributes or designs within a region that have precedents outside that region. Because of the differences in material culture evident from site to site, the detection of migration in the archaeological record can be somewhat case-specific. But even then, several general patterns can be recommended for directing studies of migration in different regions. One basic cautionary note, as Rouse warns us, is not to confuse migration with other processes such as acculturation and independent development that can produce similar patterns of intrusive material, making the presence of alien artifacts insufficient proof. While Rouse has recommended the use of information provided from other disciplines to solve this dilemma, Clark (2001) has recommended the use of more refined studies of material culture, particularly those that can distinguish between behaviors that produce artifact patterns that can be used to track migration and those that produce patterns that can be mistaken for migration.

After considering several options (ethnicity, trade, and emulation), Clark suggests the use of evidence of *enculturation* to track migrations, since it normally embodies common frameworks for transmitting cultural knowledge from one generation to the next. This knowledge, especially unconscious aspects, represents a shared tradition that in many cases is more stable than ethnicity itself and more resistant to assimilation and acculturation than do other symbols of identity. In order to measure this archaeologically, Clark makes use of stylistic theory developed by Carr (1995a, 1995b) and follows the suggestion that attributes with low physical and contextual visibility are more stable through time, less subject to careful scrutiny and self-reflection, less likely to be imitated or emulated, and reflect a shared settlement history and a common enculturative background. Thus, differences of these attributes are the result of stylistic or cultural drift between noninteracting groups. Following Carr's line of thinking he concludes that the more fundamental and mundane the artifact or characteristic, the more likely it is to passively reflect enculturative background. After comparing various "mundane" types of material culture among several ethnographic cases of migrant groups, he came up with the following material markers to identify cultural groups in diverse settings:

1. Textile manufacture (nondecorative steps)
2. Domestic architecture layout and spatial organization
3. Foodway preferences
4. Ceramic manufacture (nondecorative steps)
5. Construction of domestic installations
6. Wall and roof construction techniques

Interestingly, several pieces of evidence used traditionally in archaeology to identify ethnic groups produced less than acceptable results. Some of these types of data are burial practices, personal ornamentation, decorative techniques and designs, and projectile points. Decorative techniques and designs are of special interest for the Caribbean since ceramic decoration is par excellence the main trait used by many archaeologists to identify ethnic groups and, by default, migrations.

Of all the markers that produced acceptable results, foodway preference and ceramic manufacture are the only ones that can be assessed in the Caribbean with the information available to date. However, a growing body of evidence is becoming more accessible that will allow the assessment in the future of domestic architecture layout and spatial organization and the construction of domestic installations.

TOWARD AN ANTHROPOLOGICAL THEORY OF MIGRATION

Migration is of necessity woven into every Caribbeanist's perspective on the history of this island archipelago. Population movements began at least 5,000 years ago and continue into the present. Unfortunately, the view that became prevalent in academic circles in the mid-twentieth century of migration as an event has had the effect of clouding the historical studies and slowing work on reconstructing the narrative of the population movement of ancient societies or cultures. A recent example indicates the prevalence that migration-as-event still has on researchers' perspective on past population movements:

> Native American colonization of the West Indian archipelago was fraught with uncertainties. These early colonists faced distant ocean voyages to islands with unfamiliar plants and animals. They did not know whether they would find resources they were accustomed to using in sufficient quantities to sustain life. All of the resources they required for food, medicine, and the raw materials for construction of tools, equipment, shelter, and clothing had to be met by the plants and animals of the island, its surrounding waters, and whatever was imported" [Wing and Wing 1995:120].

As implied from this not uncommon statement on the Caribbean, the prevailing view of migration in the region is almost anecdotal, where one day a group of people for whatever reason decided to move without going through a decision-making process. They packed their belongings, loaded their canoes and went in search of a new home without any previous knowledge of where they were going. Little is said about the process of decision making, information gathering, and reasons for migrating. The view of migration in most archaeological studies does not take into consideration the multiple and complex social dimensions involved in this process. The result is an incomplete and, on some occasions, distorted narrative of migration in the Caribbean.

This chapter has sought to counter the view of migration as event by detailing its strongly processual character, then by placing migration within a larger narrative of cultural change resulting from population movements. A great number of factors and dimensions—social, political, economic, ecological, and ideological—have to be considered in order to understand migration as process. While this complexity makes it very difficult to predict specific migrational behavior, some general patterns and decision-making sequences do emerge. As Anthony (1990:896) has noted, "[f]rom a processual perspective, examining constraints and regularities in longer-term patterns of behavior, migration can be viewed as a process that tends to develop in a broadly predictable manner once it begins." Thus, whereas the characteristics of a migration may be specific to the individual case, once migrations are under way, regularities emerge in how the subsequent course of the migration plays out.

By emphasizing the social and demographic side of migration, I have tried in this chapter to provide a relatively complete, alternative view to the traditional view. Based on the theoretical and archaeological evidence, I believe that migration is a social process that includes a number of factors and occurs within a cultural context. Thus, by emphasizing the cultural context and virtually ignoring social factors, traditional approaches to migration leave out important pieces of the puzzle. Without these pieces, our potential as social scientists to understand and explain this type of behavior and its impact in the cultural and social history of a group is limited. This is not a trivial issue, because once these omitted pieces are included in our analysis a new and more complete narrative of migration and its impact on population can be reconstructed. This new kind of narrative may help resolve, or at least cast in a new light, many ongoing debates in Caribbean archaeology. Other debates may prove to be insignificant. This may be the case for La Hueca and the Archaic-Saladoid interaction. Some of these issues and debates are discussed in the next chapter in the context of two of the "migrations" more directly related to Puerto Rico.

4 / Ancient Migrations in Puerto Rico

Issues and Possible Explanations

Due to the nature of islands, migration and colonization are major topics that have been present not only in Caribbean archaeology but also in studies of islands throughout the world. In the case of the Caribbean, archaeologists and historians have proposed at least five major migrations or colonizations: (1) the Archaic colonizations of the islands, (2) the Saladoid–La Hueca migration, mostly to the Lesser Antilles and Puerto Rico, (3) the Ostionoid expansion from Puerto Rico to the Greater Antilles and northern Lesser Antilles, (4) the colonization of the Bahamas, and (5) the supposed Carib migration before 1492. Only two of these migrations are discussed more intensively in this chapter: the Saladoid–La Hueca migration and the Ostionoid expansion. The main approach in this discussion is to focus on many of the issues related to the processes of migration and colonization from the perspective presented in the previous chapter. However, in many instances the information necessary to discuss some aspects of the structure of migration process or to reach some viable conclusions is not available, and only working hypotheses are suggested in these instances. Since the amount and type of information at hand in each of the two case studies (i.e., the Saladoid–La Hueca migration and the Ostionoid expansion) are not comparable, different issues will be discussed in each example. In the case of the Saladoid migration, I am particularly interested in addressing issues related to the social processes and consequences involved in these migrations. In the case of the Ostionoid expansion, I focus on processes other than migration that can help explain this swift movement of cultural traits. I argue that in order to understand the processes and dynamics involved in both cases, we have to gain a better understanding of the role of Archaic populations before, during, and after these developments.

THE SALADOID–LA HUECA MIGRATION

In the Caribbean some researchers have suggested the possibility of at least two migrations during the early Ceramic Age, the Saladoid and La Hueca migrations. Both migrations are seen as originating in the continent although admittedly in different regions (Chanlatte Baik 1981; Chanlatte Baik and Narganes Storde 1983, 1985; see also Keegan 1995). It should be mentioned, however, that not all Caribbeanists agree that these assemblages actually represent two different cultural groups, and by default they are not two different migrations. Several archaeologists still argue that La Hueca materials, even though they are somewhat different, still should be considered part of the Saladoid series, perhaps as a different subseries or style as suggested by Rouse (1992). However, recent lithic analyses (Rodríguez Ramos 2001a, 2001b), combined with the enormous amount of ceramic, subsistence, and settlement-pattern data, have convinced me that these two assemblages represent two different groups of people above the level of style, and perhaps subseries or series. Although more discussion is needed to determine the level of distinction, I temporarily treat these two archaeological cultures as markedly different. In this book the archaeological remains that some people have called La Hueca complex (Curet 2003; Oliver 1999) are considered as a different cultural tradition from the Saladoid styles.

For the purpose of this study, however, it is irrelevant if this interpretation changes in the future or not, since the issue of migration is treated at the social level, and not at the cultural level. The important point here is that we are dealing with two different social groups that interacted with each other in several islands of the Caribbean and who may have migrated together or separately to occupy the same locations. On the one hand, the fact that in the Lesser Antilles the artifact assemblages of these two groups appear to be mixed in the same deposits (Hofman and Hoogland 1999) while in Puerto Rico and Vieques they are spatially segregated does not necessarily mean that we are dealing with the same or different people. It rather suggests that diverse types of interactions existed between both of them. More interesting is that early Saladoid sites have been found in several of the Lesser Antilles without a considerable contribution of La Hueca material (Watters and Petersen 1999), indicating that not only the degree of interaction should be studied but also the presence or absence of evidence of interaction. On the other hand, no site containing solely La Hueca materials (i.e., without Saladoid deposits) has been discovered, yet. Thus, more studies considering a variety of behavioral models are needed to explain this diversity in archaeological assemblages.

Summarizing, the important issue for this study is the presence of early Saladoid and La Hueca people (social groups, not cultures) in many islands of the Caribbean spanning from Venezuela to Puerto Rico. The migration evidence suggests three possibilities in terms of the relation between the Saladoid and the La Hueca people. The first one is that in some instances Saladoid groups of people migrated alone and did not interact closely with the La Hueca people. The second is that some Saladoid and La Hueca groups migrated and settled in a new site together. This situation implies a strong interaction between both groups, but their relationship may have varied from site to site; sometimes living together, as the tantalizing evidence from the Lesser Antilles shows, while in others they settled next to each other in discrete spaces. Finally, it is possible that in some occasions one group migrated first followed by the other shortly thereafter. In this case, following the patterns discussed above—that people do not normally migrate to places they do not have information of—it can be assumed that the interaction was present since at least before the movement of the second group. Moreover, these three possibilities are not mutually exclusive at the level of the Caribbean, and all three could have taken place at different places and times, depending on the conditions of the social interactions between both local communities, not styles, subseries, or series. One problem with these arguments is that no consideration is given to the effect or role of the local populations that inhabited some of the locations prior the Saladoid-Huecoid migration, the Archaic people. This issue is discussed in several places in this section.

While these suggestions are plausible at a theoretical level, they are difficult to test at an empirical level for a number of reasons. First, there is more ample information available for the Saladoid people than for the La Hueca. Second, even for the cases where information is available the type of data is more directed to cultural and ethnic issues that tend not to be appropriate for dealing with social issues (i.e., very few domestic units have been investigated, burial data and osteological studies are sparse, intrasite distribution of features and artifacts, etc.). Finally, the margins of error of our chronometric techniques (i.e., radiocarbon dating) are too coarse to distinguish between contemporary events and events that happened sequentially but close to each other in time. Nevertheless, by looking at certain broad and general patterns in migration trends discussed in Chapter 3, several suggestions and working hypotheses can be proposed. Because of the amount of information available for Saladoid sites, however, this discussion is skewed against the La Hueca migrations.

Despite the drawbacks of Rouse's approach to migrations, he was considerably successful in tracking the Saladoid population movement from the Middle Orinoco all the way to Puerto Rico and other parts of the coast of South America. There are two main reasons for his success despite the methodological problems already mentioned. The first one is that while his approach is not comprehensive and uses the wrong units of analysis or observation, it is designed mostly to detect migrations that are inherently clear-cut cases such as island migration. Cases that involve more complex issues and different mechanisms of culture change are more difficult, if not impossible, to detect with Rouse's approach. The second one is that he used ceramics as the main marker of migrations, a type of material culture not present in most of the islands before the Saladoid migration. While it is possible that the Archaic and Saladoid people's interaction may have included some form of transculturation, affecting in this manner their material culture and somewhat "blurring" the evidence for migration, pottery was probably one of the least affected types of artifacts. This is so, because the Archaic people did not adopt this technology in a considerable manner at that time. A conclusion from this is that future studies interested in the interaction between the early ceramic and Archaic groups should concentrate on studying material culture other than ceramics, such as subsistence remains, stone, bone, and shell artifacts.

In addition to Rouse's arguments on how and when the Saladoid and Huecoid migrations took place, some suggestions have been developed to explain the causes of migration from the continental, lowland tropical forest to the islands (Goodwin 1979, 1980; Keegan 1985; Roe 1989; Siegel 1991a). Although these models disagree with each other on the process of migration, they concur on the causal factor: social and environmental circumscription or competition for resources in an increasingly crowded Orinoco Basin. None of these models, however, has been systematically tested using archaeological data from either the Orinoco Basin or any Caribbean island. Considering that population density was extremely low compared to later times, it is difficult to visualize that population-resource imbalance or circumscription had that much of an impact in local populations or in the decision for migration (see also Heckenberger 2002). Another reason has been suggested by Rouse (1986, 1992), where he argued that the development of the subsequent Barrancoid series in the Middle Orinoco encroached on the Saladoid people, forcing them to move down river and eventually along the continental coast and the islands. A problem with this suggestion is that, to the best of my knowledge, no strong evidence has been reported for warfare or any kind of interethnic conflict in this region. However, it should be recognized that most studies of Saladoid-Barrancoid interaction in the Orinoco Basin and in the southern Lesser Antilles have focused almost exclusively on ceramic attributes, while little attention has been paid to site structures and features. Future research that expands their interests to other areas of the archaeological record may produce better information on the possibility of conflictive or peaceful relationships between these two groups. On this topic, Heckenberger (2002) has suggested that reasons for the Arawak diaspora in South America, which includes the Saladoid migration to the islands, were probably produced not so much by economic factors or population pressure but by political and social motivations of factions or emerging elites. However, while I tend to agree with his general perspective, we do not have the contextual data to test this suggestion.

Keegan (1985), estimating populations and population growth rates, has suggested that the migration was rather fast, an argument that has been supported by the relatively early dates in the northernmost end of the migration wave. Haviser (1997:68) also noticed that many of the earlier dates for Saladoid sites concentrate on the northeastern Caribbean giving the impression that early Saladoid–La Hueca people targeted this area intentionally as their place of destination. If true, this has major implications in the interpretation of the migration data for the early Ceramic Age in the Caribbean. This would tend to imply that these early migrants had previous information about the region and knew where they were going, and that probably they were intentionally targeting a particular region, two aspects that were predicted by the cross-cultural comparative approach presented in Chapter 3. To be able to accomplish this, both the Saladoid and La Hueca people had to have a considerable amount of information about these islands in order to make the decision to move there and to know what to expect once settled. In general, the only ways of acquiring this information would have been through exploring expeditions, fishing or hunting trips, trade or some other kind of interaction with the people already inhabiting the region, the Archaic people, or through a combination of all of them.

One problem with these early dates is that it is unclear how many of them represent colonies or fully established migrant settlements and how many of them represent seasonal location of "scouts" in the form of traders, fishing, or gathering groups. In other words, it is possible that some of the early dates from Saladoid–La Hueca settlements may belong to a time when these locations were used as seasonal "camps" or temporary settlements in their interaction with the insular Archaic groups before the actual migration. Due to the traditional view of treating migration as an event, this possibility has never been considered in the Caribbean before for the Saladoid–La Hueca migration. Contextual data to distinguish between these early, ephemeral incursions, and later serious settling attempts are not available to date.

Unfortunately, for a variety of reasons we have very little understanding of the Archaic cultures in the Lesser Antilles and Puerto Rico. For example, the evidence for Archaic sites in the Lesser Antilles, critical to understand this issue, is sparse and with few exceptions (i.e., Davis 2000; Hofman and Hoogland 2003; Lundberg 1991; Walker 1980), it has been poorly studied. Archaic sites are difficult to find and on many occasions they may have been destroyed by changes in sea level or recent cultural activities (i.e., plowing, modern development). Once found, Archaic sites produce relatively few artifacts in proportion to the large amount of faunal remains. Moreover, generalizations about the Archaic culture in the Lesser Antilles is difficult because of the differential intensity in which the different islands have been studied. Despite the scarcity of information, the evidence at hand shows an almost complete absence of Archaic sites in the southern Lesser Antilles and a relative abundance of such sites in the northern islands, including Puerto Rico (Keegan 1994:266–267).

Interestingly, the locations of the early Saladoid–La Hueca dates in the islands considerably overlap with the distribution of Archaic sites in the region. The fact that the early Saladoid–La Hueca groups settled in areas with relatively higher density of Archaic sites such as Puerto Rico and the Virgin Islands seems to indicate that some serious and perhaps strong relationship was present between the Archaics and the Saladoid people prior to and after the movement of the latter. Although Rouse (1992:69–70) suggested the possible existences of this relationship before the Saladoid migration occurred, to a certain point this contradicts what he has speculated for decades about the nature of the interaction between the Saladoid and the Archaic after the former "invaded" the islands of the latter. For some time now, Rouse (1986, 1992) has hypothesized that once the Saladoid culture migrated to the islands they either pushed, eradicated, or absorbed the Archaic culture. Even though these conclusions were based on unfounded assumptions or "common sense" they have been repeated and perpetuated by innumerable researchers without providing the necessary confirming evidence (e.g., Keegan 1991:441; Roe 1995:163; Siegel 1989:205). However, when evidence of the migration process (not just the event) is considered, another picture emerges where these two groups interacted in a nonconflictive way.

Thus, while direct evidence is not available, the chronology and distribution of early Saladoid communities indicates that they may have been interacting in some ways with Archaic groups before they migrated to the islands. It is possible that this interaction followed previous Archaic migrations and interaction routes that the Saladoid may have learned from other continental Archaic groups as they met in the delta of the Orinoco River. Interestingly, Rouse (1964a) has argued that it was in the continental coast and through their interaction with the local Archaic groups that the Saladoid people learned seafaring. Hence, the Saladoid learned the marine way of life from continental Archaic groups. Although I do not think that the interaction between these two groups was that simple, the possibility of relationship on the continent makes the idea of a nonconflictive interaction with of other Archaic groups in the islands very plausible.

The peaceful interaction between primarily foraging societies and cultivating groups is nothing new or uncommon. Both the ethnohistoric and ethnographic records are full of examples where, once they come in contact, hunter-gatherers and cultivators tend to establish amicable relationships, which in some instances are described as a "symbiotic" relationship (Spielmann 1991a, 1991b; see also Cornejo B. and Sanhueza R. 2003 for an archaeological example). In many of these cases, foragers provide some wild products to farmers, while farmers provide some cultivated products to the former.

The lack of evidence for systematic conflict or warfare also undermines Rouse's arguments about the fate of the Archaic groups. To the best of my knowledge, there is no evidence of the construction of defensive structures such as palisades, or changes in settlement patterns where strategic positions are favored over other locations. In addition, while the burial data is much more abundant for Saladoid settlements than for Archaic sites, there are very few indications of physical violence (e.g., broken arms, evidence for blows on head, etc.) in the osteological remains (for example, see Crespo Torres's osteological analysis of the human remains from Punta Candelero and Paso del Indio [2000] and Tibes [1998]). Interestingly, Heckenberger (2002) has argued recently that peaceful migration to new regions is one of the landmark features of what is known as the Arawak diaspora (migration of Arawak groups throughout the South American continent and the Caribbean).

Another phenomenon that the traditional perspective has not been able to explain satisfactorily, but that can be better explained by this Archaic-Saladoid interaction, is the reasons for the apparent cessation of the Saladoid migration in Puerto Rico. Rouse and others have argued that the Saladoid migration stopped in Puerto Rico because of the "formidable" Archaic population in Hispaniola. According to them, the high density of Archaic groups in this latter island would have either discouraged or defeated any attempt to "invade" it. This argument has two major flaws. The first one is the actual question. The fact that the question is why the migration stopped is assuming that the migration had a mind of itself and that the Saladoid groups were going to keep expanding for no reason whatsoever. In general, this gives the impression that the traditional view considers the Saladoid migration like an expansionist state or empire, instead of small, autonomous communities that somehow interacted forming the Saladoid archaeological culture. Even if it is agreed that they were forced to migrate to the islands due to push factors such as population pressure or pressure from other groups, it still has to be explained why it is assumed that these groups had the inevitable urge to keep moving west until they were stopped by another "push" force, the Archaic populations from Hispaniola.

The second flaw has to do with the assumptions of the differences between Archaic and Saladoid groups in military terms. Population and population density in this argument are important since it is assumed that both groups had similar military technology, and any possible advantage of either group had to be at the demographic level. So, the number of warriors would have been a determinant factor in the face of conflict. While it is possible that Hispaniola had a larger number of Archaic people and higher population densities than other islands to the east and southeast, in terms of absolute number of people Puerto Rico and several of the Lesser Antilles most probably also had larger populations than any migrant, Saladoid group. Considering that many migrant groups tend to be relatively small compared to established communities, there is no reason to believe that the first Saladoid groups to arrive on the beaches of the Lesser Antilles and Puerto Rico were larger than the Archaic groups that already inhabited these islands, independently of their population density. It is highly improbable that the Saladoid people arrived with an army-type of group "conquering" the early inhabitants of the islands.

It will be interesting if future studies can determine in some ways the size and composition of the early migrant Saladoid groups.

An alternative explanation of the apparent cessation of the Saladoid migration in Puerto Rico is that this region (the northeastern area of the Caribbean) might have been their intentional target destination; thus, they stopped in this region because this is where they wanted to go and settle. To a certain point this argument, again, is linked to the one presented before on the strong relationship between Archaic and Saladoid people, where the latter decided to move to Puerto Rico and adjacent areas because of their already established relationship with the Archaic groups from these islands, and from whom they acquired, directly or indirectly, the information needed to make the decision to move or not. While this does not explain the reasons for the migration of Saladoid people to the northeast Caribbean, it does explain many of the issues dealing with their migration process. This explanation is strengthened by the fact that it uses the premises of modern anthropological theory on migration based on cross-cultural generalizations discussed in Chapter 3. Most interesting is that by considering the different stages of the process of migrations, alternative explanations can be reached for certain issues where the traditional view has not been able to provide definite answers.

The suggestion of the existence of a close relationship between the Archaic and the Saladoid migrants prior, during, and after the population movement is supported by the few pieces of evidence we have available from some Archaic sites from Puerto Rico. While some extremely early Archaic sites have been found in Puerto Rico (i.e., earlier than 2000 B.C.; Ayes [1989]; Moscoso [1999]; Rodríguez [1997, 1999]), others have produced dates that are contemporaneous with or later than the earlier dates available for the Saladoid migration to this island. The Cueva María de la Cruz in the northeastern coast of Puerto Rico has provided two noncalibrated dates of A.D. 30 ± 120 and A.D. 40 ± 100 (Alegría et al. 1955; Rouse and Alegría 1990). This site is interesting because Cueva María de la Cruz is located a few hundred meters from the site of Hacienda Grande, the site type for the early Saladoid style in Puerto Rico. The earliest date obtained for the Hacienda Grande style at this site is 110 B.C. ± 70, strongly suggesting that both Archaic and Saladoid groups lived next to each other for hundreds of years. The archaeological material discovered in Cueva María de la Cruz is also suggestive of some type of interaction between these two groups. In this cave, for example, Saladoid pottery was discovered mixed with Archaic lithics or faunal remains in the same level (Rouse and Alegría 1990). Preliminary and general analysis of the stone artifacts from Hacienda Grande found considerable similarities on the lithic assemblages of both sites. However, little detailed lithic analysis has been performed on the assemblages to establish more accurately the nature of the relationship between both groups. Despite this overwhelming evidence, Rouse and Alegría concluded the following about the Saladoid and Archaic interaction:

> The original dates for these two sites indicate that they were occupied sequentially, the cave until the year 40 and the village site after 120, both of the Christian era. The dates subsequently obtained at Hacienda Grande make the two populations overlap for 150 years, from 110 B.C. to 40 A.D. This creates a problem. The Coroso people may well have continued to occupy parts of Puerto Rico for some time after the arrival of the Hacienda Grande people, but the two peoples *can hardly have lived side by side* at María de la Cruz and Hacienda Grande for over a hundred years. It is more likely that the Corosans abandoned the cave upon the arrival of the Hacienda Grande. . . . The median values of the dates for the cave and the village site are thus incompatible. They may be reconciled by assuming that the true values of the cave's dates are toward the lower ends of their ranges of probable variation, that is, about 75 B.C., and that the earliest date for the village site is at the upper end of its range, or around 50 B.C. Alternatively, it can be argued that one or both sets of samples were contaminated or, since neither of them was accompanied by diagnostic artifacts, that they were actually laid down during temporary occupation of the cave by villagers from Hacienda Grande" [Rouse and Alegría 1990:60; emphasis added].

Thus, for reasons that are difficult to visualize, Rouse and Alegría found it unconceivable for Archaic and Saladoid groups to coexist in the same location or nearby to each other. For them, it is easier to accept that their radiocarbon dates are wrong rather than admit that these two groups interacted in the same place. The admittance of more than one "culture" in one geographic region, however, goes against Rouse's definition of series as regions that are culturally homogeneous.

Finally, another piece of evidence is the exotic stones found in the site of Punta Candelero (Rodríguez 1991), one of the earliest La Hueca and Saladoid sites in Puerto Rico, including serpentine from western Puerto Rico and amber and chert from Hispaniola, both areas heavily inhabited by Archaic groups at this time. The presence of these stones tends to suggest some type of trading interaction between both groups after the migration of the Saladoid communities.

Another way of asking the question of why the Saladoid people stopped their migration in Puerto Rico is by asking instead why didn't they continue their migration to Hispaniola. This may be explained by arguing that the Saladoid had stronger relations with the Puerto Rican Archaic than those from Hispaniola possibly because of their differences in ancestry. Although more detailed studies are needed, the archaeological data available suggests that, at the time of the Saladoid–La Hueca migration, the Archaic people from Hispaniola may have been predominantly descendants of the early groups that may have migrated from the Yucatán peninsula, southeastern U.S., lower Central America, or the Caribbean coast of Colombia (Callaghan 2003; Veloz Maggiolo 1991, 1993; Wilson et al. 1998). Contrarily, most of the Archaics for this period in Puerto Rico seem to have descended from the early hunter-gatherer migrants that originated from the delta of the Orinoco River and Trinidad. At best, it is possible that both traditions met somewhere in Puerto Rico, possibly in its western half. Nevertheless, considering their ancestry, it is possible that, after their migrations to the islands, the Archaics from Puerto Rico and the northern Lesser Antilles had maintained some kind of interaction with groups from the South American continent. Once the Saladoid established a relationship with the latter in the coasts near the Orinoco delta, they also became part of the sphere of interaction between the Archaic groups from both regions. This interaction possibly was a conduit eventually used by Saladoid communities to collect information that led to the eventual migration, including the selection of their final destination (see also Rodríguez Ramos 2002a).

While many studies have been conducted in early Saladoid–La Hueca sites throughout the Caribbean, interestingly no one has raised the question on the rate of success of migration or how long they took to become established (Graves and Addison 1995). What is more surprising is how some of these questions have not been asked even though some of the well-known early Saladoid–La Hueca sites in the Caribbean are single-component, seemingly being abandoned well before the end of the cultural period. In Puerto Rico some of these sites are Punta Candelero in Humacao and El Convento in Old San Juan. Similar sites are also present in several of the Lesser Antilles such as La Hueca–Sorcé in Vieques, Golden Rock in St. Eustatius, the site of Morel in Guadeloupe, Hope Estate in St. Martin, Trants in Montserrat, and Prosperity in St. Thomas. This is not to say, however, that all the early Saladoid sites were abandoned during the Saladoid period since multicomponent sites can also be found such as Hacienda Grande, Maisabel, Caracoles, La Gallera, Tecla, and Cana in Puerto Rico, and Martineau in Vieques. But, the question is, why were some early settlements successful in becoming established communities while others were eventually abandoned? What conditions were present in some sites to make them long-lasting and what conditions made other sites short-lasting? Do these short-lasting communities represent colonizing attempts that failed, even though some of them lasted for several centuries? Or, do they represent early, successful settlements that later moved to better areas, after getting to know the location of social and physical resources? (See several papers in Rockman and Steele 2003.) Do all of these sites throughout the Caribbean represent a leapfrogging type of migration or few groups sequentially moving from one location to another in a matter of few generalizations?

Since the studies conducted in many of the short-lasting (single-component) Saladoid sites have concentrated in defining the cultural groups and, at best, their lifeways, the information needed to answer many of the major questions is lacking. However, we can use what we know of migrant communities and their limitations to develop some working hypotheses. Technically speaking, the early Saladoid population movements that arrived in Puerto Rico cannot be considered an initial island colonization since the island was inhabited already. Rouse (1986, 1992) has called this process repeopling (vs. peopling or colonization). Although seemingly trivial, this difference is important because the social and economic dynamics in each process can be markedly different. However, as a heuristic exercise, let us suppose that the Saladoid–La Hueca communities were actually colonizing the islands. If these groups were colonizing Puerto Rico and some of the Lesser Antilles, several factors are important in determining the success of these groups becoming well-established communities. The conditions, size, and composition of the first group(s) that arrived are critical to the final success or failure of this enterprise. As discussed before, biogeographical principles tell us that because of their nature, these groups, also known as beachheads, are extremely susceptible to stochastic or random events, especially those of catastrophic magnitude (Keegan and Diamond 1987; Moore 2001). The probabilities of success are also a function of the size of the group, the distance from the "parent" community, and the presence of other communities. Human populations have several options to mitigate these effects that other terrestrial animals do not have, such as maintaining contact with the parent community or at least one other community from a nearby island (Moore 2001) in the form of trade, exchange of marital partners, military alliances, and such. Thus, through the use of social and cultural mechanisms, relatively small migrant communities can increase their chances of survival even when their biological odds are relatively low. This is not to say that all human migrations and "colonizations" are successful, but that human communities have more strategic options than other species of animals, increasing in this way the odds of survival. In the case of the Saladoid migrant communities, these options included relationship with other Saladoid communities or with some Archaic groups. This interaction could have reduced immensely the effects of catastrophic or stochastic processes, and increased markedly the chances of survival (Moore 2001). Without the interactions with the parent community or Archaic groups, the small migrant Saladoid groups would have had a slant chance of becoming an established population. Considering the distances between islands and from the continent, the easiest interaction appears to have been at least initially with the Archaic groups rather than with the parent community, especially if they already had some type of relationship with the former before migrating.

A final issue that needs to be assessed is the demographic structure and composition of the Saladoid communities that migrated to the islands. It is difficult to assess this with the information at hand since the best type of evidence to determine sex and age distribution comes from human remains. Unfortunately, few samples with large enough sizes have been unearthed for the early Saladoid period, and even fewer of the existing ones have been studied properly. For Puerto Rico, the burials from Punta Candelero (late Saladoid), a possible failed colonization (see Chapter 7), is the best-studied osteological population of this period (Crespo Torres 2000). The information obtained from this sample can be used to compare with the results of cross-cultural studies on migrant groups and to propose some working hypotheses about the structure and composition of the Saladoid migrant groups. In fact, the burial sample from this site includes an unusual higher number of young male adults and lower number of younger and older individuals, a pattern predicted by the cross-cultural generalizations on the structure of migrant groups. This issue, however, will be discussed later in Chapter 7, when aspects of local populations are discussed.

The Saladoid–La Hueca migration is an important historical process that set the conditions for later social, political, and cultural changes, and should not be dealt with in a loose or light manner. In order to gain a better understanding of the process of their migration we have to gather more detailed and appropriate data about the actual conditions of the population movement. We have to determine more precisely, for example, the Saladoid–La Hueca–Archaic relationship. At what level did they interact, through trade of exotic materials and food, exchanging mates, and so forth? How did they influence each other in terms of cultural and social practices? How did this interaction compare with the interaction with the parent community? What were the specifics of the Saladoid migration? Did it consist of large or small groups of people? What was the structure of the groups? What kind of migration type did they follow? Were all Saladoid migrant groups related to each other? How often and what was the intensity of the interaction among the various Saladoid migrant groups? Were later Saladoid migrations related to the original migration(s), or did they represent new migration waves? Are they related to the return migration? And, what was the magnitude and impact of return migrations?

One can say correctly that instead of clarifying the narrative of this early migration the approach used here has produced more questions than answers. Although this is true in many ways, we also have to admit that by considering migration as a process and revising some of the assumptions and premises of the traditional views of migrations in the Caribbean, we are leading the narrative to becoming more complete, accurate, and realistic. In fact, instead of producing more questions, this approach has shifted the emphasis on the perspective of Caribbean migrations producing a replacement of old questions, from one focused more on culture history and culture areas, to one that stresses social processes and behaviors. Perhaps, the main contribution of this topic under this view is the role the Archaic groups and the Archaic-Saladoid interaction had in the successful migration of the Saladoid people. While the traditional view tended to assume that these groups were passive actors (or "extras") in the drama of Saladoid migration, the analogies taken from the anthropology of migrations combined with some tantalizing archaeological evidence, tends to indicate that they had a more active role in this process, perhaps even long before the canoes began to be loaded. Because the Saladoids are traditionally considered as the only origin of most of the social and cultural groups that succeeded them, the inclusion of a more dynamic role of the Archaic groups in the picture changes this panorama. Future modeling of post-Saladoid social and cultural processes will have to take into consideration the contribution by Archaic peoples to many of these issues, as suggested by other researchers (e.g., Chanlatte Baik 1986; Keegan 2000; Rodríguez Ramos

2002a). One of these sociocultural processes is the expansion of agricultural and ceramic traditions throughout the Greater Antilles and northern Lesser Antilles during the Ostionoid period.

THE OSTIONOID EXPANSION

According to the traditional view of the culture history of ancient Puerto Rico, around A.D. 600/650 the Saladoid culture gave way to a new ceramic tradition that is known in the Greater Antilles as the Ostionoid series. As with the Saladoids, the Ostionoids are seen as agricultural groups who lived in permanent villages. By this time, it is implied that all of the Archaic groups from Puerto Rico are long gone, probably because they were eradicated, assimilated, or acculturated by the earlier Saladoid groups.

While many people discuss the Ostionoid series as a cultural unit, it has to be recognized that this term hides an immense degree of diversity and variability. It contains at least four subseries and an even larger number of styles, altogether covering more than 900 years over at least Puerto Rico, Hispaniola, Jamaica, parts of Cuba, the Bahamian archipelago, and a number of the Lesser Antilles. Further, although most of the identification of Ostionoid people has been done from the perspective of the ceramic assemblages, in many instances it is difficult to determine the degree of similarity or differences between the assemblages from different islands or even within the same islands. For example, to the best of my knowledge I do not know of any formal study focusing on a stylistic comparison between the ceramics from western Puerto Rico and those from Hispaniola, the Bahamian archipelago, Cuba, and Jamaica. No one has yet determined the relationship between these different assemblages. To complicate matters even more, the term Ostionoid is not used in some of the islands such as Cuba and Hispaniola. In Cuba, these assemblages are called subtaínos and, at a superficial level, the ceramics seem to be somewhat different from the contemporary ones from Puerto Rico. Yet, it is accepted as a fact by many, including Rouse, that, with the exception of the Meillacan subseries, the early Ostionoid people developed in Puerto Rico and migrated to all of these islands.

In this section I concentrate on the Ostionan Ostionoid people that existed in western Puerto Rico, the rest of the Greater Antilles, and the Bahamian archipelago between A.D. 600 and A.D. 900. Thus, most of the discussion concentrates specifically on the spread of the Ostionan Ostionoid tradition west of Puerto Rico since this is the other major proposed migration for

Puerto Rican prehistory. Nevertheless, some of the discussion in general terms is also applicable to the expansion of the Elenan Ostionoid toward the east and southeast. Finally, it should be made clear that while I refer to the Ostionoid culture and series I am assuming that it is smaller social groups, not the whole culture, that may have migrated, interacted, and made the decisions responsible for the major changes that we detect in the archaeological record. As a point of clarification, for comparative purposes I use only uncalibrated dates, especially because Rouse's charts used extensively here were prepared using these dates.

Rouse (1964a, 1986, 1992) sees most of the Ostionoid series as emerging from the Saladoid people through culture change and eventually spreading eastward to the Virgin Islands and westward to Hispaniola, Cuba, Jamaica, and the Bahamian archipelago. The appearance of the Ostionoid people in most of the Greater Antilles, with the exception of the Meillacan Ostionoid, and some of the Lesser Antilles is seen as the resumption of the migration of farming groups from Puerto Rico into territories traditionally considered Archaic. This presumption has been repeated and adopted in one way or another by many Caribbeanists, as well (e.g., Cassá 1995; Curet 1992a, 1996; Keegan 2000; Tabío 1988; Veloz Maggiolo 1991, 1993). Contrarily, Chanlatte Baik (1986, 2000) has argued that the development of the Ostionoid series is the product of the interaction between the Archaic and the Saladoid–La Hueca people. Particularly, he suggests that the Saladoid-Archaic interaction produced what Rouse calls the Ostionan Ostionoid subseries of western Puerto Rico, while the La Hueca–Archaic interaction produced the Elenan Ostionoid on the eastern side of the same island.

The differences between these two propositions are not trivial since the selection of one over the other implies the acceptance of a series of assumptions about the social behavior and dynamics of the groups in question. In fact, the two models diametrically oppose each other in many ways. The first model assumes that by the time of the Saladoid people the Archaic populations were disappearing almost completely as a cultural group and that the Ostionoid people emerged from the Saladoid without much influence from other groups. The second model, however, assumes that the Archaic people stayed around longer than expected, and that they actually were actively interacting with the Saladoids, influencing each other in one way or another. Thus, the first model suggests that the Archaics were assimilated and had little impact (i.e., a passive role; assimilation, acculturation) on the cultural history of the Saladoid people, while from Chanlatte Baik's perspective they had a more active and dynamic role in culture change, and through the particular social and cultural process of transculturation.

Rouse's model is the most accepted one in Caribbean literature even though he presents very little evidence to support it. Contrary to his discussion of the Saladoid migration, Rouse does not test his assumption that the Ostionoid expansion actually represents a migration. Despite his insistence on evaluating multiple hypotheses simultaneously, he did not rule out the two other competing hypotheses to migration that he warned us about, acculturation and local development. The main basis of Rouse's model is the cultural situation of Hispaniola, Cuba, Jamaica, and the Bahamian archipelago at the time of contact. With few exceptions, most of the people from these islands were composed of groups that spoke a form of Arawak language originally from South America. Noble (1955) has traced the origins of this family of languages to the Central Amazon Basin and migrated up the Negro River through the Caciquiare Canal to the Middle Orinoco Basin. These languages made it up and down the river, and eventually to the delta of the Orinoco and to the islands. Using the results of glottochronology, Rouse (1986, 1992) supposedly has been able to correlate in a gross manner the changes in language with changes in the archaeological record.

Rouse's (1986) main assumption in this model is that it is possible to equate the "movements" of these languages with the migration of actual people and cultures; he argues that the Arawak people (as biological entities), their cultures, and languages migrated together. Another assumption is that the language that prevails after two cultures come in contact is the language of the "dominant" group; in this case, the survival of Arawak languages in most of the Caribbean is enough evidence that these groups either absorbed or acculturated most of the Archaic societies. Furthermore, Rouse used outdated models developed from the colonial experience of the European countries to explain culture change produced by interaction between cultures. In fact, in multiple occasions Rouse uses the European conquest of the Caribbean as analogy of earlier indigenous migrations. These "colonial" models developed during the early times of anthropology assumed that in most instances when two cultures come in contact, one of them is dominant and eventually will impose their own culture and language over the other, submissive culture. Thus, and following this way of thinking, it is possible for archaeologists to determine the particulars of the process by studying the end results since the dominant language and culture are the ones that prevailed over time. From this perspective, it seems obvious that since the Spanish encountered mostly

Arawak-speaking people with tropical forest cultures, the dominant cultures were the agricultural cultures that migrated from South America, replacing the Archaic cultures. In the case of the Ostionoid people and using the classic (colonial) model, then it was they with the culture and language inherited from the Saladoids who migrated to the rest of the Greater Antilles and to the Bahamian archipelago.

Today, however, anthropologists know that the mechanisms and dynamics involved in situations of cultural contact are more complicated than the traditional view. The traditional, classic models seem appropriate mostly (if not only) when one of the groups is an expansionist polity or society that is trying to increase their territory, but not for other situations. Unfortunately, due to the emphasis on colonial and state societies in studies of culture contact, little is known for situations when two nonstate, relatively egalitarian societies come into contact and coexist in the same region (see various papers in Cusick 1998). Nevertheless, now we know that it cannot be assumed that all situations of culture contact follow the same patterns present in colonial settings, as assumed by Rouse and other early students of culture contact (e.g., Willey et al. 1956).

Another problem with the traditional model is the idea that culture, language, and people always migrate or move together. Normally, in this type of situation we tend to underestimate the power and severity of sociohistorical processes such as emulation, ethnogenesis, transculturation, and diffusion that can produce the differential movement of culture, language, and population. This is a problem that has baffled anthropologists at least since Franz Boas's times, and little progress has been done since then. At this point, the anthropological theory of culture contact and migration cannot predict under what circumstances these three institutions will move together and under which others they will disconnect from each other (Terrell 1986, 2001). What is clear now, however, is that culture, language, and populations do not necessarily move together in every situation, especially when dealing with tribal societies where autonomous communities and even households can interact with other groups independently from the rest of their culture. This is a premise that complicates in many folds the issues of migration and culture contact and change, as it is evidenced by the case of the ancient South Pacific. In this case supposedly only two types of languages carried by two types of biological populations have resulted in an amazing and unpredictable diversity, where biology, culture, and languages have been mixed in any imaginably possible way and new trends were created (e.g., Terrell 1986; see also various papers in Terrell 2001 [editor]). Things can get even more complicated if we add the ingredients of time and localized history, where "hybrid" groups can come in contact with other "pure" or "hybrid" populations at different times and in various social and cultural conditions.

Therefore, the co-movement of language, culture, and populations cannot be assumed for all situations, and it is something that has to be determined empirically. The assumption that they all move together all the time is unfounded and can lead to the wrong conclusions. I am not suggesting here that the Ostionoid expansion did not involve the movement of people, languages, and culture together; the point is that to date this has not been proven, and that we have tended to underestimate other mechanisms (i.e., transculturation, emulation) that may have been involved, as well. It cannot be assumed that the social processes involved when two or more Caribbean, tribal, and perhaps segmentary societies came into contact are the same that are present in the cases of imperial or colonial expansion that witnessed many areas of Africa, Asia, and the Americas as a consequence of the colonial politics of European nations.

Chanlatte Baik's model (1986) is not unique and is similar to other ones proposed by several Cuban and Dominican archaeologists (e.g., Ulloa Hung 1999; Veloz Maggiolo 1991, 1993), especially under the rubric of transculturation. Unfortunately, this type of model has received little attention in the Caribbean, especially from people working in Puerto Rico and the Lesser Antilles. While Chanlatte Baik's model was presented in a very general way and without specifying the details of the social mechanisms and dynamics involved in the Saladoid–La Hueca–Archaic interaction, it proposes some possibilities that deserve more research. The model does not assume that the Archaic peoples or cultures were eradicated from Puerto Rico once the Saladoid–La Hueca people arrived on the island. On the contrary, it proposes that they came into contact with each other and established a relationship that lasted for some time, as discussed in the preceding section. From this interaction, it is proposed, the two main Ostionoid subseries developed for this time in Puerto Rico. Particularly, he argues that the Ostionoid people are no other than the Archaic groups acculturated by their contact with the Saladoid–La Hueca migrant groups that moved to Puerto Rico. The Ostionan subseries developed from the interaction between the Saladoid and the Archaic groups, while the Elenan subseries arose from the contact between La Hueca and the Archaic groups. However, once the Ostionoid formed (or Agro-III using

Chanlatte Baik's terminology), Chanlatte Baik argues that the Ostionoid expansion took place through a combination of migration of Puerto Rican Ostionoid groups to the neighboring islands and the acculturation of resident Archaics in those islands.

Beside the evidence for interaction between Saladoid–La Hueca people and Archaic groups, there is some archaeological evidence from Ostionoid deposits that tends to support this model. For example, in Puerto Rico some of the dietary preferences such as the presence of large amounts of seashells in Ostionoid deposits is a characteristic that is shared by many Archaic deposits, but not that much by the Saladoid–La Hueca assemblages (Reniel Rodríguez Ramos, personal communication). Moreover, studies performed on the stone artifacts of all groups seem to indicate that the Ostionoid groups tended to follow the Archaic lithic technology more than the one carried by the Saladoid–La Hueca people (Rodríguez Ramos 2002a, 2002b).

The model, as presented by Chanlatte Baik, however, raises several issues. First, as is the case with Rouse, Chanlatte Baik puts the interaction between all the groups at the level of culture and not at lower levels. If the Saladoid and La Hueca people were tribal societies with communities being more or less autonomous, then the interaction should have happened at the community, descent group, or even at the household level. Furthermore, Chanlatte Baik does not specify the nature and scale of the interaction; he only implies that it must have been strong enough to create some kind of cultural "hybridization." The possibility that various communities or even that the La Hueca and Saladoid cultures had different types of interactions is not raised at all, and it is implied that all interactions were similar in nature and magnitude. Also, it has not been explained how the Ostionan and Elenan subseries developed mostly on opposite ends of the island, when all the La Hueca assemblages discovered to date are always associated in one way or another to Saladoid deposits. In other words, how can the spatial separation of the two Ostionoid subseries be explained when two of the precursors were always present in the same location? Moreover, while Chanlatte Baik argues that the Ostionoid people are "acculturated" Archaics, he does not explain what happened to the Saladoid and La Hueca groups when the Archaic people "turned" into the Ostionoids. He does not consider transculturation as a possibility, where the Ostionoids emerged from a "give and take" between the Saladoid-Huecoid and the Archaic peoples. Finally, from Chanlatte Baik's writings it is difficult to determine why migration is a necessary ingredient to explain the whole process of the Ostionoid expansion. As mentioned above for the case of Rouse's model, the migration of Ostionoid people from Puerto Rico to other islands has not been tested properly.

Another suggestion, not so much to account for the development of the Ostionoid series but to explain the spread of Ostionoid pottery making in the northern Caribbean, has been proposed by Keegan (2000:150). In this paper Keegan suggests that the spread of the Ostionoid series and its diversity can be explained by a combination of diffusion, migration, and hybridization. His model starts with the diffusion of ceramic technology from the Saladoid groups from Puerto Rico to the Archaic groups of Hispaniola and possibly Cuba, creating what is referred to as the protoceramic or protoagricultural (Archaic sites containing relatively crude ceramics, see Godo [1997, 2001], Ulloa Hung [1999], Ulloa Hung and Valcárcel Rojas [2003], Veloz Maggiolo [1991, 1993], Veloz Maggiolo et al. [1993], Veloz Maggiolo et al. [1976]). Around A.D. 600, although some Chican and Meillacan modes are present since 350 B.C., this diffusion eventually led to the creation of a hybrid culture later known as Meillacan Ostionoid. At the same time, the Ostionoid series developed in Puerto Rico and began migrating, establishing "colonies" in Hispaniola, Haiti, Jamaica, Cuba, and the Bahamian archipelago. Keegan (2000:150) argues that "the speed with which this expansion took place suggests that settlements were small and widely scattered and that in some places these people interacted with the Meillacan people."

The model proposed by Keegan seems to be more realistic and plausible than the ones presented by Rouse and Chanlatte Baik to explain the Ostionoid expansion. While I agree with most aspects of the model, especially the ones dealing with interaction and transculturation between Archaic and ceramic groups, I have some reservations with some minor points. First, Keegan assumes that the interaction between the groups occurred between islands and not within Puerto Rico itself; or, the Saladoid people did not interact with the Puerto Rican Archaic groups. Second, he argues that the Ostionoid series developed directly from the Saladoid series without any apparent influence from other groups. Third, by claiming diffusion as the only process involved he sees the Archaic groups as having a passive role, where they received ceramic technology without having any effect on the donor group. And, finally, he suggests that the spread of the Ostionan Ostionoid subseries was produced by a fast and swift migration out of Puerto Rico. In fact, he suggests that this migration reached Hispaniola, Cuba, the Bahamian archipelago, and Jamaica within a matter of decades. He does not specify, however, the reasons for or the mechanisms of this migration. Nevertheless, Keegan's model is the most complete one that tries to explain not only the spread or expansion of the Ostionoid series but also the diversity observed in the archaeological record.

A related and important issue that has been treated loosely when discussing the Ostionoid expansion is the matter of chronology. Most of us have accepted, at one time or another, that both the Ostionan and Elenan Ostionoid subseries first appeared in Puerto Rico since the earliest dates obtained so far come from this island. The accepted beginning date for these subseries is around A.D. 600/650 for Puerto Rico while other islands show slightly later dates. However, this date differs very little for the early Ostionoid dates from neighboring islands to the point that, for Rouse (1992:Figure 14), the Ostionoid began in Hispaniola and the Virgin Islands at the same time as in Puerto Rico. This small difference between the early dates for the Ostionoid series from all of the islands raises several additional issues. The first one is that, in the case of the western side of the "expansion," the dates from Puerto Rico, the rest of the Greater Antilles, and the Bahamian archipelago differ very little if it is considered that the Ostionoid expansion had to involve the migration of one or more communities to other islands, and reproduced fast enough to populate the whole island of Hispaniola, and begin populating the Bahamian archipelago and parts of Cuba in less than 200 years. For example, the occupation of the Bahamian archipelago has been dated as early as A.D. 685 (Berman and Gnivecki 1995:430) to A.D. 700 (Keegan 1997:21); in other words 100 years or less after the development of the Ostionan Ostionoid groups in Puerto Rico. Due to the scarcity of radiocarbon dates, the beginning of the Ostionoid series in Cuba cannot be determined more precisely. While many early dates have been obtained around A.D. 900 for the presence of Ostionoid in this island (Berman and Gnivecki 1995), some researchers claim that they were present in Cuba at a much earlier time (e.g., A.D. 700 [Calvera et al. 1996:60] or A.D. 700–800 [Tabío 1988:56, 159]). Keegan (2000), citing Martínez Gabino et al. (1993), argues that ceramics with Ostionoid characteristics found near Havana have been dated to A.D. 620. Finally, dates as early as A.D. 650 have been obtained from Jamaica (Rouse and Allaire 1978).

This far from perfect chronological information can be used to conduct a heuristic exercise where we can estimate in a gross manner hypothetical population growth rates needed for small Ostionoid groups migrating from Puerto Rico to the island of Hispaniola and push the Archaic groups out as suggested by Rouse and Chanlatte Baik. A premise of this argument is that the Archaic populations did not contribute reproductively to Ostionoid populations. Let us suppose that the Ostionoid Ostionan subseries developed in Puerto Rico around A.D. 600 and it began migrating almost immediately. In addition, let us suppose that the early dates for the Bahamian archipelago, Cuba, and Jamaica represent the beginning of the colonization of these islands. For sake of this exercise let us round that date to A.D. 800 (an extremely generous number considering that many of the dates reported above are more than 100 years earlier). Further, let us assume that all regions of the island of Hispaniola had to be somewhat populated before the colonization of the Bahamian archipelago, Cuba, and Jamaica took place. This does not mean that the island had to be fully and equally populated in terms of population density and carrying capacity, but that all regions had some population that called the place home. For our exercise we need to estimate the population of Hispaniola around A.D. 800. Needless to say, at present the information to estimate this population is nonexistent. However, relatively conservative estimates can be used to prove our point. For the sake of the argument let's assume that Hispaniola at this time had a population density of 1.5 persons per km^2 giving a total of about 114,000 people (Hispaniola has a total area of 76,500 km^2). Compared to other regions around the world and to estimates based on ethnohistoric evidence (e.g., Cook and Borah 1971–1974; see other estimates in Anderson Córdova 1990, 1995), this population density can be considered very low and reasonable for our purposes. Arbitrarily, let us also assume that four groups of Ostionoid people each composed of 50 people (a total of 200 people) migrated from Puerto Rico to Hispaniola and began the Ostionoid expansion.

If these 200 people are the ones responsible to push out the Archaic groups and reproduce to reach a population of 114,000 in less than 200 years, then they must have needed a population growth rate of at least 3.1 percent or 31 per 1,000 per year, an extremely high rate that many would consider impossible for the biological limits of human reproduction. If instead the original number of people were 500, then the new rate would have been 2.7 percent or 27 per 1,000 per year, not an impossible rate but still a relatively high value that has been observed only in recent years among third-world countries. If we increase the numbers of years to 300 (i.e., assuming that the peopling of the Bahamian archipelago, Cuba, and Jamaica began around A.D. 900) and the starting population to 1,000 people, then the rate is reduced to 1.6 percent or 16 per 1,000 per year, still a high rate for preindustrial, non-Christian populations in historical terms. As mentioned above, these estimates are far from perfect but they are relatively conservative since a density of 1.5 persons per km² is relatively low and the amount of time allowed is pretty generous. These growth rates are considered high not merely in terms of the reproductive capacity of humans, but they are also very difficult to maintain for long periods of time considering the wide range of factors that affect them (e.g., changes in population structure, small variations in mortality and/or fertility, stochastic processes). Therefore, it is difficult to conceive (or find a historical example of) a population that could have maintained such a growth for such a long time. It is important to point out that these calculations do not include the number of people that migrated to the other islands (i.e., Cuba, Jamaica, and Bahamas), only the ones needed to populate Hispaniola before migration occurred. Of course, the inclusion of the early migrant populations of these other islands will make the Ostionoid expansion more questionable.

All of these numbers deserve further discussion since they can be explained or their integrity questioned in a number of ways. First of all, a possible drawback of this "simulation" is that the original migrant population is underestimated and that migrants from Puerto Rico kept moving into Hispaniola well after A.D. 600. Hence, the figure of 1,000 people is too small, and probably considerable larger populations migrated from Puerto Rico to Hispaniola and/or for longer periods of time. This possibility implies that high population growth rates could have been maintained by immigration from Puerto Rico, but it cannot be either discarded or supported with the information available. However, if larger numbers of people migrated to Hispaniola and/or for sustained periods of time, then relatively large population growth rates should have been experienced instead by the groups from western Puerto Rico. As shown in the next two chapters, the little regional evidence available for western Puerto Rico suggests an increase in the number of sites between A.D. 600 and A.D. 900. If so, this means that the population growth rates of Puerto Rican populations had to be high enough to produce this local increase in population and, at the same time, compensate for a relatively large number of immigrants moving to Hispaniola. While more specific estimates of population growth rates necessary for this are difficult to calculate, an educated estimate is that it would have been much higher than the genetic and biological limit of human populations. Thus, depending on which argument is chosen, a considerable high population growth rate had to be present either in Hispaniola or in Puerto Rico during the early Ostionoid times and is needed to explain the increase in population and the eventual simultaneous colonization of Jamaica, Cuba, and the Bahamian archipelago. That is, without considering any possible contribution of Archaic populations to these numbers. If true, this situation has to explain at least two things: (1) why and how either the Hispaniolan, the Puerto Rican, or both populations grew at those extremely fast rates? And, (2) how were these small groups able to maintain high population growth rates for such a long period of time?

Another plausible problem with the simulation is that the population density of 1.5 persons per km^2 is too high, and it causes us to overestimate the population growth rates. If the population density is reduced to one person per km^2 (i.e., a population of 76,500 people) and an initial population of 1,000 for 300 years is kept, the population growth rate is 1.4 percent or 14 per 1,000 per year. This is still a relatively high growth rate that in some pre-industrialized cases is on the high end of early migrant communities that are colonizing a previously uninhabited area, a situation not applicable to Hispaniola since a significant Archaic population was already present prior to the suggested migration of Ostionoid groups. However, it is still possible that Hispaniola had an even smaller population density (i.e., < 1 persons per km^2). But, assuming that they still had the capacity to expel or push the Archaic groups out of the island as the traditional model states, then it has to be explained why some Ostionoid groups migrated to Jamaica, the Bahamian archipelago, and eventually to Cuba, when, at least theoretically, there was plenty of land (and resources) available in Hispaniola.

A final problem, and the most critical point with the simulation, is the assumption or premise that the Archaic populations did not contribute to the general growth rate. Since prior to the Ostionoid "migration," Hispaniola seems to have had a considerable Archaic population, it is difficult to visualize how some migrant Ostionoid groups were able to settle without the consent of some of these communities and eventually push them out of the island toward Cuba. Even more difficult to understand is how these two groups existed together without any kind of interaction with the exception of a conflictive relationship as traditionally suggested. As mentioned before in the case of the Saladoid-Archaic interaction, amicable relations between farmers and foragers are a strong possibility supported cross-culturally by historical and ethnographic information, and these relations should not be discarded a priori. Of all the assumptions of the simulation, this is probably the weakest and more difficult to defend. A relationship between these two regions (i.e., western Puerto Rico and Hispaniola) must have been present before the so-called expansion, and possibly even earlier than the arrival of the Saladoid–La Hueca people to Puerto Rico. There is some indication (e.g., lithic material

Ancient Migrations in Puerto Rico / 87

from the site of Maruca [Rodríguez 1997, 1999]), for example, that Puerto Rico is where the Archaic groups from the traditions from Hispaniola and possibly Cuba met with Archaic groups migrating from South America. Also, as mentioned in the preceding section, in the early Saladoid–La Hueca site of Punta Candelero (eastern Puerto Rico), Rodríguez (1991:611) unearthed pieces of serpentine, amber, and chert that probably originated in Hispaniola and western Puerto Rico (see also Rodríguez Ramos 2002a, 2002b for some other evidence). Although this does not mean direct contact between early ceramic groups and the foraging groups from Hispaniola and western Puerto Rico, it indicates that there was some flow of materials that probably was accompanied by some social relations between both islands. Consequently, it is hard to accept that these relations were not present in later times. This relationship is also suggested by the settling of late Saladoid groups in southeastern Hispaniola, where Saladoid ceramics have been found (Veloz Maggiolo 1991, 1993).

In addition, several Archaic assemblages with relatively crude and modeled ceramics dating between 500 B.C. and A.D. 500 have been discovered in Hispaniola and Cuba. Some researchers (e.g., Keegan 2000; Rouse 1992) have argued that the adoption of ceramics by Archaic people was the result of diffusion from the Puerto Rican Saladoid communities to the Archaic communities. Other archaeologists (Godo 1997, 2001; Guarch Delmonte 2001; Ulloa Hung 1999; Ulloa Hung and Valcárcel Rojas 2003; Veloz Maggiolo and Ortega 1996; Veloz Maggiolo et al. 1993; Veloz Maggiolo 1976) argue against the diffusionary perspective and suggest that these ceramics were the products of local independent developments. However, a third possibility is that the development or adoption of ceramic technology by Archaic groups resulted from the interaction (transculturation) with ceramic groups. This is different from the idea of diffusion since it normally implies that the receiving culture normally has a passive role, while the donor culture is seen as a dominant one. In this case, the protoagricultural or protoceramic assemblages were the result of mutual influence between the Archaic and ceramic groups, where the former adopted the technology and reinterpreted it within their own cultural canons and conditions. It is interesting, however, that while normally the early Saladoid groups of Puerto Rico, with their elaborated painted ceramics, are blamed as the responsible party for the diffusion, the ceramics of most of the protoagricultural assemblages make use only of plastic forms of decorations (incisions) and not paint. This tends to support the idea that, if true, the technology was not diffuse in an indiscriminate manner, but it was consciously adopted and reinterpreted by the Archaic groups.

In fact, if these relations were present before the development of the Ostionoid series and, as argued before, if the Saladoid–La Hueca–Archaic interaction may have had a role in this development, then it is possible that these relations were also involved in the Ostionoid expansion. If so, it can be argued that the Ostionoid did not start first in Puerto Rico (as an event), but it may have developed (as a process) concurrently in Puerto Rico and the neighboring islands. In the process of this development, these interactions, combined with other internal and external factors, may have had a major role. In this interaction different groups influenced each other (i.e., transculturation) at a lower level of society (communities, kinship groups, households) through a number of mechanisms such as intermarriage, exchange, alliances, peer-polity relations, emulation, migration, and so forth. If this argument is correct, then it will explain the small or nonexistent differences in chronology between, for example, eastern Hispaniola and western Puerto Rico. Further, it will explain how the Ostionan Ostionoid subseries was able to expand so fast throughout the western Caribbean without requiring extremely high population growth rates. Hence, it is suggested here that the Archaic populations from at least Hispaniola (and perhaps Puerto Rico, too) contributed reproductively and culturally to the Ostionan expansion to the west, and, therefore, this expansion can be explained without summoning migration as the sole process involved.

An implication of this argument then is that not all "Taíno" or Chicoid groups from Hispaniola are neither direct biological nor cultural descendants of the Saladoid–La Hueca groups. If true, and considering that most of the groups from Hispaniola at the time of contact spoke a form of Arawak language, then the Caribbean may be a case similar to the South Pacific (but in smaller scale) where in some instances the evidence shows culture, language, and "biology" moving differentially throughout the islands. A future study of this phenomenon will be a great contribution to a still ongoing anthropological debate of when and under what circumstances culture, language, and "biology" move together and when and under what circumstances they don't (see various papers in Terrell 2001).

Even if the Ostionoid expansion is credited mainly to migrations from Puerto Rico to Hispaniola, for example, the generalization discussed above for migrant groups suggests that these groups must have had some type of information about this island prior to the population movement. As mentioned before, there are multiple ways of collecting this information from afar including trade, exchange, exploring expeditions, and alliances. Considering that

Hispaniola was already densely populated by Archaic groups, one or more types of intergroup, social relations seem to be more plausible than the collection of information from some explorers or incidental fishers. Also, if Hispaniola was as populated as suggested by many, then the establishment of a migrant community must have received the approval of the local groups, even if a concept of territoriality did not exist strongly among the already established Archaic groups. In summary, even if migration is accepted as a major factor in the Ostionoid expansion to the west, its mere occurrence insinuates that some type of relationship between the Puerto Rican cultivating-ceramic communities and the Hispaniolan Archaic existed already. This relationship was a necessary condition to gather enough information about potential target areas and to get the acceptance of the local Archaic groups that inhabited the island. Therefore, it is possible that some form of interaction was occurring as part of the whole Ostionan Ostionoid subseries (not only for the Meillacan subseries) development and expansion even before migration took place.

While the evidence necessary to study and test many of the suggestions presented here in relation to the Ostionoid expansion is not available, the data at hand tend to indicate that the processes involved were more complex than once suspected and that they may have included multiple aspects that varied through space and time. As Keegan (2000) suggested, the Ostionoid expansion seems to have included multiple aspects of culture change such as transculturation, diffusion, and migration, none of which can be discarded with the evidence available. This is not to say that migration was not an integral part of the processes as suggested by Rouse and others; the case of the Bahamian archipelago may be a definite example of migration. But, it may not have had such a primordial role as normally believed; in other words, it was not a population movement (in Rouse's terms), but the migration of smaller groups. Further, as Chanlatte Baik (1986) proposed, the development of the Ostionoid series may have involved not only local development but also the interaction between the Saladoids, La Hueca, and the Archaic peoples of Puerto Rico and perhaps Hispaniola, too. Thus, the changes observed around A.D. 600 in the northern Caribbean can be explained without summoning a large migration of populations out of Puerto Rico to the rest of the Caribbean. Multiple and diverse forms of complex social interactions between and within islands were probably responsible by this almost synchronous development across the northwestern Caribbean.

Moreover, it is important to consider that most probably the process of "transculturation" involved more than the exchange of cultural and economic practices, since it is during this time that major changes are detected in the archaeological record reflecting shifts in the social, economic, and political organizations of these groups. Some of the shifts include changes in mortuary practices (Curet and Oliver 1998), household structure and composition (Curet 1992b), material culture (Curet 1996), settlement patterns (Curet 1992; Curet et al. 2004; Lundberg 1985; Rodríguez 1985, 1992; Torres 2001), and the development of ball courts and plazas (Alegría 1983; González Colón 1984; Oliver 1999; Siegel 1999). Several of us have seen these dramatic transformations as part of the development of new sociopolitical systems in Puerto Rico, probably related to the formation of chiefdoms or *cacicazgos* (Curet 1992a, 1992b, 1996; Curet and Oliver 1998; Moscoso 1986; Oliver 1999; Rouse 1992; Siegel 1989, 1992, 1996a, 1999). However, to date none of the models and suggestions proposed to explain these changes include the Saladoid–La Hueca–Archaic interaction as a factor in these developments. I am not implying that all the conclusions developed from these models are useless or wrong, but in order to make these models fully operational and more realistic they have to recognize or at least discard, to a greater or lesser degree, the presence and potential effects of this interaction.

It is important to recognize that most of the discussion presented here has concentrated on western Puerto Rico and its relationship with Hispaniola and other islands. Little has been said about eastern Puerto Rico and its interaction with the northern Lesser Antilles. It is highly possible that the cultural differences identified for these two regions of the island (i.e., Ostionan vs. Elenan subseries) reflect different dynamics involved in the processes of culture change. While I am not implying that the cultivator-forager interaction had nothing to do with the development of the Elenan subseries as proposed by Chanlatte Baik (1986), the evidence clearly shows that the interaction of groups from eastern Puerto Rico with Hispaniola was small compared to groups of the Ostionan subseries in the western side of the island. In fact, by this time (A.D. 600) most of the northern Lesser Antilles were inhabited by ceramic, cultivating groups, while no evidence has been discovered for the presence of Archaic groups (e.g., Hofman and Hoogland 2003). Thus, it remains to be investigated, what was the role of intergroup and interisland relations in the social and cultural developments that occurred in eastern Puerto Rico and the northern Lesser Antilles?

Summarizing, the simulation study estimating potential population growth rates and the evidence for the cohabitation of Archaic and Saladoid and Huecoid peoples suggests that the occupation of Hispaniola, and the rest of the Greater Antilles for that matter, by Ostionoid groups may have been due more to aspects of culture change produced as part of the interactions of all these groups than to migration. The details of the types, mechanisms, and dynamics of these interactions are still to be determined, however. In the search for the answers to these issues we should not discard the contribution of various and different combinations of processes (i.e., migrations, transculturation, diffusion, acculturation, emulation, alliances) that could have occurred in different places and/or different times.

CONCLUSIONS

As can be seen from the discussion presented in this chapter, Caribbean archaeologists traditionally have dealt with issues of migration and social change in very superficial ways without considering many of the social processes involved or the structures and scales of the groups that migrated. Many times, these two issues have been studied as events in the culture history of the region instead of complex processes that involve multiple and complicated aspects of social and cultural considerations. Most of the social and demographic variables and conditions engaged in migrations have serious consequences that can affect aspects of survival and future directions of culture and social change of the migrant groups, and they should not be treated in an incidental manner. On the contrary, we have to redirect many of our research approaches to be able to collect and include detailed data necessary to understand the relationship between migration and other sociocultural processes and its role in later sociopolitical and cultural developments. When phenomena such as migrations are seen from a demographic perspective, the picture that develops is different and in many cases more detailed. Using this analytical approach has consequences on many of our reconstructions not only at the interisland level but also, as shown in later chapters, on circumstances of interest at regional and community levels.

By now it should be obvious to the reader that the approach that Rouse has suggested for the study of migrations is limited and appropriate for very few clear-cut cases in the history of the Caribbean. His approach is mostly methodological and not theoretical. This method is not useful for the identification of more complex cases where migration is one of many variables included in the process. Perhaps the largest problem of this approach is that it treats migration as a simple event and not as a process that includes a series of steps, including unpredictable decision-making stages.

From the perspective presented in this chapter, it is easy to realize that the Saladoid migration was far from simple and one-directional as presented by our traditional perspectives. This population movement was not a random migration where the migrants were explorers at the same time. The whole process probably involved multiple steps, including information gathering and several decision-making stages. The information we have at hand, while far from being ideal, can be used to develop several working hypotheses for future studies. First, as suggested by Haviser's (1997) observations, the early Saladoid migration wave purposefully aimed at the northeastern Caribbean as their place of destination. This, at the same time, suggests that they had available a considerable amount of information about this area, and probably they had established some strong relations with the local Archaic populations before moving into these islands.

Second, we cannot assume a priori that Saladoid–La Hueca migrants replaced in one way or another the Archaic groups that may have inhabited several of the Lesser Antilles and Puerto Rico. Quite the opposite, the evidence tends to suggest that these groups coexisted relatively peacefully in the same habitats for relatively long periods. If true, this supports the argument that the Saladoid groups had established some relations with Archaic groups even prior to their movement to the islands.

Third, judging by the presence of a number of single-component Saladoid sites, it is possible that many of the migrant communities never became fully established settlements. In other words, they were failed attempts to settle many of the regions. Ironically, many of these sites are the ones used as "pure" examples of the early Saladoid–La Hueca societies in the Caribbean islands; in many cases we are defining the Saladoid–La Hueca cultures on the unsuccessful communities that probably were going through at least demographic stress, instead of on the successful ones. The reasons for their failures can include ecological disasters, lack of vital resources in the region settled, demographic and genetic problems, and others.

Fourth, it is suggested that the early Saladoid migration stopped in Puerto Rico not so much because it encountered strong resistance from Archaic groups in Hispaniola but because this was their target destination. Following Rouse's (1964, 1986) suggestion that Saladoid and Archaic groups had established some relations in the coasts of South America, it is hypothesized here that these spheres of interaction extended further to groups in other areas including the Archaics from the northeastern Caribbean. This interaction could have been stronger with the groups from Puerto Rico than Hispaniola since the historical ancestors of the former probably came from South America, while the latter seem to belong to a different cultural tradition. It is possible that the Saladoid migrants acquired some information about the region from these Archaic groups prior to the population movement (e.g., through trade or exploration of friendly territories).

Cross-cultural generalizations about human migrations can be combined with some information available to also make some suggestions about the Ostionoid expansion. This expansion traditionally has been closely related to the development of the series in Puerto Rico. With the exception of the Meillacan subseries, the Ostionoid was normally seen as a local development that sprouted out of the Saladoid people, and, once developed, it immediately resumed the migration west. However, contrary to Rouse's own suggestions, other possibilities to explain its development and eventual spread to other islands have not been ruled out at all. In fact, some of the evidence, as pointed out by Chanlatte Baik and Keegan, tends to suggest that other processes may have been present, as well. Particularly of interest is the argument that the Archaic–Saladoid–La Hueca interaction may have had a key role in the development of the Ostionoid series and its eventual expansion. Archaeological studies in Puerto Rico and the Lesser Antilles have all but ignored this possibility and the impact of this interaction in complex historical processes. Ironically, the works of scholars from Hispaniola and Cuba have been recognizing these possibilities for years, receiving little attention from archaeologists working in other islands (e.g., Godo 1997; Guarch Delmonte 2001; Ulloa Hung 1999; Ulloa Hung and Valcárcel Rojas 2002).

So, combining some of the suggestions from Chanlatte Baik (1986) and Keegan (2000) with some general observations made in the previous sections the following working hypotheses can be proposed. First, it is highly possible that the factors that led to the development of the Ostionoid series in Puerto Rico included the foragers-cultivators interaction. However, while I have been emphasizing this interaction as having a major role in culture change, I want to make it clear that I do not believe this interaction was the only major source of the shifts we see in the archaeological record. My argument here is that it probably was one of several major factors and that the role of Archaic groups may have had into these processes have been overtly overseen by previous research. Obviously, many of the internal and external factors that have been proposed to explain cultural and social changes in the Greater Antilles were also active during this time, including intraisland peer polity interactions, internal conflict, environmental changes, competition for status, alliances, emulation, intermarriage relations, changes in subsistence and economic strategies, internal factionalism, exchange and trade, and others. Our challenge is to determine which ones of these factors had more weight than others, when and in what situations, and how all of them interacted to produce the changes that we observe in the archaeological record.

Second, the fact that this development happened almost simultaneously in the neighboring islands suggests that the Ostionoid series may have not originated exclusively in Puerto Rico, but, instead, it was a multi-island process. If so then, third, some form of interaction was present between the populations from Puerto Rico and those from the neighboring islands, as in the relations suggested by Keegan and Chanlatte Baik between the Saladoid groups and the Archaic groups from Puerto Rico and Hispaniola. Finally, processes other than large-scale migration can explain the Ostionoid expansion, and large-scale migration may or may not have been part of this general process.

Perhaps most of these hypotheses can be summarized by saying that a key piece in understanding two of the very important phenomena in ancient Puerto Rico is the role of Archaic populations. From the perspective presented here the Archaic may have been responsible for or at least contributed considerably to many of the roles normally assigned to the Saladoid or Ostionan Ostionoid people. For example, it is highly improbable that the Saladoid people actually explored the Caribbean without any previous knowledge. In my opinion, the credit for this belongs to the Archaic groups that actually ventured into uncharted territory. Further, while many of us tend to see Archaic social and cultural life as sort of static for hundreds of years and over large expanses, in reality their history probably included many dynamic and influential social and political processes. When migrating to Puerto Rico, the Saladoid social groups were most probably exposed to these processes and dynamics, which eventually contributed to later social, cultural, and political developments such as the development of the Ostionan and Elenan Ostionoid subseries and stratified societies. Hence, future research and modeling of human behavior in the Caribbean should account for the possibility of strong Archaic–Saladoid–La Hueca interaction as a powerful factor involved in many of the ancient social and political processes. It will be interesting, for example, to see how future research on this interaction changes our perspectives of many of the political developments such as the rise of chiefdoms in the Caribbean.

5 / Intraisland Population Trends

Regional Analysis

Long-distance migration between the continent and the islands and between the islands themselves, such as we saw in Chapters 3 and 4, offers an opportunity to examine demographic processes at work on a large scale. The next step in reconstructing the behavior of the ancients is to narrow our focus an additional degree and look at developments co-occurring at different sites on the same island. In this chapter, therefore, population dynamics are discussed at the intraisland level. A comparative analysis of population trends across three regions in Puerto Rico and the adjoining Vieques Sound area provides the basic demographic data for reconstructing the social and political organization in discrete areas of the Caribbean archipelago.

Intraisland processes have received little attention in Puerto Rican and Caribbean archaeology. In large part this situation reflects Caribbeanists' adherence to Irving Rouse's cultural chronology for the Caribbean, which emphasizes cultural and supracultural units (i.e., the subseries or series). These units are generally equated with social units at the level of a large part of or whole island, or a group of islands. However, the use of cultural categories in an analysis of social processes at any smaller geographic area is beset with problems. Among other effects, use of these categories in an indiscriminate manner has the propensity to create a process of homogenization, where the same cultural, social, or demographic processes are seen as occurring at the same time over the totality of each of the "culture areas." Based on this perspective, many of the social and cultural models developed cover these relatively large areas without taking into consideration the variability and diversity of processes that have taken place within it and the possibility of localized groups developing independent and diverse demographic strategies and responses. For example, many of the models developed to explain several social changes in Puerto Rico assume that either Puerto Rico as a whole or the eastern side of the island is homogeneous enough to be considered as a single demographic, social, and political unit (e.g., Curet 1992a, 1992b, 1996; Curet and Oliver 1998; Oliver 1998; Rodríguez 1992; Siegel 1991b, 1992, 1996, 1999). Needless to say, this approach obscures the possibility that different regions in either Puerto Rico or the eastern part of the island may in fact have different demographic and social histories. Some demographic aspects of this internal variability are presented in this chapter by comparing population trends in size and distribution of various culture areas of Puerto Rico.

To counteract prevailing beliefs, and to establish a foundation for further regional comparative work, this chapter examines the patterns and variability in population dynamics in four regions of eastern Puerto Rico for which sufficient data are available. Three of the regions are located within what Rouse has identified as the Vieques Sound area (eastern Puerto Rico and adjacent islands); these are the Loíza River Basin, the Salinas River Basin, and the Vieques Naval Reservation. The fourth region, the Yauco River Basin, is in the Mona Passage in western Puerto Rico. A careful examination of the data shows that the regions present both differences and similarities in respect to ancient settlement patterns and implied population trends through time. I argue, therefore, that the diverse demographic trends observable in the archaeological record reflect major differences in social and political processes that were likely operating at the same time in different parts of this area; the historical processes, therefore, were different. A corollary is that eastern Puerto Rico, and for that matter the Vieques Sound, cannot be considered a single social, political, and demographic unit. Only by first understanding the local political and social history of specific regions can we make broader generalizations about eastern Puerto Rico and construct a more complete picture of these ancient groups.

Eastern Puerto Rico is emphasized for a couple of reasons. First, this area has been defined as culturally distinct from western Puerto Rico on the basis of the different archaeological materials found on the two halves of the island. Second, this area has received more research attention than western Puerto Rico, partly as a result of several academic projects that have taken place there, but also because of various projects related to cultural resource management. In particular, more specifically regional studies have been conducted in eastern Puerto Rico than in western Puerto Rico. Data from Vieques are also examined because this island is part of the Vieques Sound culture area (see Rouse) and to demonstrate that the processes also differ from one island to another. The Yauco River Basin (western Puerto Rico) is included because it is one of the few areas in western Puerto Rico (and for that matter, in the greater Mona Passage as a whole) where regional studies have been conducted.

It should be noted that the limitations of regional data available for Puerto Rico do not allow as thorough an analysis of population dynamics as one might like; we simply lack sufficiently detailed data on population estimates and distribution with good chronological control. However, some settlement pattern data collected in specific regions are available, and these data can be used to help delineate regional trends. So, it is at the regional level of analysis that we can begin to hypothesize a political history and economy, and by comparing their differences and similarities we can gain a better understanding not only of the idiosyncrasies of each region but also of their converging or diverging paths. The contribution of this chapter, then, is to use demographic and population dynamics to understand the range of political organizations and political economies that developed within the same culture area.

THE FOUR REGIONS

The four regions considered in this study are shown in Figure 5.1. Three of the regions are river basins, and the fourth is the island of Vieques, adjacent to Puerto Rico. River basins were selected because site distributions throughout Puerto Rico for all periods display a propensity for communities to be oriented in major river valleys or at the confluence of major drainages, as observed by many regional studies (Curet 1992a; Curet et al. 2004; Lundberg 1985; Rodríguez 1984, 1985, 1992; Torres 2001). Moreover, an ethnohistoric document describes Puerto Rico at the time of the Conquest as divided in small *cacicazgos* ruling small river valleys (Ponce de León y Troche and Santa Clara 1582 [1914]). It is within these river valleys that further shifts in site distributions seem to have occurred throughout the sequence (Torres 2001).

Before reviewing and discussing the data provided for each region there are several considerations that have to be kept in mind. It is clear that the studies and the data they generated have some differences that can affect our final results. These differences include the origin of the data (e.g., survey vs. archival information), chronological units (e.g., styles vs. subseries), scale (i.e., river basins vs. the Vieques island), physiographic characteristics, and the different

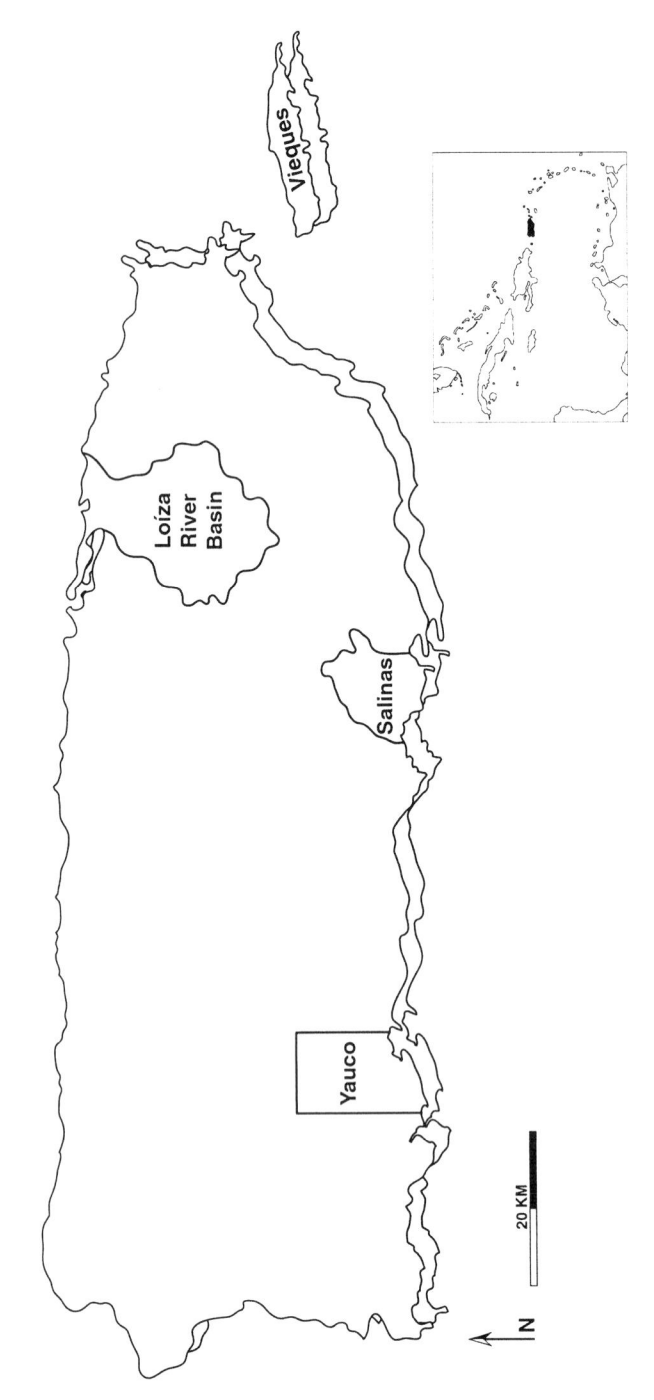

Figure 5.1. Map of Puerto Rico showing the four regions included in the intraisland study.

processes of site discovery and the period of time during which the various data sets were recorded. Despite these issues, however, it is believed that when the scales of the projects are considered, the problems with the data do not preclude their utility for exploring regional demographic patterns, and social and political organization through settlement pattern analysis. My intention here is to define and show differences of gross demographic trends or patterns in the record of the regions, and to detect major changes in those patterns through time. Thus, considering the units of observation and the scale of analysis, these areas are comparable for the purpose of exploring regional variation for the development of working hypotheses for future studies and the modeling of past human behavior. Interpretations of the data flow from the assumption that the spatial pattern of material culture is a reflection of human behavior, which is influenced by environmental, demographic, and social variables. In the discussion that follows, these patterns are manifested through the distribution of sites across the landscape and their spatial relationships to one another through time.

Loíza River Basin

The Loíza River Basin is located on the northeastern coast of Puerto Rico. Covering an area of 788 square km, and 42 km long, it is the largest basin in the island (Picó 1974). The river rises in the Central Mountain Range and flows north, crossing the interior Valley of Caguas, the humid foothills, and the karstic topography, characterized by hills and caves, to finally reach the coastal plains. Many parts of the plains are so low that drainage is deficient, forming swamps, marshes, and the Piñones lagoon west of the river's mouth, the largest estuary in the northeast. Most of the river is included in the Subtropical Moist Forest of Ewel and Whitmore (1973), while the upper reaches of the river are located in Lower Montane Wet and Subtropical Wet Forest.

The information used in this analysis was provided by Rodríguez (1990, 1992). Using information from his own research (e.g., Rodríguez 1984) and from the archives in the State Historic Preservation Office (SHPO) and the Instituto de Cultura Puertorriqueña, Rodríguez reconstructed changes and trends in settlement patterns through time for the basin. For this study he divided the basin into three physiographic regions, which will also be used in this work. The first one is the Upper area, which includes land traversed by the river from its origin through the Central Mountains and valleys. The second one, the Intermediate area, is in the northern foothills of the Central Mountain Range and incorporates the upper part of the karstic topography.

The third area is the Lower area, which is concentrated on the coastal plains and includes the lower part of the karstic topography. Rodríguez also differentiated between three different sizes of sites, which he represented on his maps by three different sizes of symbols. Although the criteria he used to define both the physiographic areas and the designation of site size are not mentioned in the publications, I follow Rodríguez's categories to differentiate between the various parts of the basin and the different site types (i.e., villages, hamlets, isolated households).

The Loíza River Basin is one of the archaeologically best-studied regions of Puerto Rico, yielding evidence of continuous human occupation from Archaic to modern times. In this discussion I will focus strictly on Ceramic Age sites from the Hacienda Grande (or early Saladoid) to the Esperanza (Chican Ostionoid) styles.

The settlement pattern through time for the region, as observed from the distribution maps (Figures 5.2 to 5.6), consists of an increase in number of sites simultaneous with new occupations in the interior. However, a closer look at these distributions and at the sizes of sites shows some variations in this general tendency (Figure 5.7). The number of sites increased gradually between the Hacienda Grande style (300 B.C.–A.D. 400) and the Monserrate style (A.D. 600–900). This gradual increase changed toward the Santa Elena style (A.D. 900–1200), when the data show a marked increase in the number of sites. When the size of sites is considered, however, the increase is seen to result not so much from the formation of large sites as from the appearance of more small and medium-sized sites, as shown on the map. At the end of the sequence (Esperanza style, A.D. 1200–1500) the general trend is reversed and the number of sites shows a slight reduction, most of it due to a decrease in medium-sized sites, since small and large sites increase in numbers.

A second trend is apparent in the distribution of sites between physiographic regions (Figure 5.8). In general, during the early Saladoid series (Hacienda Grande style) settlements were environmentally and geographically bound to the coastal Low areas. However, during the Cuevas style, people seem to have made incursions farther inland, into the Intermediate and High areas of the Loíza River Basin, including the Valley of Caguas, one of the largest valleys of central Puerto Rico. During the Monserrate style a shift in population density occurred, with the Intermediate area having more sites than either the Low or the High area. In contrast, in the second half of this period, during the Santa Elena style, site densities seem to have been polarized between the Low and High areas, with the fewest sites in the Intermediate

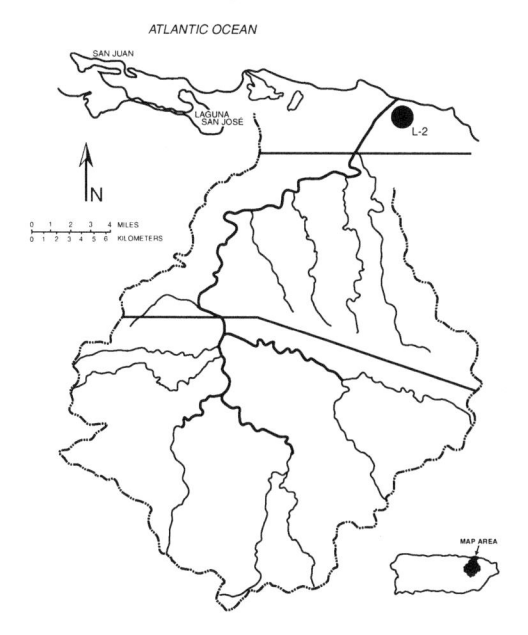

CEDAROSAN SALADOID SUBSERIES - HACIENDA GRANDE STYLE
PERIOD II-A
(250 BC - AD 400)

Figure 5.2. Map of the Loíza River Basin showing the location of sites belonging to the Hacienda Grande style (adopted from Rodríguez 1992).

area. The polarization of the distribution of populations within the Loíza River Basin is also present during the next period, although a small decrease in the number of sites (i.e., only by three sites) is registered for the Low area.

Other distributional patterns are observed for both areas beyond those based on physiographic divisions, particularly the frequencies of the different site types (Figure 5.9). During Saladoid times most of the sites tended to be relatively large villages, while during the Elenan Ostionoid subseries, a general trend began in which smaller sites became more prevalent, finally becoming a majority at the end of the Esperanza style. These trends together resulted in a combination of nucleated and dispersed settlement patterns. However, the distribution of small sites varies through time. During the Monserrate style, small sites are found exclusively in the Intermediate area, but they are not present in the Low or High areas. This pattern reverses during the next two styles, when small sites are missing from the Intermediate area but are present in larger numbers in the Low and High areas. Furthermore, several clusters of

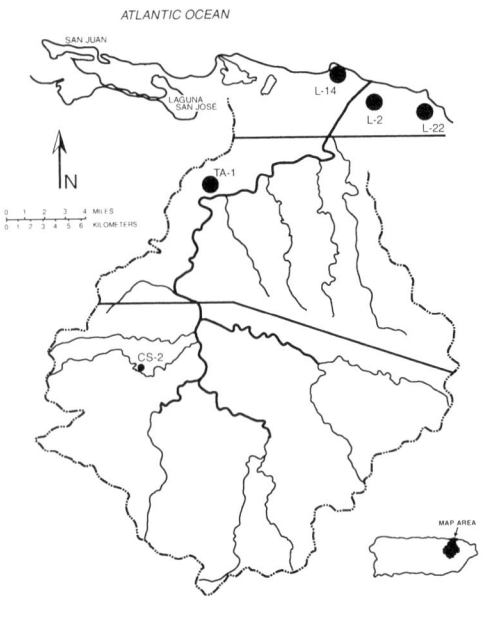

CEDROSAN SALADOID SUBSERIES - CUEVAS STYLE
PERIOD II-B
(AD 400 - 600)

Figure 5.3 Map of the Loíza River Basin showing the location of sites belonging to the Cuevas style (adopted from Rodríguez 1992).

sites appear in the Santa Elena style, mainly in the Intermediate and High areas. Many of these clusters show an arrangement of sites following a centralized pattern, in which large sites are surrounded by smaller settlements, including some dispersed domestic units or hamlets.

A small number of Chican Ostionoid sites—two or three—with monumental structures (e.g., ball courts and plazas) have been reported for this region, and some of them may have been built during the Santa Elena style. However, the chronological data needed to securely date these structures to the Santa Elena style are not available. Another pattern is observable in the Low areas of the Loíza River Basin, where numerous occupations belonging to the Santa Elena style are distributed along the coast, in marshy areas, and around lagoons (i.e., in the Low area), often forming lineal arrangements. This variation in settlement patterns strongly suggests the presence of different kinds of site *types*. Different site types could have resulted as a matter of differences in the physical environments of the localities, but they could also

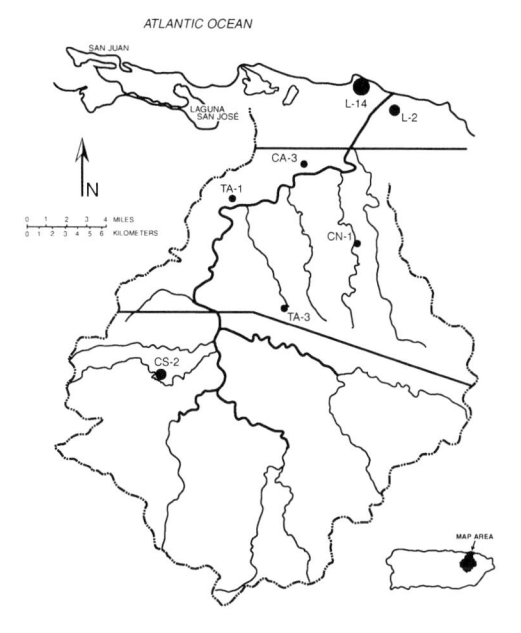

ELENAN OSTIONOID SUBSERIES - MONSERRATE STYLE
PERIOD III-A
(AD 600 - 900)

Figure 5.4. Map of the Loíza River Basin showing the location of sites belonging to the Monserrate style (adopted from Rodríguez 1992).

have resulted from changes in the groups' social and political organization. Such an alternative explanation gains support from archaeological evidence and, as we will see toward the end of this discussion/chapter, provides an exciting glimpse into the nature of prehistoric societies.

The Esperanza style saw the abandonment of some sites in the region, but compared with the magnitude and nature of the reduction in the number of sites in other regions of the island (see below), the changes in Loíza River Basin are insignificant. Most of the sites that were abandoned during this period were small and medium-sized. The abandonment of these relatively small sites was compensated for by the formation of new small and large sites. Interestingly, while medium-sized sites decreased by more than 50 percent during this period, small and large sites increased by 20 percent and 100 percent, respectively. In addition, most of the abandoned sites seem to have been founded during the Santa Elena style; large and older sites continued to be inhabited. Therefore, considering the size of the abandoned sites and the for-

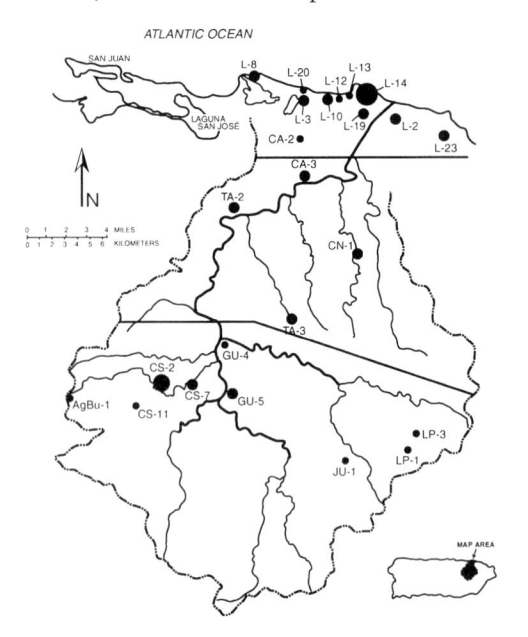

ELENAN OSTIONOID SUBSERIES - SANTA ELENA STYLE
PERIOD III-B
(AD 900 - 1200)

Figure 5.5. Map of the Loíza River Basin showing the location of sites belonging to the Santa Elena style (adopted from Rodríguez 1992).

mation of new small and large sites, the decrease in number of sites in the Loíza River Basin may not be indicative of a decrease in population.

The number of sites in the Intermediate and High areas during the Esperanza style remained constant, and some centralized settlement patterns are still visible. Interestingly, and in contradistinction to other regions along the southern coast of eastern Puerto Rico, the few sites with ball courts, plazas, and even ceremonial centers are still present in the region during this time. In fact, it seems that most, if not all, of the few sites with monumental architecture were still being inhabited during this time.

The Island of Vieques

Vieques is a relatively small island located about 11 km southeast of Puerto Rico. It has a long, narrow shape and covers approximately 133 square km in area. The topography of the island is characterized by low hills and small valleys, with an average elevation of 75 meters above sea level (masl). The

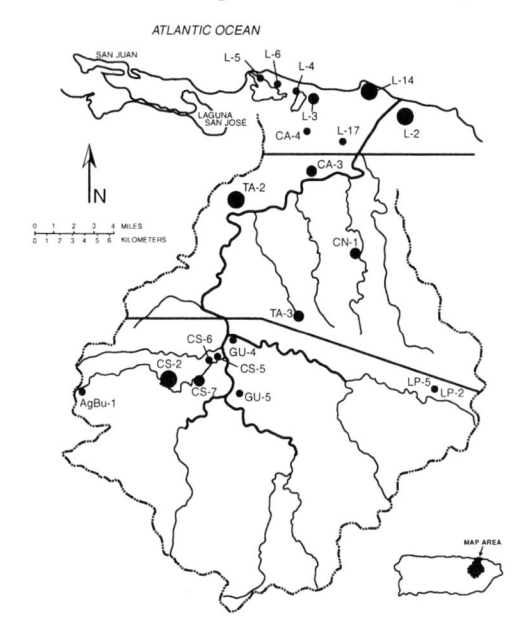

CHICAN OSTIONOID SUBSERIES - ESPERANZA STYLE
PERIOD IV-A
(AD 1200 - 1500)

Figure 5.6. Map of the Loíza River Basin showing the location of sites belonging to the Esperanza style (adopted from Rodríguez 1992).

western end of the island is typified by rolling hills and deeper soil profiles, while the eastern end tends to have more angular and rugged hills and has a greater amount of exposed rock surface. The highest point of the island, Monte Pirata (elevation 301 masl), is located on the western side. Low-lying coastal zones of sedimentary deposits are common and generally contain lagoons and swamps. Waterways flow from the high points of the island in both north and south directions to the sea, but most of these streams form small and short (< 1.6 km long) drainage basins. The vegetation of Vieques is characteristic of Subtropical Dry zones, although the western end tends to be more humid and to have some Subtropical Moist Forest regions (Ewel and Whitmore 1973). Mangrove forests and lagoons are present in several areas along the coast. Since the 1940s until 2003, the island has been divided in three sections, two of which (9,000 hectares) are owned by the U.S. Navy, mostly for naval training activities. The rest of the island is owned by individuals or by the government of Puerto Rico.

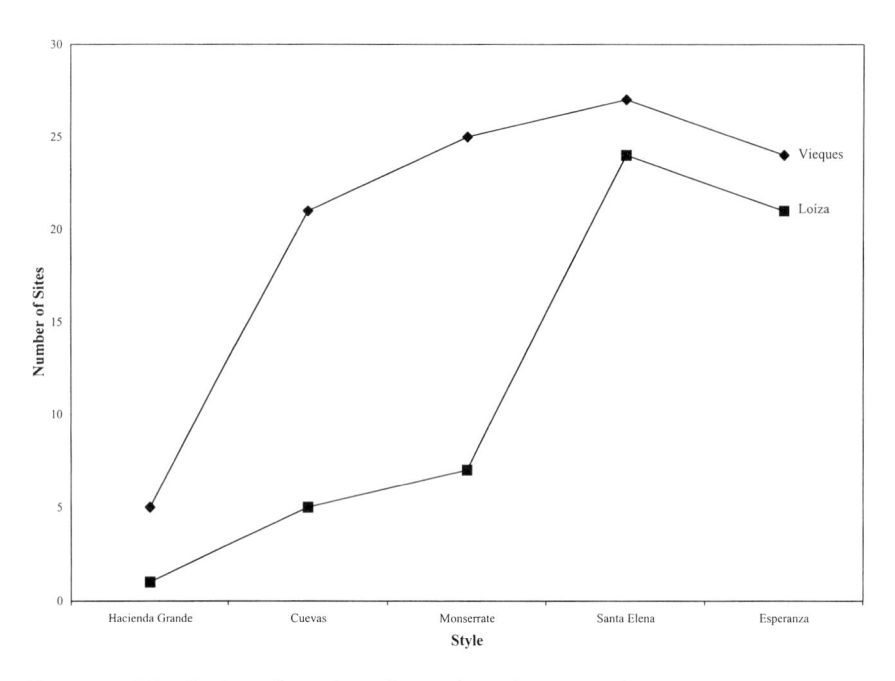

Figure 5.7. Distribution of number of sites through time in the Loíza River Basin and Vieques Island.

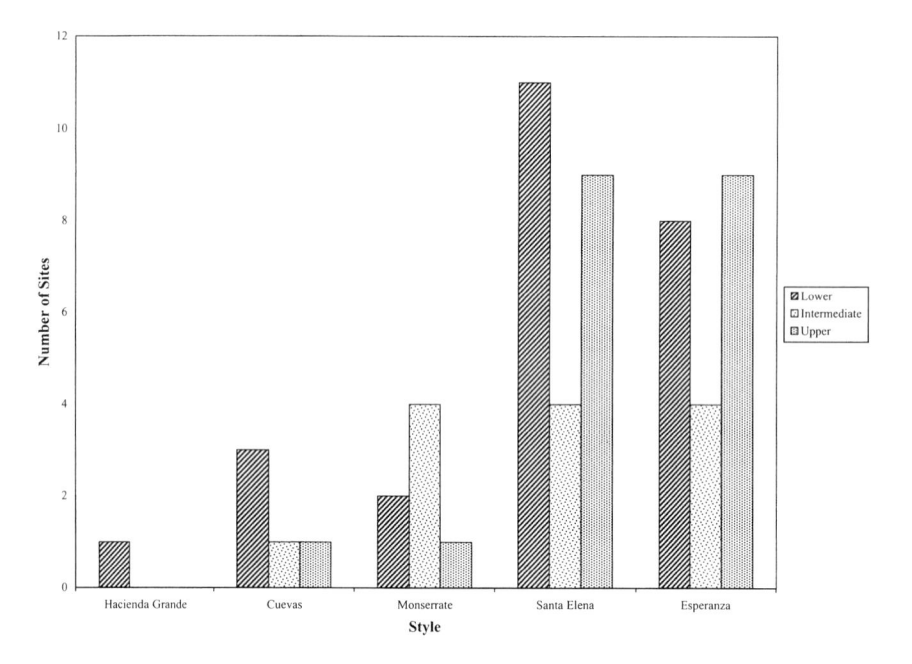

Figure 5.8. Distribution of sites across physiographic regions in the Loíza River Basin.

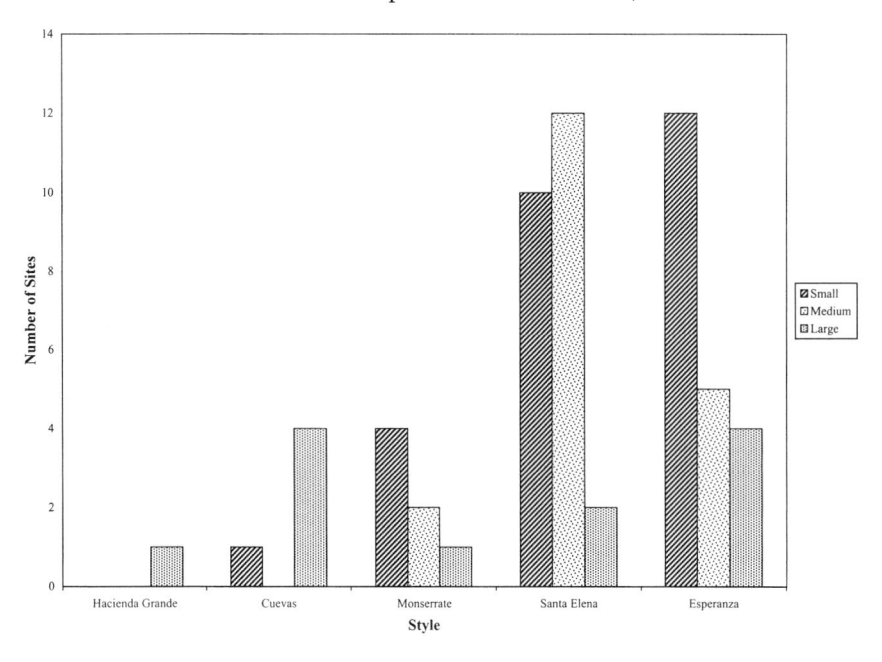

Figure 5.9. Distribution of site types through time in the Loíza River Basin.

The island of Vieques is another region of Puerto Rico that has been studied extensively. The island seems to have been occupied for a very long time, with dates for some Archaic sites going back to as early as 1500 B.C. (Figueredo 1976; Tronolone et al. 1984, 1990). The discussion that follows begins with 300 B.C., because I concentrate on the developments during the Ceramic Age. The bulk of the information on Vieques used in this chapter comes from a sampling survey conducted on U.S. Navy property in the late 1970s and early 1980s (Tronolone et al. 1984, 1990). The project divided the navy properties into 500-meter-square sectors. A total of 405 out of a possible 504 sectors were investigated in the field. The surveyed area totaled approximately 7,600 hectares, or 85 percent of the properties owned by the navy. In addition to the data from the navy properties, information provided by Rouse (1952), López Sotomayor (1975), Chanlatte Baik and Narganes Storde (1983), and Curet (1987) is used to reconstruct population dynamics for Vieques.

A total of 52 sites belonging to the Ceramic Age were selected for the study, and the dates assigned by Curet (1987) based on ceramic modes and types were used. Site classification was done in two dimensions. The first dimension was the possible function of the site, and for this I followed the definitions used by Tronolone et al. to discriminate between villages, hamlets, and campsites (even though the authors did not specify the criteria used to define these site categories). From the reports, the field notes, and my analysis of the materials, I suspect that some of the terms may not accurately reflect the true nature of many of the sites, particularly the hamlets and campsites. In Puerto Rico and in other parts of the Caribbean, permanent, single-dwelling localities have been found away from nucleated sites, especially for the Elenan and Chican Ostionoid periods (Curet 1992a; Rodríguez 1984, 1985, 1992; Rivera and Rodríguez 1991). In my opinion, many similar sites are present in Vieques, and they may have been misclassified by Tronolone and colleagues as campsites or hamlets. Therefore, it seems likely that small, single-dwelling sites or possibly special-activity sites have been miscategorized. For the sake of consistency with Tronolone's work, and because it is often quite difficult to discriminate accurately among a handful of different small sites, I retain Tronolone's site assignments, but without necessarily accepting the functions they imply.

The second dimension had to do with the physiographic characteristics of the sites. Because of the relatively low elevation of Vieques, sites were classified as inland or coastal, again using terms developed by Tronolone et al. (1984). Although Tronolone et al. (1984) did not define these terms, I here consider as coastal sites those sites located within 500 m of the coast and at elevations of less than 20 masl. Similarly, inland sites I consider to be sites located more than 500 m from the coast or at elevations of 25 masl or higher.

From the distribution maps for each period (Figures 5.10 to 5.14), it is obvious that Vieques shows a general tendency toward an increase in number of sites over time. While these general tendencies seem to indicate some similarities with the population and demographic trends identified for the Loíza River Basin, some significant differences can be observed. First, contrary to the Loíza River Basin, where the initial increase in the number of sites is gradual, becoming faster later during the Santa Elena style, in Vieques, the relatively fast rate of increase seems to have occurred early in the sequence, during Period II-b or the Cuevas style (see Figure 5.7). After this time, the curve reaches more or less a plateau, where the number of settlements continues increasing gradually until the Santa Elena style and then decreasing slightly during the Esperanza style. The rate and magnitude in the decrease in number of sites is similar to the one identified in the Loíza River Basin for this last period. Early in the sequence, the numbers of coastal and inland sites are more or less similar, with coastal sites being somewhat more abundant during the

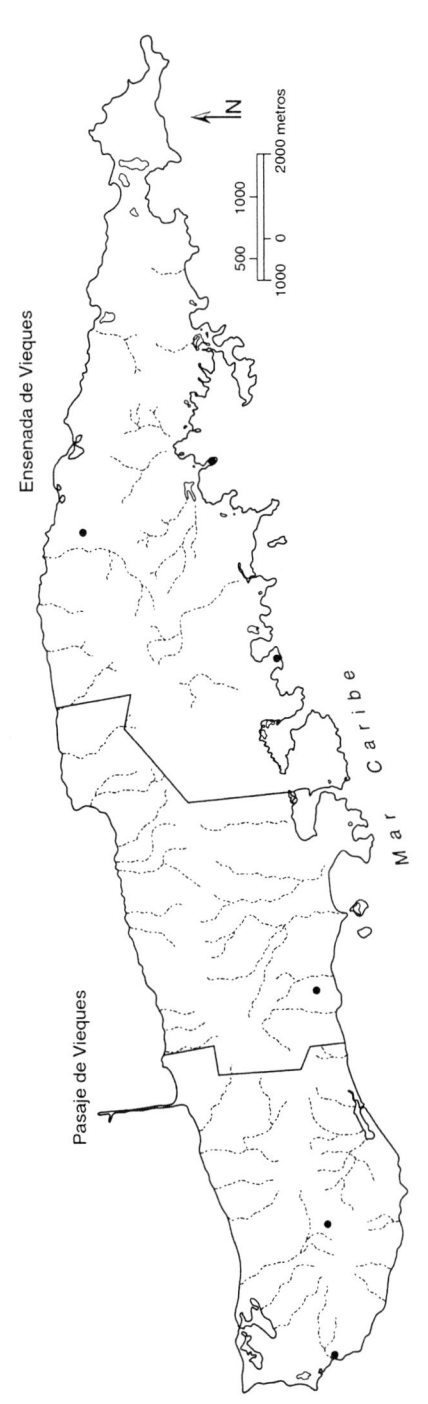

Figure 5.10. Map of Vieques showing the location of sites belonging to the Hacienda Grande style.

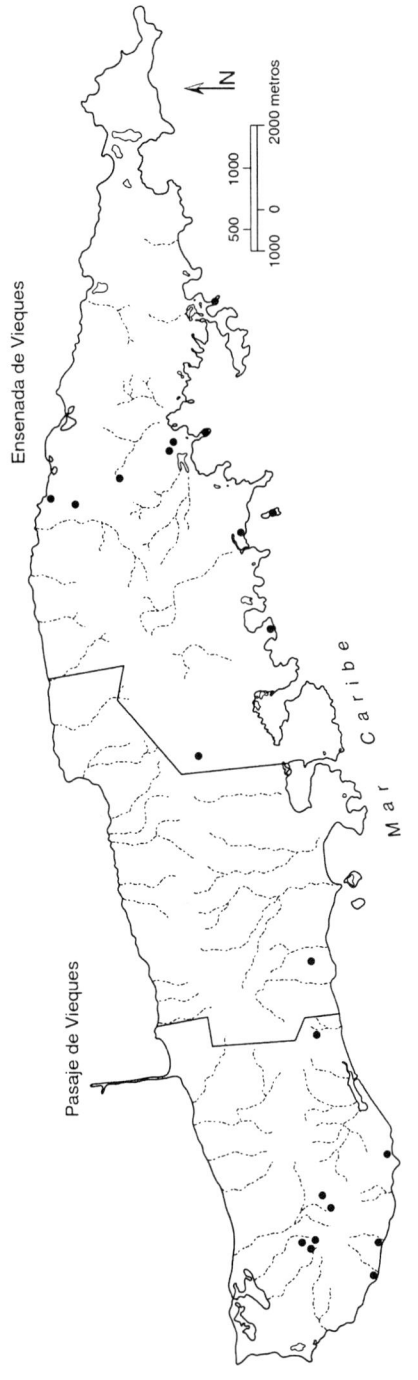

Figure 5.11. Map of Vieques showing the location of sites belonging to the Cuevas style.

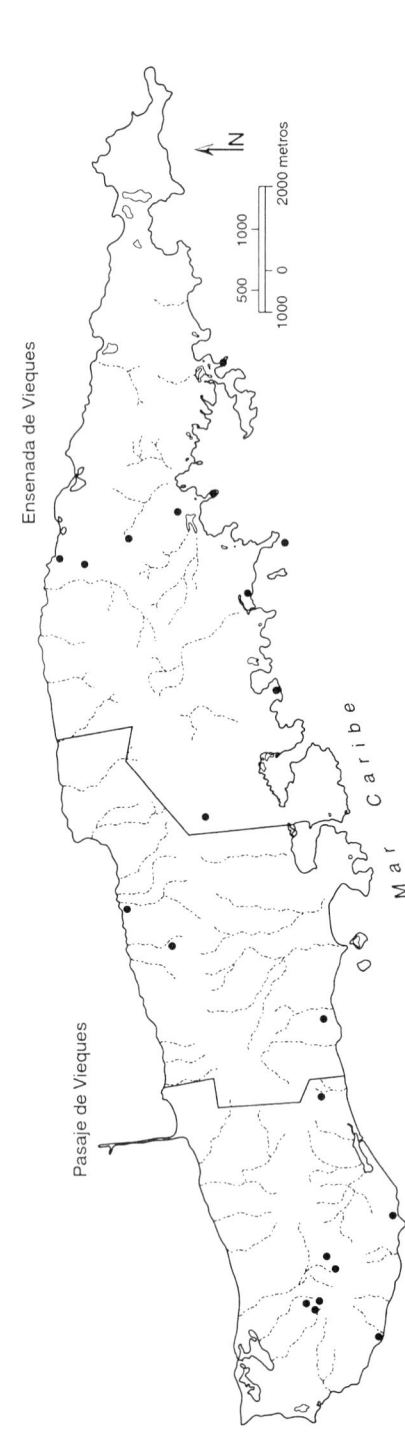

Figure 5.12. Map of Vieques showing the location of sites belonging to the Monserrate style.

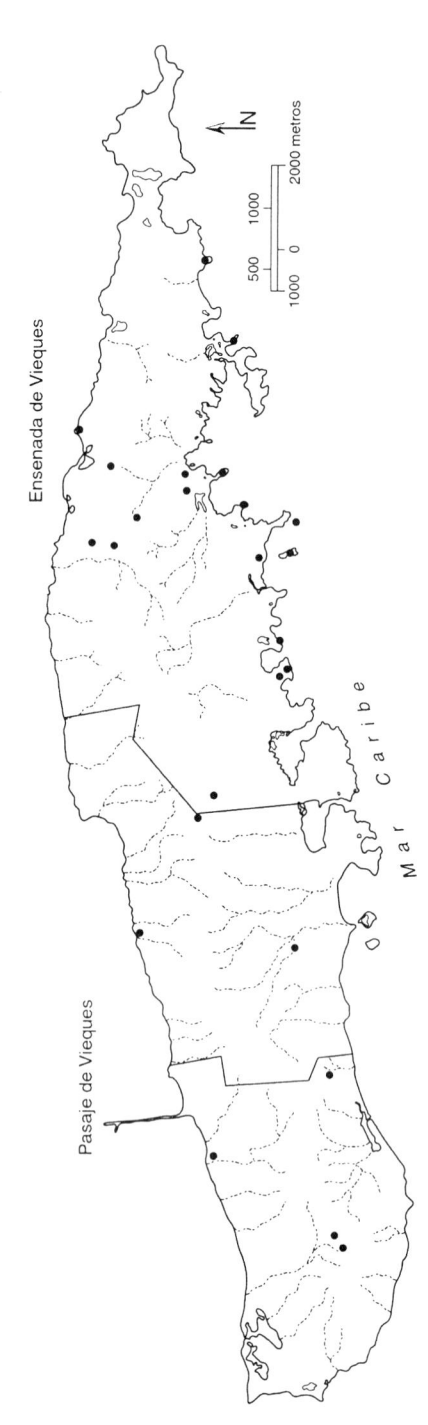

Figure 5.13. Map of Vieques showing the location of sites belonging to the Santa Elena style.

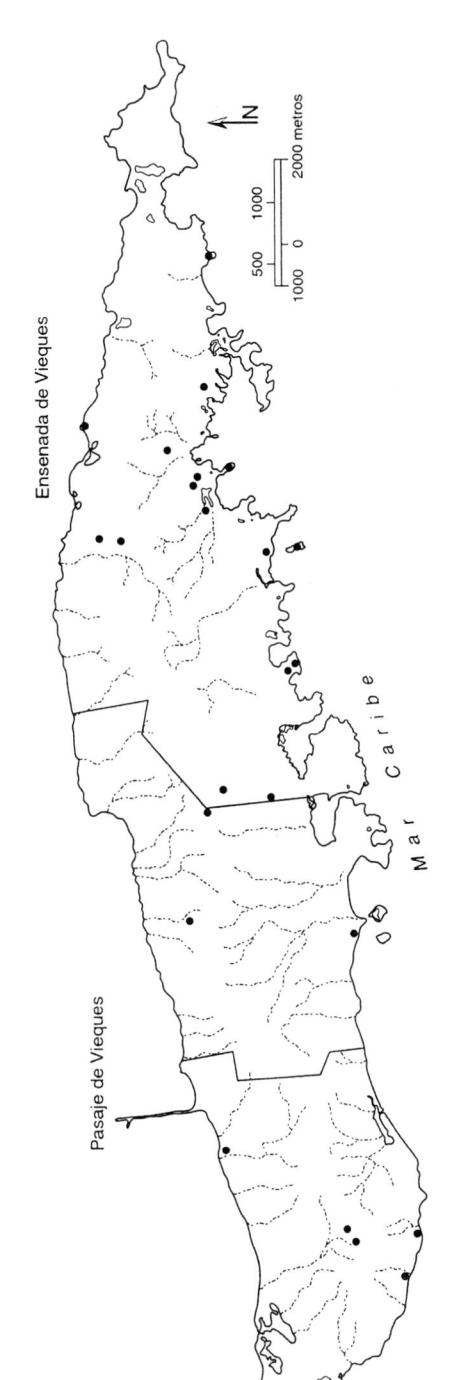

Figure 5.14. Map of Vieques showing the location of sites belonging to the Esperanza style.

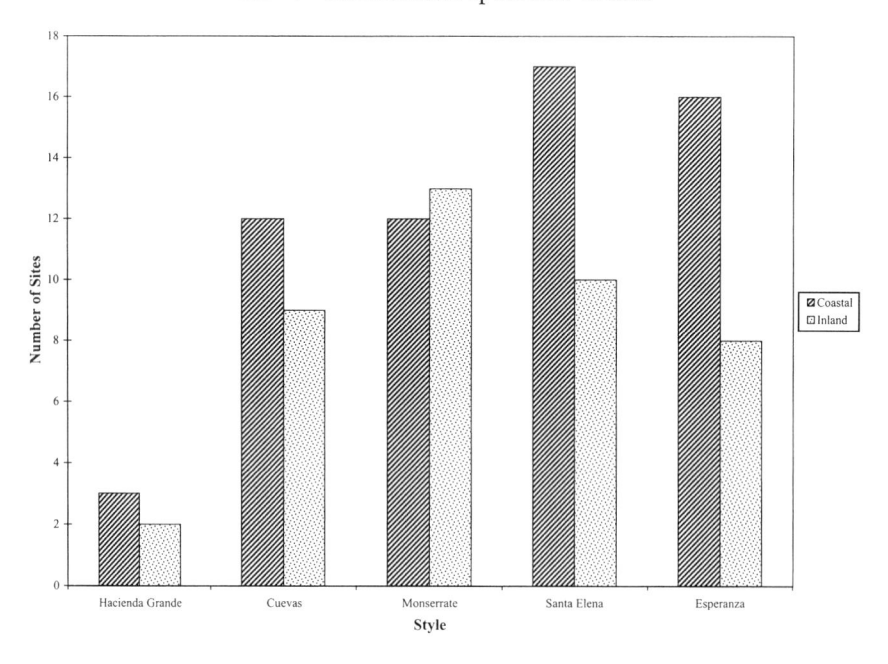

Figure 5.15. Distribution of sites across physiographic regions in the Island of Vieques.

Cuevas style. However, there is a tendency for inland sites to be a little more prevalent than coastal settlements during the Monserrate style (Figure 5.15). This trend is reversed in the Santa Elena and Esperanza styles, where the number of inland sites decreases sharply and the prevalence of coastal sites increases to more than double the amount of inland sites.

Site types also vary through time, but not as drastically as in the case of Loíza. During the early Saladoid series, sites were either villages or hamlets; small sites or camps do not appear until the Cuevas style, when they are the most common type of settlement, closely followed by hamlets. Similar to Loíza during the Monserrate style, the Cuevas style in Vieques shows a combination of dispersed and nucleated settlement patterns. This preponderance of small sites and hamlets (vs. villages) characterizes the rest of the sequence. Indeed, the drastic increase in number of sites registered for the Cuevas style (Figure 5.16) is mostly due to the proliferation of campsites and hamlets. Large sites or villages remain more or less constant (between three and seven villages) through the whole sequence, although they reach a maximum of seven villages during the Santa Elena style.

Interestingly, during the entire sequence, camps are located almost exclu-

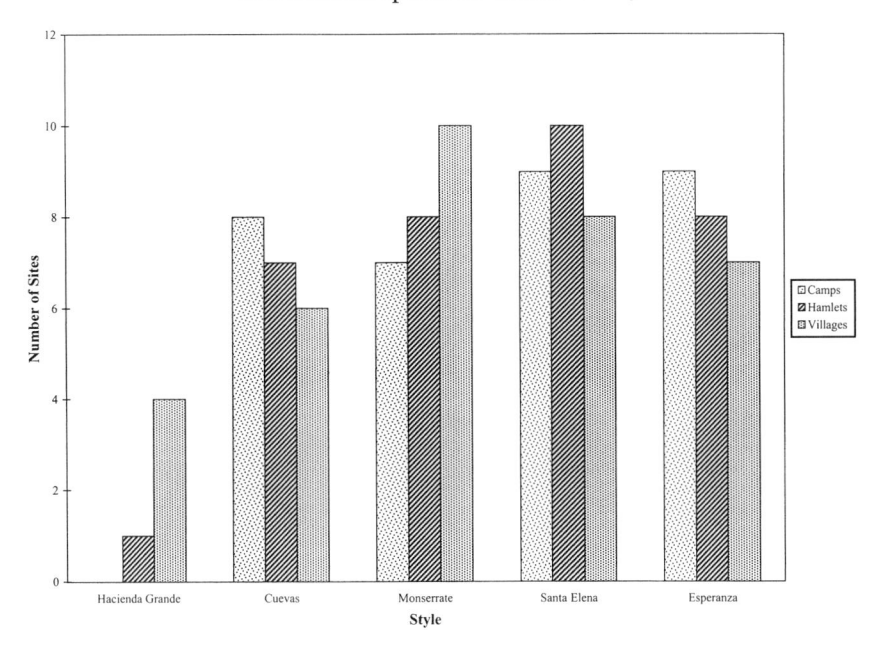

Figure 5.16. Distribution of site types through time in the Island of Vieques.

sively on the coast. Hamlets, on the other hand, are absent in coastal areas between the Hacienda Grande and the Monserrate styles. During the Santa Elena they are more abundant in coastal areas, but in the Esperanza style they are equally distributed (two hamlets each) between both areas. To the best of my knowledge only one site with a monumental structure has been reported (Rodríguez and Rivera 1983). This site, the site of Destino, belongs to the Esperanza style and is located on top of a steep hill almost in the center of the island. No other settlement with monumental architecture has been reported for any period.

Summarizing, the demographic trends in the island of Vieques seem to be characterized by an early increase in the number of sites during the Cuevas style. An increase in number of hamlets and small sites or camps is responsible for this dramatic surge in the total number of sites. The population more or less leveled off after this period, although, as in the case of the Loíza River Basin, the Santa Elena has the largest number of sites. This trend is reversed in the last period (the Esperanza style), when the total number of sites decreased slightly. The general distribution of site types was retained, with hamlets and campsites more prevalent than villages. However, from the Hacienda

Grande style to the Monserrate style, sites were distributed more or less equally between coastal and inland locations. It is not until the Santa Elena style that coastal sites are more dominant than inland sites. Thus, contrary to the Loíza River Basin, there is a general coastal tendency in Vieques during this time. In the Esperanza style, hamlets and villages are, again, equally distributed between both physiographic areas.

The Salinas River Region

The Salinas River region is located in the south-central coastal region of the island. The river originates in the Central Mountain Range of the island, flows southwest, and empties into the Bay of Rincón, just southwest of the town of Salinas. The river follows a similar hydrologic pattern as other rivers on the southern coast of Puerto Rico; they are short rivers with deep and sometimes shifting channels and with dry riverbeds most of the year. At times of intense rainfall these rivers flood. The Salinas River drains a total of 136 square kilometers and is considered one of the largest basins of the southern coast. The lower part of the area is included in the Subtropical Dry Forest zone, while the mountain range falls in the Subtropical Moist Forest zone of Ewel and Whitmore (1973). The physiography of the area can be divided in four regions. The first one is the littoral located along the Caribbean Sea and includes three large bays, Rincón, Salinas, and Jobos Bays. The bays are mined with chains of keys and coral reefs, and in some places the shoreline is edged with mangrove forests. The second region is the coastal plain, which averages 5.5 kilometers wide and is covered by ancient, fertile soils. The region is composed of lowlands, terraces, and fans of alluvial origin. The third region is the semidry foothills of the south coast. These foothills average 8 kilometers in width and are characterized by gently sloping hills, discrete river valleys, and stony, clayey loam soils. The last region is the Central Mountain Range, which crosses the island from east to west. This region consists of steep slopes and relatively high elevations.

The information used below on this region came from two regional studies. The first one was a probabilistic, stratified sampling survey of a military base located in the Coastal Plains and Foothills of the region (Rodríguez 1985). The study covered about 10 percent of the 12,000 acres that composed the military reservation, by dividing the area into 500 m sectors. A total of 22 pre-Hispanic sites were discovered within the limits of the installation. To categorize the location of sites, Rodríguez developed a formula that considered the particular river system where the site is located, the physiographic zone, and the type of soil.

The second study was conducted by Torres (2001), who included the Salinas River Basin as part of a larger region of the south-central coast of Puerto Rico. Using GIS (geographic information system) to analyze the data collected from the State Historic Preservation Office, Torres investigated the relationship between the location of the sites, their attributes, and other ecological, economic, and social variables. In addition to the sites reported by Rodríguez, Torres's study adds sites located on the coastal plains, littoral, and the mountains. In this case, Torres divided the region in four subdivisions based on their physiographic characteristics. The first region is the Coastal Plain, which extends from the coast to approximately 70 masl and embraces the littoral and coastal plains. The second region is the Foothills, which is delimited by elevations of 70 and 225 masl. The third and fourth regions consist of the highlands of the Central Mountain Range, with the Upland region located between 225 and 450 masl and the Mountain region between 450 and 1,300 masl. The study presented in this chapter uses Torres's subdivisions of the area with one modification. Because of difficulty in distinguishing between the Upland and Mountain regions, I have decided to combine them in one category. Thus, sites in this study will be considered to be located in one of the following three regions: Coastal Plains, Foothills, and the Uplands/Mountains.

Using the information obtained from Rodríguez's (1985) study and the site forms from the State Historic Preservation Office, Torres developed a site typology. The first type is called Hamlet/Special Activity sites, where he combined mostly small sites, some of which were recorded in SHPO as campsites. There are two reasons for combining these two categories. First, many of the small sites may represent misidentified settlements that, while small, may actually represent one-house locations as part of a dispersed settlement pattern common all over the south coast of Puerto Rico (e.g., Rodríguez 1986). Second, from the information provided it was difficult to determine what criteria were used to classify sites as camp or special activity sites. The second site type is Villages with Monumental Architecture Absent. These refer to clearly nucleated settlements that can be considered villages. The third type, Villages with Monumental Architecture Present, is similar to the second but has a ball court or plaza. The last site type consists of Monumental Architecture without evidence of domestic habitation, a type of site not uncommon in some regions of Puerto Rico (Oliver 1999). I use these four categories in the present study.

The distributions of sites for the Salinas River region are shown in Figures 5.17 to 5.19. In contradistinction to the fine chronological control available for

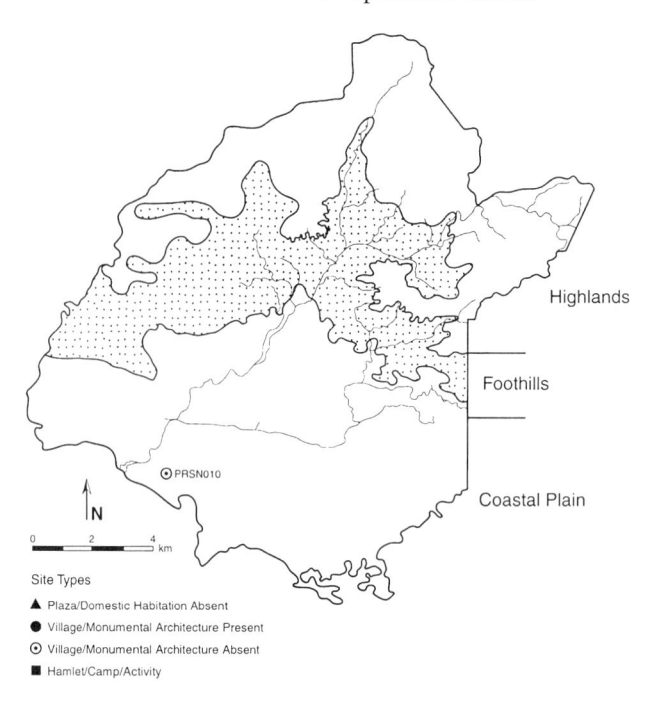

Figure 5.17. Map of the Salinas River Basin showing location of sites belonging to the Saladoid series.

the Loíza River Basin and Vieques, the sociotemporal information from this region is not based on styles but on subseries—broader cultural units. This is in part due to the nature of survey coverage for this portion of the island as well as the resultant documented data generated by such projects through time. Although some of the fine details are lost due to this lack of chronological precision, the general trends in settlement patterns are still comparable to the ones from the Loíza River Basin and Vieques and provide the basis for developing working hypotheses and further debates and research. To compensate for this lack of precision, however, the discussion on regional data is complemented below with more detailed information from particular sites studied in the south-central region of Puerto Rico.

General trends in the number of sites for this region through time indicate a notable population increase during the Elenan Ostionoid subseries (A.D. 600–1200) (Figures 5.18 and 5.20). Information available from many of the Elenan sites suggests that the bulk of the increase occurred mainly during the second half of the period, during the Santa Elena style (Curet et al. 2004;

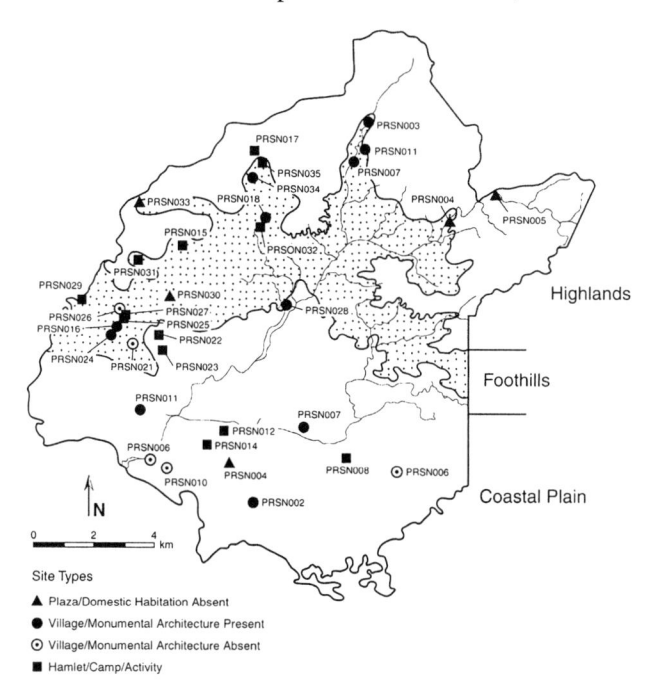

Figure 5.18. Map of the Salinas River Basin showing location of sites belonging to Elenan Ostionoid subseries.

Lundberg 1985; Rodríguez 1983, 1985). As in the case of the Loíza River Basin, but more pronounced, this seems to indicate a considerable growth of population during the Santa Elena style. An additional observation made by Torres (2001; see also Curet et al. 2004) on the settlement pattern for the South-Central region during this period is that three major clusters of sites separated by areas with low site densities seem to be apparent. The Salinas River Basin is one of these clusters. Further research conducted by Torres (2001) has suggested that these clusters, which begin to become apparent by the end of the Cedrosan Saladoid subseries (300 B.C.–A.D. 600), may indicate localized spheres of sociopolitical interaction.

Another comparable trend is the decrease in the number of sites during the Esperanza style or Chican Ostionoid subseries (A.D. 1200–1500) (Figures 5.19 and 5.20). However, the drop in these figures is more drastic than in the other two previous cases (see below), and several of the sites seem to have included one or more ball courts and/or plazas. The abandonment of sites appears to have affected more the Foothills than the Coastal Plains (Figure 5.21) and

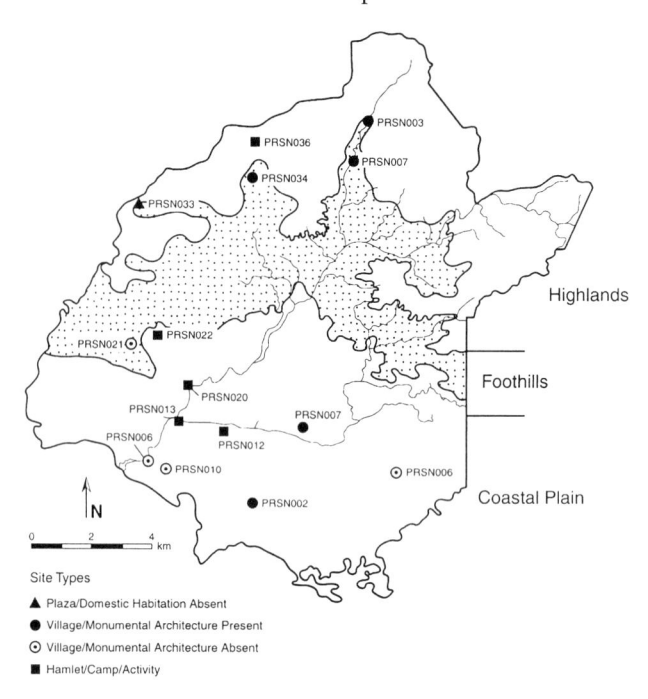

Figure 5.19. Map of the Salinas River Basin showing locations of sites belonging to Chican Ostionoid subseries.

seems to have been a widespread phenomenon through the southern coast of Puerto Rico (Lundberg 1985; M. Rodríguez 1983, 1985; Torres 2001).

In terms of site types, the Cedrosan Saladoid subseries is represented in the Salinas River Basin only by one hamlet (see Figures 5.17 and 5.20). A wide range of site types, including small sites, sites composed simply of monumental structures, and villages with monumental architecture, developed during the Elenan Ostionoid subseries, indicating a diversification of the function of many sites. This suggests the formation of a complicated settlement pattern that included more than just a dispersed and nucleated distribution of settlements. The number of site types decreased slightly during the Esperanza style, but the settlement pattern still seems to be complicated (Figure 5.22).

The general population pattern (as suggested by site distributions) through time is also similar to the one observed in the Loíza River Basin (Figures 5.9 and 5.21). Saladoid settlements are located primarily in lower elevations close to the coast, while during the Elenan Ostionoid subseries communities were founded at higher elevations and farther inland as the population grew. How-

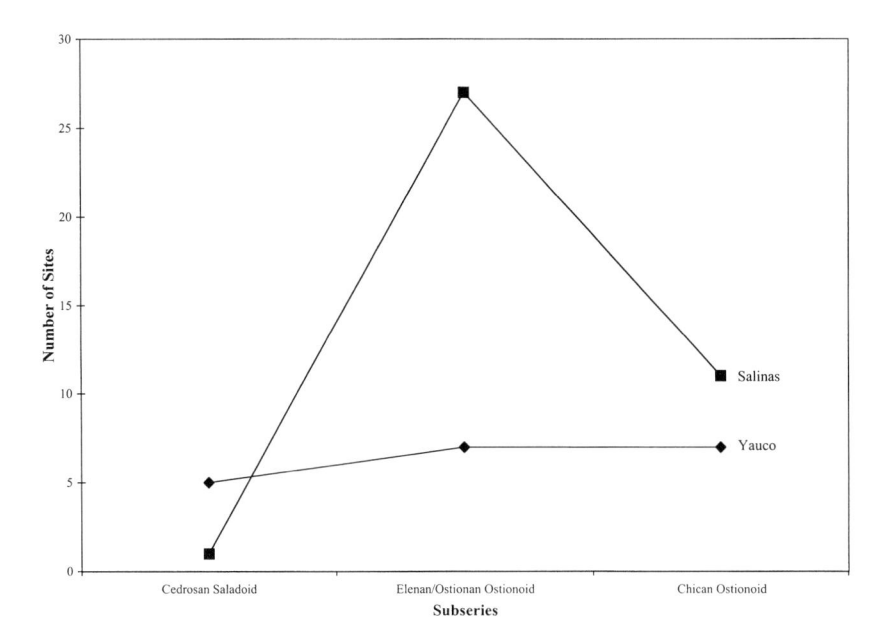

Figure 5.20. Distribution of number of sites through time in the Salinas and Yauco River Basins.

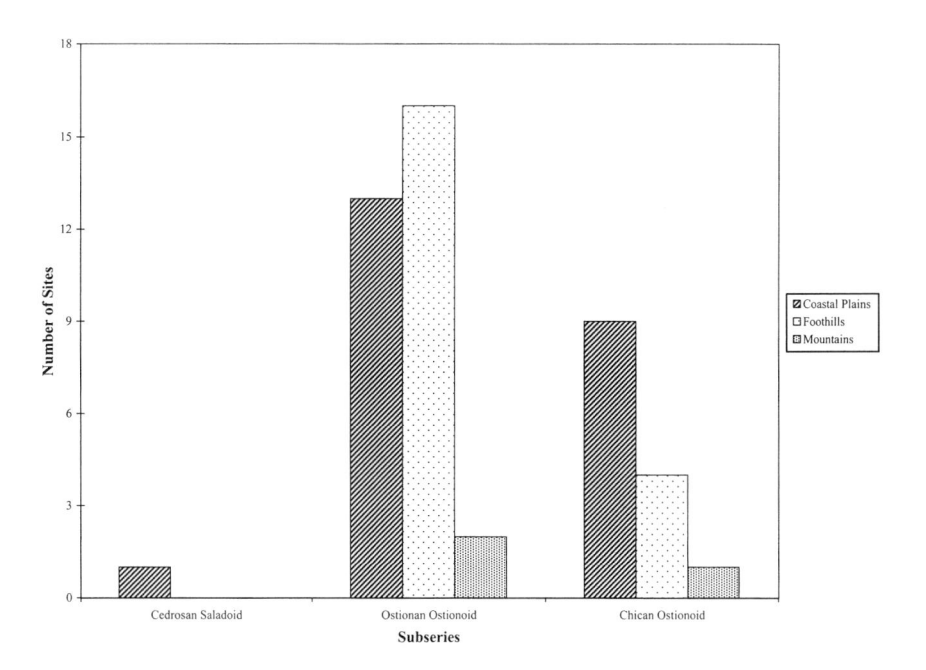

Figure 5.21. Distribution of sites across physiographic regions in the Salinas River Basin.

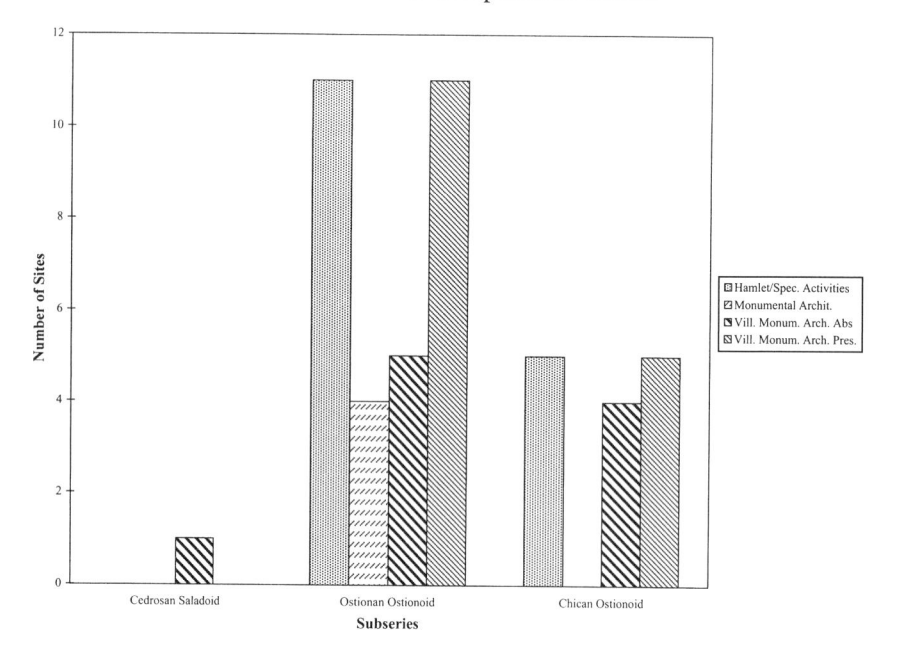

Figure 5.22. Distribution of site types through time in the Salinas River Basin.

ever, evidence from a number of sites located in the foothills of other river basins of south-central Puerto Rico suggests that the beginning of population movement to the interior may have occurred during the early Saladoid series or the Hacienda Grande style (Curet et al. 2003; Curet et al. 2004; González Colón 1984; Maiz 1996:91, 2002). This would have been several centuries earlier than the movement inland in the Loíza River Basin. This distribution may reflect opportunistic subsistence strategies (Siegel 1991) that took advantage of multiple ecological zones by locating community sites midway between the coast and the upland regions. An alternative explanation is that it may represent early stages of the colonization process (e.g., exploration, hunting trips, etc.) as described in the previous chapters.

Sites located in the foothills are more prevalent during the Elenan Ostionoid subseries, a pattern produced by the increase in the number of sites and possibly the economic importance of access to multiple resource locations. During this time monumental architecture in the form of ball courts and plazas is built in many sites, more than half of them in the foothills. More of these structures may have been present in lower elevations, but they may have been destroyed by agricultural and other cultural activities in recent times (Alegría 1983). Some of the sites that include communities with monumental architecture in general show a centralized pattern with smaller settlements surrounding them.

As mentioned above, during the Chican Ostionoid subseries a number of sites in the foothill areas, including several with monumental architecture, were abandoned, and most of the population became concentrated in the coastal plains. Although a drop in the number of sites is observable among all site types, the bulk of the reduction is composed of Hamlet/Special Activity sites located mostly in the foothills. Furthermore, all of the abandoned sites with monumental architecture are located in this latter area. In addition, some centralized distribution is also apparent during this time.

Summarizing, as in the Loíza River Basin, the general trend in the distribution of sites through time in the Salinas River Basin is a tendency of early sites concentrating in coastal plains, and a later movement to the interior foothills. During the Elenan Ostionoid subseries most of the sites were located in the foothills with a ratio of 2 to 1 compared to the number of settlements in the coastal plains. However, in later times and contrary to Loíza, there is a general tendency of locating sites near the coast. Coastal sites in the Chican Ostionoid subseries more than double the number of sites in the foothills. This change in emphasis of site location occurred concomitantly with a drastic drop in site numbers and the abandonment of many settlements in the foothills, including several with monumental architecture.

Yauco River Basin

I am using the term Yauco River Basin to refer to this region, but in reality it includes two river systems that I have decided to combine to increase the sample size. These river systems are the Yauco River, of course, and the Guayanilla River. Although they can be considered separate hydraulic systems and their points of origin are far apart, they are much closer together in the coastal plains (< 5 km) being separated by relatively low hills. Further, their river mouths open to the same bay (Guayanilla Bay) at about two kilometers apart. Thus, even though geographically these basins are two different systems, considering their proximity in the coastal plains where most of the indigenous population concentrated and the fact that they are also connected by another body of water (Guayanilla Bay), I have decided to combine them in this study. This is not to say that both basins were part of the same social, economic, and political system. This may or may not be true, but more information is needed to make such a statement.

The Yauco and the Guayanilla River Basins are located in the southwestern coast of Puerto Rico on the south side of the Cordillera Central, or Central

Mountain Range. The Yauco River originates on the Central Mountain Range and flows from northwest to southeast, emptying into the Bay of Guayanilla. The Guayanilla River originates in the same Central Mountain Range but farther east, flowing from the north to the south and converging with the Yauco River in Guayanilla Bay. The total area of the Yauco Basin is 120 km^2, while the Guayanilla Basin is smaller. Both systems include three geographic regions as defined by Picó (1974): the western wet zone, the southern dry hills, and the south coastal plains. The basins also include two different ecological life zones as defined by Ewel and Whitmore (1973): the Subtropical Moist Forest, represented in the high part of the basin, and the Subtropical Dry Forest, found mostly in the Foothills and the Coastal Plains.

The Yauco River begins in the steep mountains of the volcanic Central Mountain Range at an elevation of about 680 masl. It flows down to the limestone foothills, where the average elevation drops relatively quickly to 150 masl. Throughout these hills several small tributaries empty into the Yauco River. The river eventually reaches the Coastal Plains, which can be divided in two areas, one immediately adjacent to the coast, with an average elevation of 5 masl, and the other an area that rises slowly to an elevation of 25 masl. The Guayanilla River follows a similar route, although it does not flow near the low sedimentary rises in the Coastal Plains. Both rivers form part of a system of mangrove forests that surround most of the shoreline of Guayanilla Bay.

Most of the information used in this study was obtained from the reports of Maíz López and Questell Rodríguez (1984, 1990), who conducted a stratified sampling survey. The authors of this project divided the Yauco River Basin into five strata:

Stratum A: coastal plain, < 5 masl
Stratum B: lower basin, between 5 and 25 masl
Stratum C: middle basin, between 25 and 160 masl
Stratum D: upper basin, between 160 masl and 680 masl
Stratum E: the coastal dry forest and limestone bluffs along the coast

Between 17 percent and 23 percent of the area of each stratum was surveyed, with a total average of approximately 20 percent of the whole basin. Although the authors did not create a site typology, in their discussion they distinguished between possible habitation sites and temporary campsites.

Additional information was obtained from Torres (2001), who also included the Yauco and Guayanilla River Basins in his study of the south-central coast of Puerto Rico. In this case, he added sites from the archives of the State Historic Preservation Office to the ones reported by Maíz López and Questell Rodríguez. In his analysis, however, he used the same physiographic regions mentioned for Salinas. To retain some level of consistency with the Salinas River Basin, I have decided here to use Torres's physiographic regions. Thus, the Yauco River Basin was divided into three sections: the Coastal Plains (0–70 masl); the Foothills (70–25 masl), and the Uplands/Mountains (> 225 masl). Furthermore, I use the same site typology developed by Torres and mentioned for the Salinas River Basin, although not all of the types are present in the sample from the Yauco and Guayanilla River Basins. Finally, rock shelters and caves were eliminated from the analysis, since they may not have been used as habitation sites. Even if they were, their contribution to the general populations of the region should have been minimal.

In general, the site sample from this region is relatively small, in part because the regional study that collected the data used a stratified sampling strategy and not a full-coverage survey. In addition, the region has not been studied as intensively as other parts of the island. Although the trends in population dynamics for this region are not as clear as for the other three examples, I have decided to include them in this comparative analysis to form a wider and more complete picture of the different population processes that may have been active throughout the island, including the various cultural regions. The Yauco River Basin is the only region included in this chapter that theoretically does not belong to the Elenan Ostionoid, or the culture area named for the Vieques Sound by Rouse. It is actually located in the Mona Passage culture area, belonging to the Ostionan Ostionoid, which tends to share some cultural trends with eastern Hispaniola. A general difference between the distribution of sites in the Yauco River Basin compared to the other regions is that all habitation sites from all periods are located exclusively in the Coastal Plains.

The distributions of sites across time in the Yauco River Basin are shown in Figures 5.23 to 5.25. On the one hand, the general pattern of number of sites through time is very different from the pattern for the Salinas River Basin and, to a lesser degree, the pattern for the Loíza River Basin, but on a smaller scale because of the small sample. On the other hand, the pattern is more similar to the general pattern for Vieques. The frequency of sites increases from the Cedrosan Saladoid (300 B.C.–A.D. 900) to the Ostionan Ostionoid (A.D. 600–1200) and remains unchanged in the Chican Ostionoid (A.D. 1200–1500).

During the Cedrosan Saladoid subseries, and similar to other regions, the

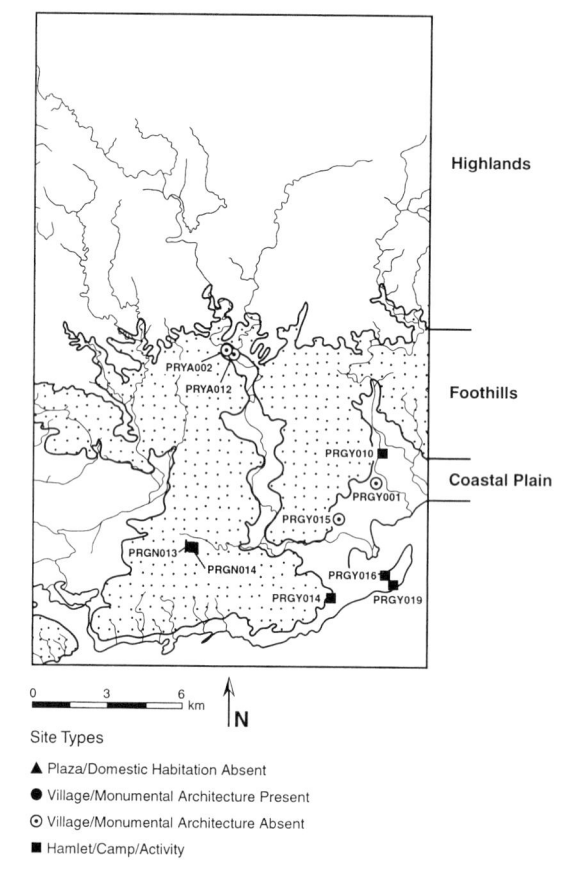

Figure 5.23. Map of the Yauco River Basin showing locations of sites belonging to Saladoid series.

number of villages or large sites exceeded the number of smaller settlements (see Figure 5.23). An interesting trend observable for this period, however, is that while all of the early sites are concentrated on the coastal plains as in the other three regions, two of the three largest ones (villages) are located more than 10 km away from the coast (see Figure 5.23). This suggests inland incursions earlier than in some of the other regions. This difference may be due more to differences in coastal physiography than to cultural or social reasons (see Maíz López and Questell Rodríguez 1984, 1990 for a more thorough discussion). While the coast in the Loíza and Salinas River Basins and Vieques include low beaches, the Yauco River Basin has a more abrupt coastal line, characterized in part by littoral cliffs, the prevalence of mangroves, and a lack

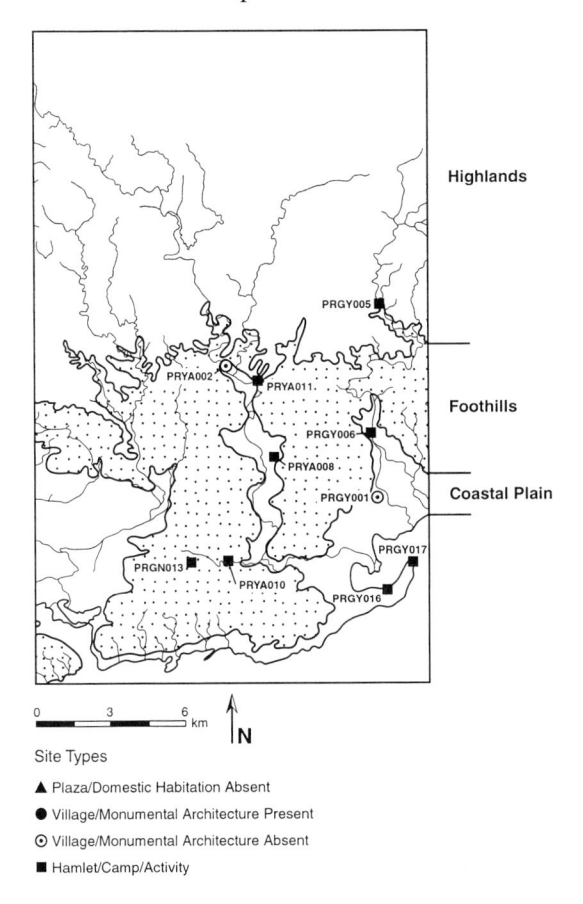

Figure 5.24. Map of the Yauco River Basin showing locations of sites belonging to Ostionan Ostionoid subseries.

of beaches suitable for landing canoes, which would have made seafaring a bit more difficult. Further, the inland soils of the coastal plains, which are volcanic in nature, are more fertile than the soils of the coastal plains, which are of sedimentary origin. Also, the littoral of the coastal plains tends to be markedly drier than the inland area, making farming more difficult in lower elevations. Alternatively, the sites may simply have been destroyed beyond recognition with the heavy development of areas around Guayanilla Bay in modern times. This explanation, although it should be kept in mind, does not address why villages and smaller sites are found for later periods closer to the coast.

During the Ostionan Ostionoid subseries (Figures 5.20 and 5.24), the total number of sites increased, but most of the increase came from the founding

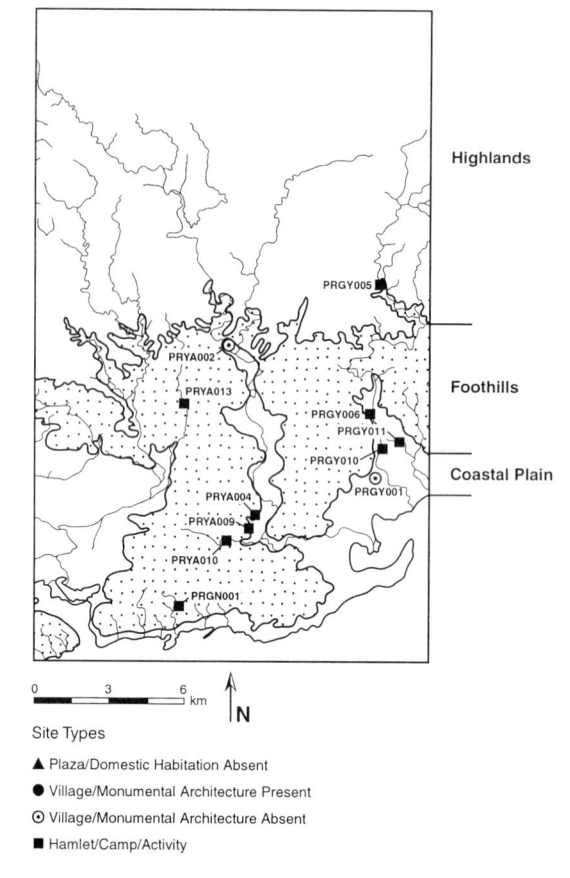

Figure 5.25. Map of the Yauco River Basin showing locations of sites belonging to Chican Ostionoid subseries.

of new, small settlements. In fact, the number of small sites (hamlets and camps) surpassed the number of villages, a pattern opposite to the one observed for the previous period. This period has only one village less than the Cedrosan Saladoid subseries.

Unlike in the other regions, the Chican Ostionoid in the Yauco River Basin shows the same number of sites as the Ostionan Ostionoid subseries (Figures 5.20 and 5.25). Although during this period hamlets and special activity sites continued being predominant and the total number of sites remains constant, the graph in Figure 5.26 shows that the proportions of site types varied. The Chican Ostionoid subseries shows a decrease of one village and an increase of one hamlet or special-activity site. This abandonment of a relatively large site

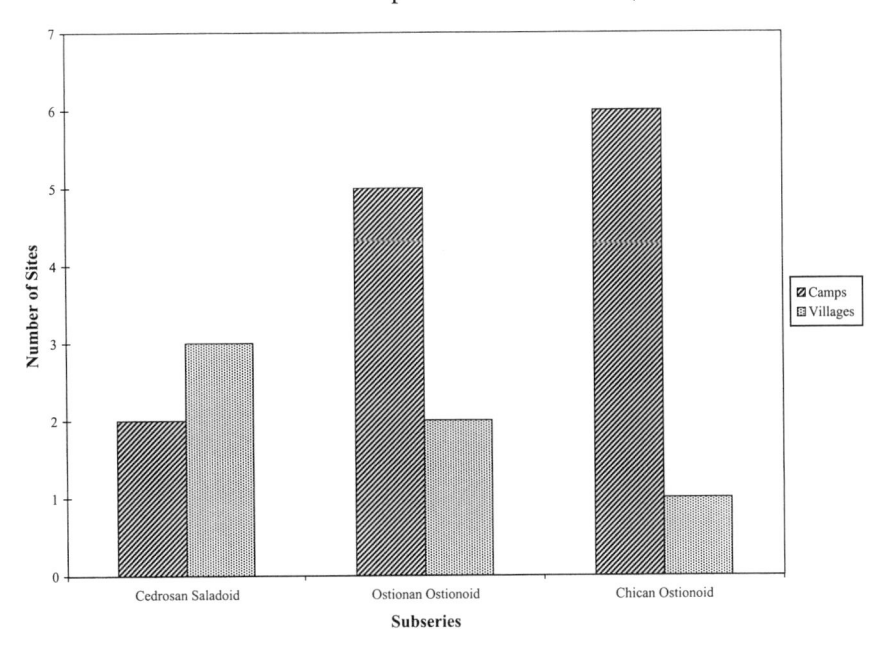

Figure 5.26. Distribution of site types through time in the Yauco River Basin.

(the site of Tecla; Chanlatte Baik 1976, 1977), and the founding of a much smaller one, suggests a general decrease in the true population of the area. The magnitude of this reduction, however, is difficult to determine with the data at hand.

There are two other important differences between the Yauco region and the Loíza and Salinas River Basins. The first is the absence of sites with ball courts and plazas in the sample. A ball court has been reported for the site of Mattei (Alegría 1983:109; Rouse 1952:537), on a river basin west of the Yauco River system, but the presence of monumental architecture in my sample has not been confirmed. Supposedly, monumental architecture has been reported for two of the sites in the region (the sites of Diego Hernández and Tecla). But after consulting the bibliographical sources cited in the case of the site of Diego Hernández and a personal communication with Luis Chanlatte, excavator of Tecla, it was concluded that these reports reflected more the perceptions of previous researchers than actual observations of strong evidence for the presence of monumental architecture. Thus, to maintain a certain degree of consistency and to be on the conservative side, these sites are here considered to be simple villages without any monumental structure.

This lack of monumental architecture in the Yauco region is not surprising. The construction of ball courts and plazas is usually but not always (e.g., Rivera Fontán and Silva Pagán 1997, 2002) connected to eastern Puerto Rico or the Elenan Ostionoid subseries (Alegría 1983), and not to western Puerto Rico or the Ostionan Ostionoid subseries to which this region belongs. Even so, these differences between nearby regions raise a question that should be addressed in future research, especially when we remember that relatively large, long-lived villages are included in the Yauco sample, some of which, it has been speculated, were the seats of powerful chiefs.

The second difference between the settlement pattern of this region and the other three regions is that there is no clear emergence of a centralized distribution of sites in which several smaller sites are located around a single larger site. It is not clear whether the lack of such a pattern reflects the actual archaeological situation or is an artifact of the small sample size. If confirmed in future studies, this lack of centralization may indicate some major and great differences in the internal organization of regional populations between the Yauco River Basin and the three other regions. It will also be interesting to determine how common the lack of this pattern was for post-Saladoid times in western Puerto Rico or the Ostionan Ostionoid subseries.

In general, then, the number of sites in the Yauco River Basin tended to follow patterns observed in other areas of Puerto Rico, but perhaps not to the same degree. The number of sites increased between the Cedrosan Saladoid and Ostionan Ostionoid subseries but remained surprisingly constant during the Chican Ostionoid subseries. If we consider that this stability between periods was temporally associated with the abandonment of one large site and the founding of a smaller one, it is possible that the region experienced a decrease in population, but probably of a smaller magnitude than the population decrease observed in the Salinas River Basin. However, while I do believe that the general trend is correct, I am not sure of the precision in terms of the magnitude of the changes because of the small sample size. Unlike the other regions, most of the early villages (Cedrosan Saladoid) in the Yauco River Basin area are not located near the coast but are farther inland in the Coastal Plains. It is unclear if the reasons for this are the differences in environmental settings, subsistence practices, cultural and/or social conditions, or the destruction of early sites along the coast by modern development. However, considering that later sites are found in the Coastal areas, it is possible that this is not so much an artifact of the sampling procedures or poor conservation, but mainly a pattern produced by other social, cultural, and/or economic reasons.

Regional Comparisons

The four regions—three in Puerto Rico, the fourth in Vieques—show a constant increase in number of sites up to the end of the Elenan and Ostionan Ostionoid subseries (A.D. 600–1200) or the Santa Elena and Ostiones styles (A.D. 900–1200), when they reached their highest number of sites. However, this increase in number of sites was neither uniform nor constant for all periods and all regions. In Loíza, although some increase in number of sites is observable during the Hacienda Grande and Monserrate styles, it is not until the Santa Elena style that the number of sites more than triples from the previous period. In Vieques, a similar large-scale increase occurred much earlier, during the Hacienda Grande style, when the number of sites quadrupled. In these two regions most of the increase reflected an increase in the number of small sites, some of which may have been special-activity sites. In Salinas the number of sites increased severalfold between the Cedrosan Saladoid and the Elenan Ostionoid subseries (i.e., between A.D. 400 and 1200), but without better chronological data it is difficult to establish more accurately the timing of this change. In this case, the increase in site number occurred across the entire range of site types—small, medium, and large—including villages with monumental architecture. In Yauco as in Salinas, the increase in sites again seems to have occurred sometime between the Cedrosan Saladoid and the Ostionan Ostionoid subseries, but it seems to have been due mostly to an increase in the number of small sites.

With the exception of Yauco, the sequences also show a decrease in the number of sites during the Chican Ostionoid subseries, but the size of the reduction and which kinds of sites decreased in number vary between the regions. The difference in the number of sites between the Santa Elena and the Esperanza style in the Loíza River Basin is only three sites, or 12.5 percent, and on Vieques Island there are two less sites, or a reduction of 8.7 percent. A more dramatic reduction is observed in the Salinas River Basin, where 17 (or 54.8 percent) fewer sites are present during the Chican Ostionoid subseries than before. The Yauco River Basin does not show a change in the number of sites for this same period.

To determine whether the drastic reduction in the number of sites in Salinas could be attributable to the broad chronological units used (i.e., subseries), I calculated the number of sites in the Loíza River Basin and on Vieques for each subseries, instead of style (see Figure 5.27). As can be observed from this figure, even when the number of sites in all regions is considered at the subseries level, Salinas still exhibits the most dramatic decrease in number of

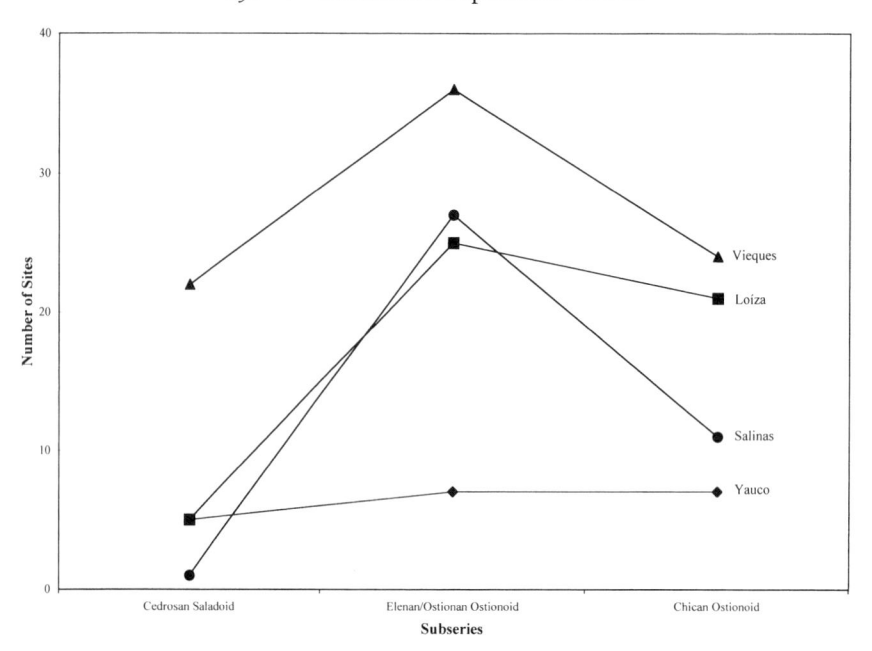

Figure 5.27. Distribution of number of sites through time in all regions.

sites between the Elenan and the Chican Ostionoid subseries, although closely followed by Vieques. Also, Yauco still presents the most stable population between these two periods. Thus, the general differences discussed in the comparisons presented in the previous section do not seem to be an artifact of differences in the chronological/cultural units used in the analysis. On the contrary, these differences seem to be real.

Most of the reduction in number of sites in the Loíza River Basin is due to the abandonment of small, dispersed sites located in the Low area of the region, especially those sites located along the coast; larger and older sites continued to be inhabited. The number of sites in the Intermediate and High areas of the south-central region remained constant, and some ball courts, plazas, and even ceremonial centers, still not common, continued to be in use, or new ones were built. No Santa Elena–style settlement with monumental architecture (if such existed) was abandoned by the Esperanza style. For the first time in the sequence, the number of sites in the High areas slightly exceeded the number of settlements in the Low areas. On Vieques, the slight reduction in the number of sites between the Santa Elena and Esperanza styles occurred exclusively at the level of hamlets; the number of villages and campsites remained constant. The general distribution of sites across physiographic regions also remained constant, with a larger number of settlements located along the coast.

In contrast, in the Salinas region a number of sites that were abandoned by the Chican Ostionoid subseries were villages located in the Foothills, many having one or more monumental structures. Interestingly, the relative proportions of the different site types remained more or less constant in this region, from the Elenan to the Chican Ostionoid subseries. So, the changes between these two periods occurred more in the absolute number of sites and in population focus, which shifted from the Foothills to the Coastal Plains. This rather dramatic decrease in site number and the abandonment of major sites, many of them with monumental architecture, characterizes other regions of the southern coast of Puerto Rico at the end of the Elenan Ostionoid period (Curet 1992a; Curet et al. 2003; Curet et al. 2004; González 1984; Lundberg 1985; Rodríguez 1983, 1985; Torres 2001). The Yauco River Basin did not experience an observable reduction in the number of sites, but considering that this apparent stability resulted from the abandonment of a large village and the formation of a small hamlet, this region probably experienced a small decrease in population, too. Interestingly, sites for all periods in this region are located in the Coastal Plains. Thus, as in the case of Loíza and Vieques, the general distribution of sites remained more or less constant in the Yauco River Basin, but with a larger concentration of sites along the coastal plains than in the upper foothills or inland. It can be concluded that while a reduction in the number of sites is observed for most of the islands of Puerto Rico and Vieques during late pre-Columbian times, the rate, magnitude, and nature of the abandonment of sites may have varied from region to region.

The distribution of settlements over the various physiographic areas also shows similarities and differences among the four regions. The general trend is one of a movement of population from the coastal plains to the interior, and then a shift in population density focusing again on the coastal plains. Yauco and Vieques are somewhat exceptions to this general pattern, since most of the Saladoid villages in the former are located within 10 km from the coast, and in the latter they are more or less equally distributed between coastal and inland areas. Later, during the Cuevas style times, people seem to have made incursions farther inland in the High areas of the Loíza River Basin, but not so much in the Salinas or Yauco region, where populations stayed mostly in the Foothills and the Coastal Plains, respectively. This discrepancy may have been produced by physiographic differences, especially those related to the accessibility to the central, intermontane valleys. The northern side of Puerto Rico has a wider coastal plain with elevations rising gradually and more distant from the coast than along the southern coast. The southern side of the Central Mountain Range tends to rise sharply at a relatively short distance from the ocean, restricting movement from the coastal plain to the interior mountains. An illustration of the difference is the average slope of several rivers in Puerto Rico flowing north and south. The average slope for seven major rivers flowing north (Picó 1974:Table 1) is 25 m/km, while the average for six major rivers in the southern half of Puerto Rico is 45 m/km. These figures indicate a relatively steep drop in elevation for rivers in the south compared to rivers in the north. The northern high regions (i.e., the north side of the highlands, or the Central Mountain Range) also have more suitable and accessible areas (i.e., relatively flat and fertile interior valleys) for human habitation than the southern side of the mountain ranges. One of these is the Valley of Caguas, in the upper Loíza River Basin. It is possible that the coarseness of the data from the Salinas and Yauco regions resulted in several distributional patterns being lumped together and hidden within the broader Period III, but we still have to consider that the different population patterns noted for the Salinas and Yauco regions may have resulted from lack of access to High areas from the southern coast. However, these patterns could have also been produced by differences in social, political, and economic factors, such as interactions with Archaic groups from Puerto Rico or Hispaniola, access to particular resources, and so on.

During the Elenan Ostionoid subseries, the Salinas River Basin shows a shift in site density, with the Foothills containing a higher number of sites than the Coastal Plains. Although from the data it is not clear whether this trend started early in this subseries, some information from other sites on the southern coast suggests that the sharp increase occurred during the second half of the Elenan Ostionoid, that is, during the Santa Elena style (Curet 1992a; Lundberg 1985; Rodríguez 1985). In Yauco, the trend during this same period is different from the one observed for Salinas, where all sites remained exclusively in the Coastal Plains region.

A similar pattern is observed in the Loíza River Basin, but here it is clear that the population increase began early in the period, in other words during the Monserrate style, when site density was higher in the Intermediate area. In contrast, during the Santa Elena style population densities seem to have become polarized between the Low and the High areas, with the Intermediate area having the lowest number of sites. The polarization of the distribution of populations within the Loíza River Basin is also present during the Esperanza style, whereas in the Salinas region the population focus shifted again from the Foothills to the Coastal Plains. The social and political implications of these trends are discussed below.

The trends in Vieques are somewhat different. From the Hacienda Grande to the Monserrate styles, sites are more or less equally distributed between the Coastal and Inland areas. This tendency changes during the Santa Elena and Esperanza styles, when most of the sites are located in the Coastal area. However, this dominance of coastal sites is produced almost completely by an increase in number of campsites or other small sites along the coast. Otherwise, hamlets and villages are more or less equally distributed between both physiographic regions.

Other distributional patterns are observable in Loíza, Salinas, and Yauco beyond the one based on physiographic divisions. A trend observed in the data sets even since early Saladoid times is the propensity for communities to settle in major river valleys. This suggests that these drainages could serve as effective cultural, social, and political units of study. A closer look at the Loíza and Salinas drainages, and to some degree Vieques, indicates the presence throughout the whole sequence of clusters of sites, many of them located at the confluence of major streams, especially during the Ostionoid series (A.D. 600–1500). During Saladoid times most of the sites composing the clusters are relatively large villages, while the Santa Elena style includes both large nucleated and small, dispersed settlements. Several of the clusters of the Santa Elena style show an arrangement of sites following a centralized pattern, where large sites are surrounded by smaller settlements, including some dispersed domestic units or hamlets. In the Salinas region, many of the central settlements tend to have one or more ceremonial structures (i.e., ball courts or plazas); similar structures may have been present in considerably smaller frequencies in the Loíza River Basin, but more precise information on this is not available. This tends to support the argument for variability in social and political processes even between river basins in the same culture area.

Finally, the distribution of sites across the different physiographic landscapes in the Loíza River Basin follows a bimodal distribution, with the populations concentrated mostly in the Low and High areas during the Santa Elena and Esperanza styles. The Intermediate area shows low population densities. This polarization of the location of sites is not observable in the other regions. As mentioned earlier, some of these differences could have resulted from the absence of habitable, accessible intermontane valleys in the region. An equally possible explanation is that this polarized distribution of sites resulted instead from social, political, and economic processes. These processes, and their effects on population dynamics, have major implications for the study of the prehistoric peoples of Puerto Rico.

REGIONAL POPULATION DYNAMICS AND DEMOGRAPHIC INFLUENCES: INTRAISLAND DIFFERENCES AND SIMILARITIES

Several marked social, economic, political, and demographic changes occurred in Puerto Rico during its ancient history. It is obvious from the discussion above that while many of these changes seem to be similar at the level of the culture area, important differences exist when a comparison is made between regions within this area. Observations offered above show that homogeneity is certainly not the case. This realization is significant since eastern and western Puerto Rico are normally considered homogeneous cultural units in many of the models developed to explain social and cultural changes in the area (see Table 5.1). This suggests that while the various regions of this area share some cultural traditions they also may have experienced different and more localized social and political processes. Although many are the issues that can be discussed, here I concentrate on three major topics: population trends, the abandonment of sites, and settlement patterns and monumental architecture. Some of the issues have been presented in a preliminary manner elsewhere (Curet et al. 2004). We could also speculate about the fine details of the relationships between the observed population trends, as informed by the number of sites, and the ancient political organization and economy, although better data are needed than are presently available to offer these working hypotheses in confidence.

Population Trends

In general, population seems to have grown gradually in all regions, from the Cedrosan Saladoid to the early Elenan and Ostionan Ostionoid subseries. In the Loíza, Salinas, and possibly Yauco River Basins a dramatic increase in the population growth rate occurred between the Monserrate and Santa Elena styles, a common development in many regions of eastern Puerto Rico (Curet 1992a, 1993; Lundberg 1985; Rodríguez 1985, 1992; Torres 2001). Interestingly, this phenomenon coincides with a possible decline in population suggested for the Virgin Islands, east of Puerto Rico (Morse 1992; Vescelius n.d., cited in

Table 5.1. Diachronic Comparison of Regional Information for the Four Regions.

Period	Loíza River Basin	Island of Vieques	Salinas River Basin	Yauco River Basin
II	Few, mostly large sites located mostly in Low areas.	Few, mostly large sites located in Coastal areas. Second half of the Period, marked increase in the number of sites and larger diversity of site types. Coastal small sites and inland hamlets become more prevalent.	One hamlet in the Coastal areas.	All sites located in the Coastal Plains. Few, large sites most of them located inland. Small sites are located closer to the coast.
III	Increase in the diversity of site types. Large increase in number of sites during the second half of the Period. Population is polarized between the Low and High areas. Centralized settlement pattern Possibly, few sites with monumental architecture.	Increase in the diversity of sites. Slight increase in the number of sites. Distribution of sites during the early part of the Period is equative between coastal and inland areas. Coastal sites became more prevalent in the second half of the Period. Camp sites and hamlets are the most common site types, but villages are also present. Possible centralized settlement pattern. No evidence of monumental architecture is available for this Period.	Increase in the diversity of site types. Large increase in number of sites. Sites concentrate in the Foothills. Hamlets and small sites are the most prevalent settlements in both physiographic regions, although villages in the Foothills are also common. Centralized settlement patterns. Large number of sites with monumental structures, including "ceremonial centers," especially in the Foothills	Villages and smaller sites are present. Increase in the number of sites. All sites are located exclusively in Coastal areas. No evidence for monumental architecture is available for this Period. No evidence for centralized settlement pattern.

Continued on the next page

Table 5.1 Continued

Period	Loíza River Basin	Island of Vieques	Salinas River Basin	Yauco River Basin
IV	Slight decrease in number of sites. Abandonment of few small or medium sites. No strong evidence for decrease in population. Population is still polarized between Low and High areas. Centralized settlement pattern still present. Monumental structures are present at least in two sites.	Slight decrease in the number of sites. Abandonment of few sites, most of them are camp sites and hamlets. Villages and hamlets are distributed equally between Coastal and Inland areas; all camp sites are located in Coastal areas. Possible centralized settlement pattern. Evidence of one site with monumental architecture.	Abandonment of large number of sites, most of them hamlets and villages located in the foothills and several with monumental structures. Strong indications of a massive depopulation of the region. Population concentration shifts from the Foothills to the Coastal Plains. Settlement pattern shows a major disruption in the organization of sites over the landscape.	No change in total number of sites. One village was abandoned and one hamlet/special activity site was founded. No evidence for monumental architecture. No evidence for centralized settlement pattern.

Lundberg et al. 1992). Although both phenomena might be correlated, reflecting interisland migrations, no direct relationship can be confirmed with the information at hand until better regional data are available for the Virgin Islands.

Vieques shows a dramatic increase in number of sites much earlier, during the Hacienda Grande style or early Cedrosan Saladoid subseries. At this point it is not clear why Vieques experienced a surge in population at such an early time compared to the Puerto Rican regions, but a likely explanation is that demographic factors during this time were markedly different on Vieques. These differences may have included different rates of population growth due to the presence of some of the earliest Saladoid communities in the region (Chanlatte Baik 1981; Chanlatte Baik and Narganes Storde 1983, 1986), different forms of interactions between Saladoid groups and the Archaic groups, and differences in the interactions with other Saladoid groups from other regions, including other Lesser Antilles and the mainland.

During the Chican Ostionoid subseries the population in the four regions studied seems to have declined, although this change is more marked in the Salinas River Basin than in Yauco, Loíza, or Vieques. Although it is possible for a population to grow constantly in the absence of extraneous elements that might affect birth or mortality rates, the negative growth rates for this period may indicate that other factors influenced the population trends. The abnormal negative population growth rate for this period suggests that some drastic sociocultural measures were taken that reduced the total population. Since to date there is no archaeological evidence for epidemics, institutionalized warfare, famines, or any other major natural catastrophe that might have increased considerably the mortality rates or reduced the fertility rates for this period in Puerto Rico, it is reasonable to suggest that prehistoric cultures either were practicing some kind of population control or were migrating to other areas. Because the early chronicles do not mention any birth control practice among the late prehistoric groups, it seems more likely that this decline in population was mainly produced by emigration to other areas within Puerto Rico, or perhaps to other islands. Peter Roe (personal communication, 1991) has suggested that the decrease in population during late prehistoric times in Puerto Rico might have been produced by migrations to the island of Hispaniola. Other possibilities have been suggested by Rodríguez (1992), especially population movements to the interior mountainous regions of Puerto Rico. Rodríguez (1992) has reported that in the Loíza River Basin, the population shifted from the coast to inland valleys through time, and this shift correlated with the development of ceremonial and political centers in these areas. This argument is supported partially by recent work conducted by Oliver (1998) in the interior region of Caguana, Utuado, where a slight increase in the number of sites is apparent for the Chican Ostionoid. However, Caguana, like the Loíza River Basin, is located on the northern side of Puerto Rico, which may show a trend different from what may have taken place in other areas of the islands, including the southern coast.

Independently of the explanation used, we have to consider that the degree and nature of the decrease in populations vary between regions. In general, the drop in population in the Salinas River Basin is larger in magnitude than in the Loíza and Yauco River Basins and Vieques. In fact, considering that the sites that were abandoned in two of the latter three cases are only three and two small settlements respectively, it is possible that none of these regions experienced a decrease in the total population, since the people that moved may have been absorbed by larger communities. More refined population estimates, however, are needed to determine the magnitude of population decrease in the Yauco and Loíza River Basins and Vieques. The situation in the Salinas River Basin, though, is clearer. This region suffered not only a large exodus of people but also the abandonment of a great number of sites with monumental architecture. This difference in population trends indicates that the demographic processes involved in the transition between Santa Elena and Esperanza styles were different in all regions (see below).

Abandonment of Sites

An issue that has to be discussed, in addition to determining where people may have gone during Chican Ostionoid times, is the catalyst for the observed population movements. The usual culprit, population-resource imbalance, long a favorite as a causal factor, has lost some support because of the lack of evidence, especially from the archaeological data for the Valley of Maunabo in the southeastern corner of Puerto Rico (Curet 1992a, 1993; see next chapter). Several suggestions, however, can be made with the information available. One possibility is that people might have been attracted to bigger political centers, either in the interior mountains of Puerto Rico or Hispaniola, which could have provided more social and subsistence opportunities to commoners. To test this proposition we would need population estimates from these regions to determine the probability of population movement into them. Further, population increase in these areas has to correlate with evidence of an increase in the size and development of the local polities, indicating a possible relationship between both processes. Unfortunately, we currently lack the evidence necessary to conduct such comparison. A second possible explanation is that people from coastal regions migrated to other areas, fleeing the raids of other groups such as the so-called Caribs from the Lesser Antilles (see various papers in Paquette and Engerman 1996; Whitehead 1995; Wilson 1997). Although this explanation is generally plausible, it does not conform very well with the evidence from all of the regions, since at least in the Salinas and Yauco River Basins and Vieques, a considerable number of the Esperanza style sites are concentrated on the coastal plains, close to the shore. Moreover, most of them do not seem to be located in strategic, defensive positions. If avoiding or defending against Carib raids was the reason for the depopulation of the regions, then we would expect to see sites located away from the coast and in defensible places, such as mountain or hilltops, difficult to access.

A third possibility is that some small sectors of society moved to other areas, fleeing from (or possibly to) the influence of certain chiefs (i.e., sociopolitical dissatisfaction or dissention). Although it is highly possible that dissent occurred in indigenous polities and that internal conflict may occasionally have led to emigration of these dissenting groups, this factor should not have produced a massive migration. Thus, this may explain small changes in populations, such as noted for the Loíza River Basin, but not the marked decrease in the number of sites visible in the Salinas River Basin.

A fourth possible factor is an environmental disaster or degradation of the regional environment that may have produced a sudden reduction in the amount of resources available, forcing people to move. Here I do not refer to short-term climatic disasters such as hurricanes, since in many ethnographic cases people return after a short period of time. Instead, I am referring to long-term natural disasters, such as pervasive droughts, or human-induced disasters such as large-scale soil erosion and deforestation. To date, there is no strong evidence indicating that a generalized natural disaster occurred in Puerto Rico around A.D. 1200, and little data exist to determine the degree of deforestation and soil erosion due to cultural activities in pre-Hispanic times. However, information available from the Valley of Maunabo (Curet 1992a; see next chapter) in southeastern Puerto Rico does not support this argument. In this valley, where a sharp decrease in population is evident for the Esperanza style, populations never approached even the most conservative figures for the carrying capacity, even when environmental degradation is considered.

Nevertheless, the Maunabo study concentrated on agricultural production for subsistence purposes and did not consider the over-exploitation of environmental resources for political purposes (i.e., to finance chiefly projects, feastings, and the like). If an environmental disaster produced by human activities was responsible for the abandonment of sites, especially in the Salinas River Basin and more generally in the south-central region (Lundberg 1985; Torres 2001), it has to be explained how this disaster became generalized, when the exploitation of the environment takes place in the immediate area of the communities. In other words, the particular activities affecting the environment and their magnitude must have been widespread enough to affect not only the local, surrounding environment of the Salinas River Basin but also most of south-central Puerto Rico. This explanation, however, does not sufficiently account for the minimal decrease in number of sites reported for the Loíza River Basin or Vieques.

Finally, a fifth possibility is social and political collapse of the region, especially of emerging stratified societies that developed during the Santa Elena style. Early stratified societies such as chiefdoms have been described in the literature as relatively unstable polities that can rise and collapse in relatively short periods of time (e.g., Anderson 1994; Curet 1996). The development of these societies seems not to have been localized, but they developed within networks of interaction that Renfrew (1986) has called peer-polity interaction. Although the success of these polities depends on strategies dealing with both internal and external factors (Blanton et al. 1996; Feinman 1995; Feinman et al. 2000; Renfrew 1986; Spencer 1993), if some key piece of the network is affected, this may cause a collapse of the polities at the regional level. Hypothetical examples of some potential disturbances are changes in trading routes for long-distance exchange or the death of a charismatic and politically astute chief influential in the maintenance of the network. This argument explains changes at the local region and not so much at larger scales, and therefore it is more applicable to the south-central region, including the Salinas River Basin, than to the Yauco and Loíza River Basins and Vieques.

It is important to note that several of these explanations do not exclude each other, and two or more of them could have worked together to produce the abandonment of sites and the accompanying decrease in population. For example, some ruthless leader may have promoted an increase in productivity to support his or her communal and political projects, causing an environmental disaster because of the vast deforestation and erosion of soils, and eventually forcing some people to move out of the region. This strategy also may have motivated the emigration of dissenters and other discontented people. The reduction in agricultural production and in demographic support may have undermined the political power of this ruler, causing its eventual demise and a marked disruption of the peer-polity interaction network.

Summarizing, it is difficult to come up with a solid explanation for the population trends observed in each of the four regions examined in this chapter. However, it is clear that the regions of the Loíza, Salinas, and Yauco River Basins and Vieques did not follow similar paths in the transition from the end of the Elenan and Ostionan Ostionoid subseries and the beginning of the Chican Ostionoid. The south-central region presents a more dramatic reduction in the number of sites and the abandonment of several centers, many of them with monumental architecture. This is clear evidence that this region experienced not only a demographic collapse but also most probably a disruption of the social and political organization and network that spanned a relatively large region. During this transition, the Loíza River Basin shows the abandonment of only three small and medium-sized sites, and Vieques shows the abandonment of two small sites; in each case, the populations of the abandoned sites may have been absorbed by larger settlements. It cannot be said with any degree of confidence that the population in the Loíza River Basin and Vieques decreased during this time. Further, the general settlement pattern in these two regions did not experience any major change in the location of sites; most of the centers were still being occupied, and their distribution throughout the physiographic areas were similar between the Santa Elena and Esperanza styles (see below). The Yauco River Basin, though, does not show any change in number of sites between these two periods, but differences in site size show that this region may have experienced at least a slight population decrease. All this strongly suggests that the economic, social, and political processes involved in the transition between the Elenan/Ostionan and the Chican Ostionoid were different in each of the regions. In fact, this transition is marked in Salinas by a major demographic and regional disruption of the local networks, while the Yauco and Loíza River Basins and Vieques saw relatively little change in terms of the settlement patterns.

Settlement Patterns and Monumental Architecture

Differences in settlement patterns can be seen as evidence of a variety of processes operating in different regions at the same time. Two aspects are discussed here, the distribution of sites across the various physiographic regions and the construction of ball courts and plazas.

Despite similarities in the formation of site clusters and the centralized distribution of small settlements around larger ones (with the exception of Yauco), the settlement patterns of all the regions show some differences. The first major discrepancy between the regions in terms of settlement patterns is seen in the differences in the distribution of sites throughout the physiographic regions. During the post-Saladoid, most of the sites in the Salinas River Basin were concentrated between the Coastal Plains and the Foothills. By the end of the sequence, after the population collapse, sites were clustered mainly in the Coastal Plains. The Loíza River Basin presents another picture where, during the Monserrate style, sites are distributed mostly between the Low and Intermediate areas, but during the Santa Elena and Esperanza styles populations were for the most part divided between the Low and the High areas, with a low frequency of sites in the Intermediate area. In the Yauco River Basin, sites of all periods concentrated in the Coastal Plains, although some were located farther inland than others. In Vieques, the Monserrate style shows little change compared to the previous Hacienda Grande and Cuevas styles, with sites more or less equally represented in both Inland and Coastal areas. In later times (Santa Elena and Esperanza styles) Vieques presents a displacement of sites toward the coast.

If centralized, stratified polities developed in most of eastern, and perhaps western, Puerto Rico during post-Saladoid times, as evidenced by the central place of some large sites (Curet 1992a; Rodríguez 1992; Torres 2001), these differences indicate that the dynamics and interactions within and between polities at the regional level may have been more diverse than once thought. It has been suggested (Curet et al. 2004; Torres 2001) that, based on this spatial evidence, in the south-central coast of Puerto Rico the social and political separation occurred more between river basins. Contrarily, the Loíza River Basin seems to indicate that this separation was also present even within the same river basin. These differences could have been produced by a combination of factors, including differences in physiographic characteristics of the regions, where the topographic landscape in some areas facilitates communication or interaction between polities, and in others it curbs this interaction. Other possible factors include historical and social particularities within the regions, which, combined with the physiographic characteristics, could have resulted in some localized processes.

Another major difference between the regions is the widespread use of monumental architecture in the Salinas River Basin, and in the South-Central region in general, contrasting with the scarcity of structures in the Loíza and Yauco River Basins and Vieques. Furthermore, although better dating information is needed, it seems that the erection of formal ball courts and plazas began much earlier, during the Elenan Ostionoid subseries, in the South-Central region than in the Loíza River Basin and Vieques. (No monumental structure has been located for the Yauco River Basin.) In Loíza and Vieques, monumental architecture was used more during the Chican Ostionoid subseries. The role of these structures in stratified societies has been a matter of debate (Alegría 1983; Oliver 1998; Walker 1993), but it seems that they had multiple functions, ranging from religious and communal ceremonies to athletic events that included some forms of gambling and exchange, to interpolity competition for the purpose of reducing tensions between groups from different territories. It is clear that these formal structures had an important role in the internal and perhaps external relations of the stratified societies in Puerto Rico. Independent of their function, however, the differential distribution of monumental architecture between both regions suggests that through time, polities from various localities made use of different ideological strategies. If so, then models suggested for the development of social stratification in eastern Puerto Rico (e.g., Curet 1992a, 1996; Curet and Oliver 1998; Oliver 1999; Siegel 1989, 1992, 1996, 1999) have to be revised to include the diversity in political strategies.

Therefore, the abandonment of many sites with ball courts and plazas in the Salinas River Basin and in the South-Central region of Puerto Rico at the end of the Santa Elena style supports the idea of a major rearrangement of the political, social, and perhaps economic landscapes of the southern coast. This type of rearrangement is not visible with the regional data available for Yauco, Loíza, and Vieques. Nevertheless, the shifts in site densities across physiographic areas in all regions tend to indicate that some other forms of political and social organizations also happened at this time in the rest of the regions, as well.

The number and distribution of sites over the landscape are in many instances a reflection of the social, economic, or political organization of societies. The changes in these demographic variables presented in this chapter strongly suggest that, independent of their cultural affiliation, different processes may have been operating in the various regions compared. In some instances the differences may have been produced by the different physiographic characteristics of the regions, but in others the evidence points to possible social, economic, and political causal factors. Nevertheless, it has to be admitted that the variables used here provide only indirect evidence of population estimates and dynamics, and more precise methods are needed in order to refine the picture that is beginning to develop. Although number of sites may be a general reflection of the total population, this correlation can be affected by the frequency of the different site sizes. For example, two regions with a similar number of sites could have different total populations if one of them has more large sites than the other. This kind of difference becomes important when it is suggested that population/resource imbalance set the stage for the development of social hierarchy. Several models have suggested that social inequality became institutionalized because the population exceeded the number of people the local environment could support. Such arguments generally draw their strength from the large increase in number of sites noted during the Elenan Ostionoid period, when considerable archaeological evidence of social inequality appeared. In order to test these models, the total population of the region, not the total number of sites, has to be weighed against the carrying capacity of the environment. Thus, more refined data to estimate the actual number of inhabitants of a region are necessary, because we are not comparing different regions but considering a dynamic relationship between population and the absolute limitations of the environment. This comparison is the topic of the next chapter.

6 / Population, Carrying Capacity, and Population Pressure

Ancient Demography of the Valley of Maunabo

The analysis in the last chapter used crude estimates of populations based on number and location of sites to study general and gross demographic trends in several regions of Puerto Rico. While useful for comparative purposes and for generating future working hypotheses, this approach is not appropriate for dealing with more certain social, cultural, political, and economic processes at a finer scale. In order to address many of these issues, more specific and detailed data about populations and their interaction with the local environment are needed. This chapter presents a case study where more accurate population estimates are compared with the capacity of the environment to support human populations in order to test several population pressure models suggested for the development of social hierarchy in the Caribbean. Particularly, the analysis that follows evaluates whether prehistoric groups were experiencing population pressure or not prior to the development of social stratification.

In many regions of the world, archaeologists have used, in one way or another, population as an independent and dependent variable to explain many social and cultural processes. In the Caribbean many researchers have used similar arguments in which some form of population increase and population/resource imbalance triggered or were related in some ways to major changes such as population movements (e.g., Boomert 2001:61–62; Rouse 1992; Stokes 1998:69), shifts in subsistence strategies (e.g., Carlson 1999; Haviser 1991:144; Jouravleva and González 2000; Moscoso 1999:94; Roe 1995; Wing 2001a:115), and social and cultural change (e.g., Carlson 1999; Chanlatte Baik 1981; Roe

1995:158; Veloz Maggiolo 1991, 1993; Veloz Maggiolo and Ortega 1986:61). Despite this heavy reliance on demographic variables for the modeling of past human behavior, few researchers have used population in a more precise and rigorous manner (e.g., Keegan 1985, 1992). Most of the time, terms and concepts such as population estimates, dynamics, and processes (including population pressure) are used in vague, undefined, and informal ways.

In this chapter I discuss a population study I conducted in the Valley of Maunabo (Figure 6.1). I have previously published some aspects of this research in a preliminary manner (Curet 1993), and here I am presenting the final and more refined results, some of them based on using improved formulas for estimating ancient populations (Curet 1998). Although trends of this kind were presented in the previous chapter, the discussion included here has three major differences. The first one is that the population trend, the focus of this chapter, is based on actual population estimates and not on total number of sites. Second, the analysis is not conducted from an exploratory/empirical perspective, but it is framed within the empirical examination of a particular theoretical model. And, third, the trends are related to the local environment by comparing them to an estimated value of the carrying capacity of the region. Thus, archaeological data are being used to estimate populations in order to compare them to the ability of the local environment to support them as part of a test of a particular hypothesis. Despite focusing the discussion on the study of this particular social phenomenon, the chapter is also intended as an example of the intricacies and complexities of demographic issues, which traditionally tend to be dealt with in a very loose manner.

The particular model being tested is based on several demographic suggestions to explain the development of social hierarchies and inequality among Caribbean societies. At the time of Spanish contact in the late 1400s the indigenous groups of the Greater Antilles were organized in relatively stratified societies. Although ethnohistoric documents have been helpful in the study of late precolumbian societies and cultures, their contribution to the study of the causes for the development of these polities is very limited. Insofar as chiefdoms and other forms of stratified societies are almost nonexistent in the Americas today, archaeology possesses the best way to understand the development of these hierarchical social organizations (Drennan and Uribe 1987:ix). For the Caribbean, several anthropological models have been proposed to explain the rise of chiefdoms. These are often widely accepted but rarely have been tested archaeologically. While some of them may seem outdated and some people would consider them a flashback to the 1960s and 1970s, demo-

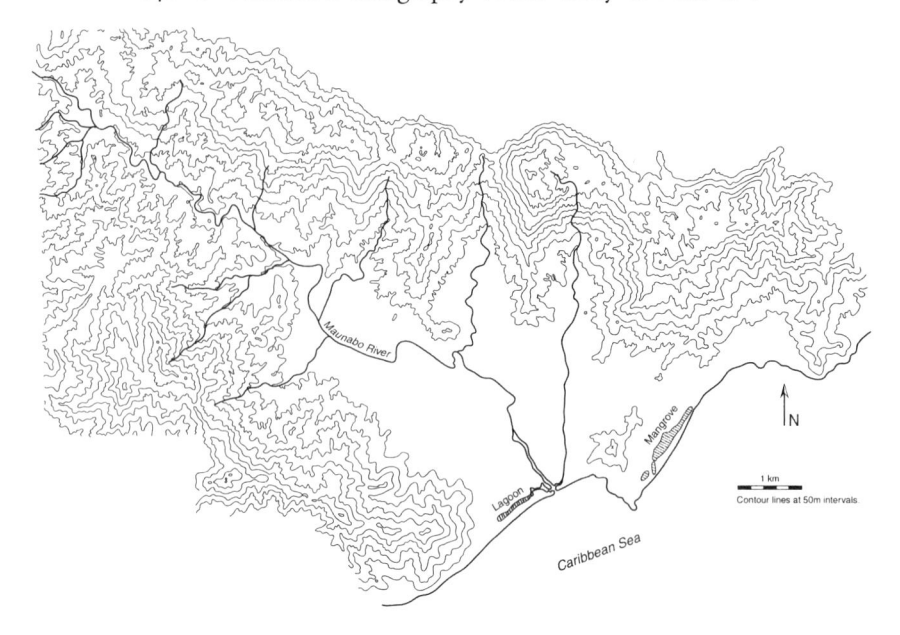

Figure 6.1. Map of the Valley of Maunabo.

graphic models of this kind are still being used in many respects, not only in this region but also throughout the world.

DEMOGRAPHIC MODELS

One of the most detailed population models developed for the Caribbean has been proposed by Veloz Maggiolo (1977–1978, 1987, 1991). In this model, Veloz Maggiolo has suggested that population growth is the major factor of change in prehistoric Caribbean societies, and therefore in the development of chiefdoms. However, his model does not merely posit a direct relationship between population pressure and the emergence of social inequality but operates indirectly through the development of intensive agricultural techniques. According to Veloz Maggiolo, the first agricultural groups that migrated from South America depended heavily on slash-and-burn agriculture, similar to the Tropical Forest groups described by Steward (1948). One of the drawbacks of this agricultural practice was the need to move whole villages when the nearby soils were exhausted, or what Veloz Maggiolo calls semi-sedentarization. But once in the larger islands, where marine and terrestrial environments offered a wider variety of resources, local groups started to diversify their subsistence patterns in response to demographic growth and to avoid a drastic environmental degradation. In general, this diversification consisted of adopting a strategy in which intensive gathering and fishing were combined with restricted use of the slash-and-burn agricultural method (Veloz Maggiolo 1977:58, 1991:171). This strategy was termed an attenuated slash-and-burn system (*sistema de roza atenuado*), which he still considered to be part of the lifeway of the tropical forest groups. Accordingly, this new subsistence strategy not only allowed for a better use of the environment by following a diversified approach without complete degradation of the soils but also allowed the full sedentarization of native groups (Veloz Maggiolo 1991:174, 176). Although some of what follows is quite detailed, it is necessary to show the rudiments of the model.

The model states that the constant population growth forced local communities to abandon the attenuated slash-and-burn system and develop more intensive agricultural techniques, which included the development and use of *montones* and irrigation systems, and a more intensive use of floodplains along rivers (Veloz Maggiolo 1977:59, 1987:78, 1991:169–170). *Montones* are earth ridges where topsoil was gathered to form a mound up to one meter high, with a perimeter of between 3 and 4 meters (Cassá 1974:34–35; Fernández de Oviedo 1959:230; Las Casas 1967, vol. 1:58–59; Moscoso 1986:419–423). The concentration of organic material from the humus stratum created a matrix of loose dirt that allowed root crops to grow faster and bigger than by simply using the traditional slash-and-burn technique. In addition, the higher elevation of the *montones* improved the drainage of the soil, avoiding contact between water and the roots for long periods of time. Although manioc can grow in all classes of soils, drier conditions have been reported as preferred for its growth (Roosevelt 1980:121–122).

The new intensive techniques produced a surplus of staple goods that generated the *need* for redistribution, which at the same time created social differentiation, increasing the stratification within social organization (Veloz Maggiolo 1987:80, 1991:175). The emerging positions of chiefs and their "aides" had some privileges over the rest of the population that were sanctioned by the new order (Veloz Maggiolo 1991:175). From Veloz Maggiolo's (1991:182) perspective, chiefs are seen as public figures acting on behalf of the group, a perspective that Brumfiel and Earle (1987) have called the adaptationist approach.

In proposing this model, Veloz Maggiolo brings to our attention not only environmental but also socioeconomic factors. For him, social stratification is not directly produced by population increase but by the intensive agricultural techniques that were developed as a response to demographic changes. These new techniques changed prehistoric societies in two ways: (1) new relations of production are developed, since leaders and managers are more useful for the construction and maintenance of the agricultural works, and (2) a manager is needed to redistribute the social product and surplus. To support his arguments Veloz Maggiolo presents an endless list of archaeological evidence, which he masterfully dominates. In general, Veloz Maggiolo's model has great resemblance to the hydraulic model developed by Wittfogel (1957), where it is argued that the state developed out of a need to manage, organize, and control the construction and maintenance of irrigation systems.

Although the model presented by Veloz Maggiolo is the most complete and one of the few that have been presented in a coherent manner for the Caribbean, it has some theoretical weaknesses. First of all, although it is true that South American tropical forest groups have to move their villages every few years due to soil depletion, it is not clear that that was the case in the Greater Antilles. There has been no evidence for continuous movement of villages in early ceramic times (i.e., during the Saladoid Series). On the contrary, it seems that sites belonging to these periods were occupied for long periods of time, in the order of centuries (see previous chapter; see also Rodríguez 1989b, 1990:292). Furthermore, as has been established by Roosevelt (1980), soil depletion in some areas of lowland South America is not a feature of the slash-and-burn technique but a deficiency of the soils. In the Greater Antilles, in contrast to lowland South America, the soils are continuously regenerated by erosion from nearby mountains, which are mostly of volcanic origin. Guarch Delmonte (1982, 1989) has presented a similar argument, explaining that the soils used by early indigenous groups in Cuba can regenerate at a faster rate than in some areas of Amazonia.

Another problem with the model has to do with the demographic premise. Veloz Maggiolo uses population increase and soil depletion as factors that initiated technological changes. To support this, he presents evidence of an increase in the number of sites between the Cuevas (A.D. 400–600) and the Santa Elena and Pure Ostiones (A.D. 600–900) in Puerto Rico, the use of new environmental niches, and the colonization of Hispaniola by Ostionan Ostionoid groups (see also Rouse 1986:181–182 for a similar argument in the explanation of Ostionan Ostionoid migrations from Puerto Rico to other islands). Nevertheless, although population increase seems to have occurred and new habitats were occupied, the connection between demographic growth and environmental degradation and/or population pressure has never been proven. Here, Cowgill's arguments against population pressure hypotheses can be echoed (Cowgill 1975). If population was growing too fast and to a point of environmental degradation, then why did they not apply cultural birth control techniques (e.g., infanticide, abortion, long lactation, abstinence, postponement of marriage, contraceptives, etc.), which have been reported even for South American groups (see Roosevelt 1980:35 for some examples)? In addition, why did not Cuevas people colonize completely the other islands of the Greater Antilles (i.e., Hispaniola, Cuba, and Jamaica) and the Bahamas before making any major change in their subsistence system and in their political, economic, social, and ideological structures?

An additional problem concerns the model. First, although it explains the development of leadership in response to the new production system, it does not provide an explanation for hereditary positions. Positions of leaders are present not only among nonegalitarian groups but also among tribal farming societies and hunters and gatherers. However, contrary to the cases of institutionalized hierarchies, among egalitarian societies, leaders are "elected" according to their ability and not their ancestry. Therefore, the need for a leader to supervise and manage the communal works and redistribution does not logically imply inherited leadership.

Furthermore, there are some problems with the assumptions of the *need* of communal work for agricultural constructions. At least for the case of the intensive technique of the *montones,* the chronicles specified that one of their advantages was the little effort needed for their construction and maintenance compared to the relatively high returns. For example, Las Casas (1967, vol. 1:65) estimated that 20 people working for one whole month in six-hour days were able to produce enough manioc to feed 300 people for two years. Cassá (1974:43–44), based on this information, has estimated that an Indian was able to make about 6 *montones* in six hours. Zuazo (1518) also reported that an Indian was able to produce up to 12 *montones* per day, although he did not specify in how many hours. Even though the figures in these statements might not be precise, they present the idea that prehistoric groups were able to produce surplus in the form of staple goods without large communal works.

This low labor requirement of the *montones* has also been supported by ethnographic evidence from modern South American groups. Carneiro (1957), for example, has reported that the Kuikuru Indians grew manioc in small hillocks of soil. According to his estimates (Carneiro 1957:137) each hillock contained between 4 and 10 plants of manioc, while there were an average of

396 hillocks per ha. These estimates are similar or even lower than the ones reported by the chronicles for the Greater Antilles (Las Casas 1967:59; Cassá 1974:39–41). Nevertheless, by using this technique the Kuikuru were able to produce about two and a half times as much manioc as they actually consumed (Carneiro 1957:159). Although more than half of the production was eaten by peccaries, wild pigs, or the *saúva* ants (Carneiro 1957:159–160), a situation not necessarily present in the Greater Antilles, it is clear that the Kuikuru Indians had the ability to produce a surplus of food without the presence of centralized and institutionalized leadership to organize the labor.

One final problem is that it is not very clear why Veloz Maggiolo considers that once surplus is produced there is a *need* for a redistributive system that has to be organized and directed by the chief. Although I recognize that surplus production might create changes in the relations of productions (i.e., social relations) I do not think that the shift is automatic, or that it is always marked enough as to change the basic social organization. Egalitarian societies, including hunters and gatherers as well as agricultural, tribal groups, have distributive systems that are mostly based on the kinship structure, and, when necessary, are supervised by an elder, or a head man (normally, a nonhereditary position). When surplus is produced or when one portion of the social system is in need, this redistributive system can be activated (e.g., Hegmon 1991). In other words, there is no *need* to develop a whole new political and social system for the distribution of the social product (Moscoso 1986:108). In general, it seems to me that Veloz Maggiolo's concept of surplus production leading to a need of a redistributive system that at the same time produces changes in relations of production is a Marxist adaptation of Sahlins's (1958) and Service's (1962) ideas on the nature of chiefdoms.

Nonetheless, the model presented by Veloz Maggiolo, although not systematically tested, is supported by some archaeological evidence (e.g., increase in the number of sites, development of intensive agricultural techniques, and the exploitation of new ecological niches). Therefore, it cannot be discarded simply on terms of a priori theoretical grounds, but it has to be tested using systematic archaeological data. To test this model archaeologically it is necessary to show that (1) population pressure (which means that population was reaching the carrying capacity of a particular region) occurred prior to cultural, technological, social, and economic changes; (2) if population was approaching the carrying capacity of the region, then it is necessary to demonstrate that the subsistence system of the early agricultural groups would have degraded the environment, if not completely, at least enough to decrease the resource returns. However, if prehistoric populations were maintained always well below the carrying capacity, then there is no evidence or reason for arguing environmental degradation in prehistoric times.

López Sotomayor (1975) has also suggested similar factors for the development of chiefdoms in Puerto Rico, although not in a formal model. She argues that the increase in population made an increase in production and the supervision of the production process necessary to assure the acquisition of food and its distribution in an adequate manner (López Sotomayor 1975:13). The increase in production is seen here as the development of new intensive agricultural techniques (i.e., the use of terraces, or *montones*), and a refinement of techniques used for fishing, hunting, and for producing other artifacts. The complexity of these techniques required leadership to supervise the communal work and the distribution of the social product. In addition, the increase in production was not even across the landscape and created an unequal development of productive forces. This inequality produced a differentiation between groups, which developed a need for protecting the interests of those who had more than others, probably strengthening the differential sociopolitical ties within a chiefdom (López Sotomayor 1975:88).

Therefore, again, in this model the position of the chiefs and their aides (or nobility) is viewed from a functional perspective: to supervise and administer the production and distribution of staples and to guarantee the security and boundaries of the chieftainship (López Sotomayor 1975:88). Due to its similarity with the model suggested by Veloz Maggiolo (1977), López Sotomayor's suggestions suffer from many of the same theoretical weaknesses, and require the same testing procedure.

Similarly, Chanlatte Baik (1981:18–20; Chanlatte Baik and Narganes Storde 1986) has argued that the cultural development of chiefdoms was the result of a demographic explosion experienced during the Elenan/Ostionan Ostionoid (or what he has called Agro-III; A.D. 600–1200). This dramatic increase in population, combined with ecological degradation and a not very advanced fishing technology, forced prehistoric groups to put more emphasis on agriculture, which, although it is not very clear how, led to the development of chiefdoms. While there are some aspects of these suggestions that are not very clear, the basic argument of the previous models is present: increase in population, ecological degradation, intensification of agriculture, and the need for leadership.

Other suggestions where population plays an important role in migration and social change have been proposed more recently in the Caribbean (Carlson 1999; Stokes 1998) and elsewhere (e.g., Cohen 1997; see also Billman 1997 for other examples in the Andean region). However, many of these studies present the possibility of population pressure as a causal factor for population movement and/or development of social complexity, but they are not integrated systematically in a model. Presumably, however, their underlining assumptions and mechanisms are similar to the ones presented above.

Conclusions and Expectations

In addition to the demographic models, several other hypotheses have been proposed for the development of Caribbean hierarchical societies that vary greatly in perspectives, coherence, and acceptance (see Curet 1992a for a review of some of these models). Some of these models emphasize warfare, long-distance, or surplus production. In general, however, demographic and/or environmental degradation models have tended to be more acceptable among Caribbeanists than those based on other factors, such as warfare and trade. One reason for this is that there is strong archaeological evidence for an increase in the number of sites and changes in subsistence strategies during the Formative period of stratified societies. However, the number of sites does not always indicate population since site size and function are important variables that must also be taken into consideration. Furthermore, population increase does not necessarily mean population pressure.

Although none of the different types of models have been formally or systematically tested, the work presented here concentrates on testing the population pressure (or population/resource imbalance) premises. This study is conducted from a regional perspective because: (1) by definition, chiefdoms are regional phenomena, and (2) the only way to test most of the variables proposed by the models (i.e., population estimates, nucleation, subsistence strategies, carrying capacity, etc.) is by using regional information.

For this purpose, the Valley of Maunabo, a coastal river valley located on the southeastern side of Puerto Rico, was chosen for the study, and a survey strategy combined with surface collections was used to measure the variables of interest. These variables included data on site size, regional and intrasite chronology, and environmental information on the valley's capability for the production of staples (i.e., for estimating its carrying capacity). Site area is used for estimating prehistoric populations, using ethnographic analogy with lowland South American groups (Curet 1992a, 1992b, 1998). The value obtained from this procedure is compared with the carrying capacity estimated

Ancient Demography of the Valley of Maunabo / 153

for the valley to evaluate whether prehistoric groups were experiencing population pressure or not, prior to the development of social inequality.

Obviously, and as suggested by many of the models, most of the evidence should be detected for the time before the Chican subseries, that is, probably during the Ostionan and Elenan subseries (i.e., A.D. 600–1200). Veloz Maggiolo (1977–1978, 1991:171) has suggested that incipient social inequality developed first in the southern area of Puerto Rico, sometime during the first half of the Elenan/Ostionan Ostionoid (A.D. 700–800), which supposedly correlates with the development of the *montones*. Moscoso (1986) also indicates that the first hierarchical societies developed in southern Puerto Rico but, following the trends in ceramic designs, he suggested a date of around A.D. 1000. Similarly, Rouse (1992:126) has recently suggested that the Formative age in the Greater Antilles started sometime during the Elenan Ostionoid series in eastern Puerto Rico. Here I partially follow Veloz Maggiolo's suggestions because they are based not only on ceramic changes but also on the appearance of intensive agricultural techniques and ceremonial centers such as Tibes (Curet et al. 2003; Curet and Rodríguez Gracia 1999; Curet et al. 2004; González Colón 1984). Thus, some forms of social inequality may have developed in the southern part of Puerto Rico sometime in the later part of the first half of the Elenan/Ostionan Ostionoid subseries (i.e., during the Pure Ostiones and Monserrate styles; A.D. 600–900), but were definitely present during the second half of the same period (i.e., during the Modified Ostiones and Santa Elena styles; A.D. 900–1200).

Therefore, to support the population/resource imbalance models, an increase in estimated population should have occurred, as reflected in site size and number of sites, during the early Ostionan/Elenan period. As demonstrated in the previous chapter, an increase in the number of sites during this period has been reported for other areas of Puerto Rico, but site sizes at different times are not normally recorded, making the comparison of population estimates between periods difficult (Curet 1987).

To test the increase in population suggested by the models and the presence of population pressure, an additional piece of supporting evidence is needed. For this reason the population estimates will be compared to the estimates for the carrying capacity of the valley. Carrying capacity is an approximation of the maximum number of people that may be supported within a given area without inducing environmental degradation (Rappaport 1968:88). This concept is very important because population increase does not necessarily equate with population pressure or a population/resource imbalance. Therefore, although theoretically the population cannot be higher than the carrying capacity, it is expected that for the population pressure hypotheses to be true, both the population and carrying capacity estimates have to be relatively close to each other for the period prior to the development of social complexity.

Due to the difficulty in coming up with precise population and carrying capacity estimates and to ensure the validity of the test, I have decided to use liberal estimates in the calculation of prehistoric populations (i.e., overestimate), while those for the carrying capacity will be conservative estimates (i.e., underestimation). The reason for this is to ensure the validity of the test and to avoid any source of error or bias, since these figures are not absolute, but "gross" estimates and they depend on the assumptions and premises made by the researcher.

It is also important to emphasize that it is *not* argued here that the Valley of Maunabo was one of the heartlands of the development of social inequality in the Caribbean or it was necessarily the location of a primary or pristine chiefdom. Nevertheless, for the demographic models to be accepted, population pressure must have been a generalized phenomenon in a large area. Otherwise, it has to be explained why people did not move to nearby, lightly populated areas, as they did in their migration through the Lesser Antilles, before dramatically changing their subsistence strategies and their political, economic, and social structures. If some areas were "overpopulated" during prehistoric times, while others were "underpopulated," then factors other than natural demographic trends might have been responsible for the high population density in certain regions (e.g., popularity of some polities, social and political factors, trade routes, the presence of valuable resources, etc.). Thus, although I have my reasons to believe that there was at least a hierarchical polity in the valley (e.g., as evidenced by the presence of stone collars, and a possible site hierarchy in the settlement pattern; see Curet 1992a), I do not consider the presence of such political organization essential for testing the demographic models since evidence for this type of organization is evident elsewhere in the island.

In summary, the test of models based on demographic premises consists of two steps: (1) the estimation of prehistoric populations at different times, and (2) comparison of these estimates with the carrying capacity of the valley. Thus, it is the purpose of this chapter to define and evaluate the population trends of prehistoric groups in Maunabo and compare them to the maximum number of people that could have been supported by the valley. First, the environment's carrying capacity is estimated to determine the maximum number of people that could have been sustained by the region. Prehistoric populations are then estimated for each of the chronological and ceramic periods by comparing the site areas with ethnographic data from lowland South American groups. Finally, population changes through prehistory are discussed and compared to the carrying capacity of the valley.

CARRYING CAPACITY: DEFINITIONS AND THEORETICAL CONSIDERATIONS

The concept of carrying capacity was first developed in ecological biology, and it was described as the equilibrial population density in a given environment (Dewar 1984; Hassan 1981:165). Later definitions referred to this concept as the maximum population size possible in a given environment without damaging the environment. With the advent of modern cultural ecology, this concept started gaining popularity among anthropologists and archaeologists. Although most of the original and current anthropological works dealing with this concept used carrying capacity to estimate the maximum possible population of hunter-gatherers in a given area (e.g., Bartholomew and Birdsell 1953; Birdsell 1953; Casteel 1972; Jochim 1976), the concept has been also applied to agrarian groups (e.g., Carneiro 1960; Conklin 1959; Cowgill and Hutchinson 1963; Keegan 1992, 1995; Keegan et al. 1985; Kowalewski 1980, 1982; Rappaport 1968; Roosevelt 1980; Zubrow 1971, 1975). Surprisingly, despite the abundance of models based on population pressure, the concept of carrying capacity has been used very little in the Caribbean (see Keegan 1992, 1995 for exceptions).

Here I define carrying capacity as an approximation of the maximum number of individuals who *may* be supported within a given area, within given technological limitations, and without inducing environmental degradation. This section contains a short discussion of the concept of carrying capacity and its theoretical considerations. More extensive reviews, criticisms, and discussions of the uses of this concept in anthropology have been published elsewhere (Brush 1975; Dewar 1984; Glassow 1978; Hassan 1981:161–175; Hayden 1975; Keegan 1985, 1995; Tolstoy 1982).

To apply the concept of carrying capacity meaningfully to human populations, slight modifications of the animal ecology models are necessary. The main reason for this is that, contrary to animals, human populations have cultural mechanisms that provide more flexibility in dealing with environmental restrictions. More anthropologically complex definitions of this concept specify that carrying capacity is a function of both cultural and environmental factors, such as (a) a particular form of land use, or level of cultural or technological development, (b) specific environmental circumstances (i.e., what resources are available, and in what amount), and (c) a specific level of exploitation such that resources are not depleted. Thus, for human populations, it is meaningless to speak of the carrying capacity of a given environment, habitat, or set of resources, since it is also a function of culturally, socially, and economically induced factors.

Most of the strongest criticisms of the use of the concept of carrying capacity in human populations concentrate their attacks on these independent factors (e.g., Hayden 1975). Specifically, the objections underscore our inability to calculate accurately the amount of potential food in an environment with a mosaic of niches, seasonal and long-term changes in the amount of available resources, and under various technologies. (However, see Terrell et al. 2003 for a different argument in terms of measuring productivity of foodstuff.) Although it is true that the use of carrying capacity as an analytical concept has its restrictions and limitations, I agree with Glassow (1978:38–40) and Hassan (1981:166) when they stress the utility of the concept. Graber (1997:264) has vowed in favor of the use of carrying capacity as of heuristic value, at the same time that he points out its lack of explanatory power. Wood (1998:108) also has argued in favor of a concept that he developed called "demographic saturation point," which, despite his insistence in being different, is very similar to the concept of carrying capacity as defined here.

Based on these criticisms, Glassow (1978:37) has listed four considerations when measuring the carrying capacity of a region: (1) what resources are exploited and their abundance, (2) how the resources are exploited (i.e., technology), (3) the degree of dependence on each resource, and (4) the viability of the resources under different levels of exploitation. Of the four factors, the first one refers to the environmental "fertility," the next two are cultural factors, and the last one alludes to the effects of culture on the environment.

As can be appreciated, the empirical measurement of these factors is very complicated and difficult to calculate, if not impossible. However, the maximum population size that a given area can support can be estimated if the least favorable circumstances for each crucial factor are considered. Following this approach, Hassan (1981:166–167; see also Tolstoy 1982) has developed a rule which states that, although it is true that many resources can be exploited by human populations, the "maximum human population size is dependent on the quantity of nutritionally critical foodstuffs, which are present in minimum amounts, at the time within the span of a few generations of their least abundance" (1981:166). Thus, according to this rule, the limiting factor that determines the carrying capacity of an area is not the most abundant resource, but the necessary (i.e., vital) foodstuffs that are least available (see Jochim 1976 and Tolstoy 1982 for a similar approach). If, in estimating the carrying capacity, the least abundant critical resource is considered, then we are controlling for the first consideration suggested by Glassow (i.e., types and quantities of resources).

In addition, if Hassan's approach of determining the conditions with lowest yields is followed, the technology of exploitation can also be determined in a more precise manner, since the least intensive or productive technique is the only one necessary to be considered. This last approach controls for Glassow's second consideration (i.e., technology). Furthermore, because this limiting resource is the only one that is being considered for estimating the carrying capacity, factors three (i.e., degree of dependency on a resource) and four (i.e., viability of resources) can be determined more accurately from the archaeological, ethnohistoric, and/or ethnographic record and from ecological studies of the region under study. In summary, by considering solely the limiting resource, we have greatly simplified the original considerations necessary for measuring the carrying capacity of a region.

The problem now is to determine the limiting resource. One way to solve this problem is to approach the concept of resources from the perspective of vital nutrients, calories and proteins being two of the most essential and most used in the anthropological literature. By establishing which one of these nutrients is less abundant than the other in the region under study, it is possible to define the limiting nutrient and to determine which of the available resources is responsible for providing it.

To demonstrate this approach let us consider the estimations of carrying capacity measured for lowland South America (Gross 1975; Roosevelt 1980), where, since the early works of Steward (1948) and Meggers and Evans (Meggers 1954; Meggers and Evans 1957), it was argued that the low productivity of the environment was responsible for the low population density and cultural development of the area. According to this argument, the shallow and easily eroded soils of Amazonia could not have produced enough food to accommodate high densities of people necessary for the development of complex societies. Later studies, however, showed that, contrary to the expectations, some areas of lowland South America were able to produce enough calories, mostly in the form of manioc, to support high populations densities (e.g., Carneiro 1957, 1960, 1961, 1970; Roosevelt 1980, 1991). The high production of manioc still did not explain why some areas of Amazonia presented higher concentrations of population than others.

Later, Lathrap (1970), Gross (1975), and Roosevelt (1980) suggested that protein, and not calories, is the limiting resource (i.e., the least abundant nutrient) in lowland South America, where the tropical forest can produce considerable quantity of manioc, while it has low densities of animal protein. Using this argument as a premise, Roosevelt (1980) has contended that high population densities were present in areas such as the floodplains, where maize (i.e., a better protein source) could be cropped. To support her argument, Roosevelt estimated and compared the carrying capacity (in terms of protein) of the floodplains and the tropical forest of the Parmana region, in Venezuela, and contrasted them with her population estimates for different prehistoric periods, and with the information available for the introduction of maize in the region. The results demonstrated a positive correlation between the increase in population and the production of maize. More recently, however, Beckerman (1994:194) has reported abundant levels of faunal protein in South American tropical forests, "suggesting that considerably denser human populations than now evident can be supported on the wild Amazonian fauna" (see also Heckenberger et al. 2003).

Once the limiting nutrient and resource is determined, the next step is to estimate the amount of such resource that can be produced by the local environment without degrading it. To do this, it is necessary to consider the fertility of all the microniches present, which have different productive capabilities. By determining the possible production in each one of the microniches the total annual production for the whole region can, in theory, be estimated. The value of the total annual production of the limiting resource can be translated into units of the limiting nutrient (either of protein or calories, depending on the case). The annual production of the limiting nutrient is then compared to the minimum amount of such nutrient needed yearly by a person to be able to survive. This process should produce the maximum number of people able to be supported by the region under the least favorable circumstances. In most instances, if the case study consists of hunters and gatherers, then the carrying capacity will be based on the natural availability of the limiting resource, while if dealing with farming societies the carrying capacity will also be based on the production of staples.

More recently, using biological formulae, Keegan (1995) has suggested that human populations probably feel the effects of population pressure and make the appropriate adjustments (in his case population dispersal) much earlier than when approaching carrying capacity. Noticing that the slope or growth rate of the theoretical logistical or S-shaped curve of population growth in colonization contexts changes from monotonically increasing to monotonically decreasing trend at half the value of carrying capacity, he argues that this reflects the early impact of overpopulation in a particular region. While this perspective can be criticized on many grounds, including against the assumptions of unchecked population increase and the use of rational behavior, my main concern is that I do not agree that, in practice, human populations will feel these early signs or even change their behavior dramatically so far away from the level of carrying capacity. Keegan's arguments are based mostly on theoretical expectations and on ecological data from other species, but it is not tested empirically for humans. If his arguments are true, then it will be difficult to explain many of the human-induced environmental disasters such as the deforestation of Spain and Haiti in the nineteenth century, or the possible degradation of the environment by many Mayan polities, the case of the Tikopia who may have lived close to their carrying capacity (Firth 1936, 1965; Kirch 1984:116–118), or even modern global warming that, despite the strong historic and scientific data, many people are still denying. Furthermore, considering that many of these changes at half the carrying capacity occur over several generations, perhaps centuries, it is difficult to believe that people were able to detect those changes. In this sense, I agree with Buikstra (1997:323) when she states that "To impute that time trends in health were perceptible to those early agriculturalists, in the throes of a process that in many cases matured over centuries, requires a level of paleopsychological inference I find difficult to accept." Thus, I still consider that to argue for the presence of population pressure, populations have to be approaching the level of carrying capacity.

In conclusion, to estimate the carrying capacity to test the population pressure hypothesis for the development of social hierarchy in the Caribbean, we have to determine (1) the least abundant critical nutrient/resource, (2) the least productive way of exploiting it (i.e., what techniques were utilized), (3) what is its viability without degrading the environment (i.e., fertility and abundance), and (4) the amounts of nutrient/resource needed by an individual to be able to survive in such environment. The measurement of the carrying capacity of the Valley of Maunabo following these steps is discussed in the next section.

PROYECTO ARQUEOLÓGICO DEL VALLE DE MAUNABO

The Valley of Maunabo is well delimited by the ocean on the southern and eastern sides, as well as two sierras on the north (Cuchilla de Panduras) and the west (Sierra de Guardarraya) (see Figure 6.1). The valley has a triangular shape, and the Maunabo River flows from the northwest, near the junction of the two sierras, to the southeast. Approximately in the middle of the valley, it turns south dividing the valley in two. In general, the valley has a wide variety of ecological habitats concentrated in a small space. It includes coastal areas, mangroves, lagoons, valley bottom, piedmonts, and mountains with tropical forests. A lagoon is located near the river mouth, although documents from the nineteenth century (Navarro 1847) report the presence of a second one farther inland, which no longer exists. Although there are some small exceptions, most of the shoreline of Maunabo is considered a high-energy coast, adverse for the proliferation of certain species of shellfish. Nevertheless, some other coastal subsistence resources, such as crabs, a few species of shells, and fish are present in abundance. This variability in such a small area was thought to facilitate the study of the relationship of social organization, demographic changes, and ecological variables.

To measure the variables of interest, in particular demography, a research design that combined intensive, stratified sampling survey work, shovel testing, and the collection of surface materials was developed. The survey provided regional-level information, including site sizes and locations, resources available for exploitation (e.g., riverine, marine, and soil resources), changes in settlement pattern through time, and site types. The shovel testing of sites and surface collections were necessary for placing the settlements in the regional chronology, estimating the site sizes, and, therefore, their populations at different periods (see Curet 1992a for more details).

A total of about 9 km^2 or 21 percent of the valley was surveyed, and 12 sites covering all periods of the Ceramic Age were discovered and studied (Figure 6.2). Of these sites, only eight were habitation settlements. The sites were dated based on the results of quantitative analysis of ceramic attributes on sherds from the surface collections (Curet 1992a). Site sizes were estimated from density maps plotted from the subsurface testings.

The Carrying Capacity of the Valley of Maunabo

As mentioned above, the concept of carrying capacity is essential for testing hypotheses based on population pressure, since "pressure" is measured in

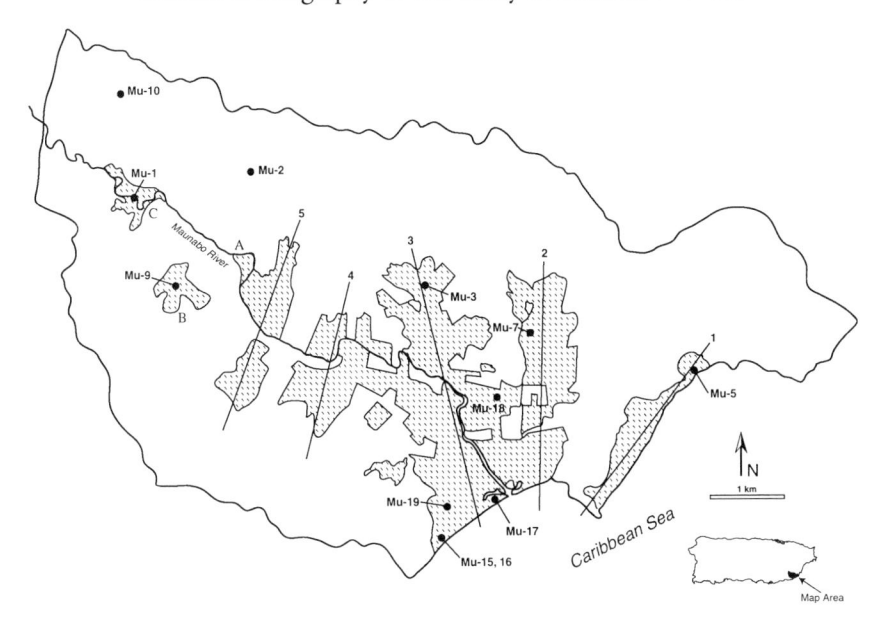

Figure 6.2. Map of the Valley of Maunabo showing the surveyed area (transects and blocks) and location of sites.

terms of the stress that human populations put on the environment, or vice versa. However, it is better to estimate the carrying capacity under the least favorable conditions since they are the ones that determine the maximum number of people who can be supported in a region. In terms of my work this approach is followed also to avoid any overestimation of the carrying capacity, which will invalidate the test of the demographic models. However, it is important to stress that calculating the carrying capacity based on the least available critical nutrient is considered as impossible by many people, since a wide range of resources can provide such nutrient in any given environment. Thus, here I am calculating a very conservative estimate in which I underestimate the carrying capacity by considering only one resource as the source of the nutrient. In other words, the estimate presented here is not even close to the actual value of the carrying capacity of the region.

The first step suggested in the previous section for calculating the carrying capacity was to determine the least abundant resource. Traditionally, ecological anthropologists have estimated the carrying capacity by using different nutrients, protein and/or calories being the most common. The decision of which nutrient should be used in this study depends on which of them is the limiting factor. While Caribbean, prehistoric agricultural groups relied somewhat on manioc to acquire the necessary calories, relatively large quantities of marine proteins were also available (i.e., fish, sea turtles, crabs, clams, shells, sea birds, and manatees), in addition to small terrestrial animals (e.g., iguanas, different kinds of rodents, and birds) (deFrance 1989; Fontánez 1991; Narganes Storde 1985; Stokes 1998; Wing 1989a, 1989b, 2001a, 2001b, 2001c; Wing and Reitz 1982; Wing and Wing 1995), and other plant resources (Newsom 1993; Vega 1996).

The abundance of animal protein in the form of marine resources might explain why Caribbean ancient groups did not have a high production of maize similar to other South American groups (Newsom and Deagan 1994; Sturtevant 1961, 1969), even when better agricultural soils (e.g., Mollisols, Alfisols, Entisols, Vertisols, Inceptisols, and others) are present in the islands for its cultivation. In this regard, Roosevelt (1980) has argued that South American groups in the floodplains adopted maize agriculture due to the scarcity of protein sources necessary for a balanced diet. This necessity seems not to have been present in coastal habitats, such as in the Caribbean islands, where protein sources are concentrated in higher densities. Furthermore, the large quantities of protein available for coastal groups have been recognized by other studies such as the one by Noli and Avery (1988). In this study, the authors noted that while prehistoric coastal groups had enormous quantities of protein accessible, they could not have depended solely on marine resources because of the risk of protein poisoning (i.e., overconsumption of protein combined with a lack of calories). Noli and Avery contend that while the diet of these groups has an abundance of protein, they were dependent on other resources to acquire the calories necessary for subsistence.

The presence of marine shells and fishing tools (i.e., net weights) in many of the surface collections from the Valley of Maunabo suggests an exploitation of coastal and river resources during all periods. Consequently, considering the intensity and technological level of development of ancient fishing techniques (Córdova Armenteros 1995; Mercado 1990) and low population densities compared to modern times, it can be assumed that marine resources were inexhaustible for the purpose of estimating the carrying capacity of the Valley of Maunabo. The early European chronicles that described in detail the intensive and extensive exploitation of marine resources also support this argument (e.g., Fernández de Oviedo 1959, vol. 118:56–57, 65–66). Local fishermen interviewed by the author further confirm this assumption. They specifically mentioned the high productivity of fish in the area, especially a sand bank, less than a mile from the coast of the valley. This fishing area is so productive that fishermen from neighboring valleys come to fish in it. To this we can add the presence of mangroves and littoral lagoons that tend to have high densities of animal protein. Further, they could have practiced other strategies to increase the amount of animal protein as for example the importation of exotic fauna such as guinea pigs, and the possibility of tendering animals such as the hutía (*Isolodobon portorricencis*), both of them reported for other parts of the Greater Antilles.

Contrary to these arguments, Keegan (1995:411) has recently criticized the use of calories as the main limiting factor and suggested instead using proteins as the main currency for calculating carrying capacity. For his argument Keegan cites his work (Keegan 1986) on the Machiguenga, where he used optimal foraging theory to explain some economic behavior among tropical horticulturalists. The Machiguenga is an Amerindian group that lives in a tributary of the Amazon River in southeastern Peru and has a mixed economy that includes cultivation, fishing, and hunting. Using estimates on maize production, faunal availability, and the costs of search and handling the preys, Keegan determined that protein availability is limited. In spite of this argument, however, it is not clear how much of his results are applicable to a different situation such as the case of Caribbean and coastal groups. While it is true that both the ancient people of the Caribbean and the modern Machiguenga are tropical forest groups that depend on slash-and-burn cultivation, hunting, and fishing, it cannot be assumed that these are enough reasons to generalize some aspects of one and apply them to the other. I am not implying that in fact Caribbean groups did not have scarce animal protein available to survive or that they did not over-exploit the environment (see Wing 2001a, 2001b, 2001c) decreasing the return rate of some marine species. But, generalizations about the availability of some resources cannot be done at a general level (e.g., neotropics) and more localized analysis has to be performed.

Other studies also suggest that Keegan's results cannot be generalized to Amazonia or the Caribbean. For example, Beckerman (1994) has concluded recently that return rates among several modern Amerindian groups from South America are high enough to produce abundant amounts of animal protein, mainly in the form of fish. Furthermore, a difference between ancient Caribbean societies and many modern Amerindian groups is the little archaeological evidence available for the use of maize among the former, indicating that maize was not used or needed as a supplemental source of protein as has been suggested for other neotropical groups (Keegan 1986; Roosevelt 1980). Although it is true that most of the early historical documents mention maize as one of the main staples of the Caribbean people, the archaeological record has produced little botanical evidence to support the written sources. In fact, maize has been positively identified in only two sites in the Caribbean, specifically in a possible chiefly context in En-Bas-Saline, Haiti (Newsom 1993; Newsom and Deagan 1994), and the site of Tutu in Saint Thomas (Righter 2003). This lack of evidence has led Newsom and Deagan (1994) to suggest that perhaps maize was an elite, high-status staple that was not available to most of the population. If so, then it will explain both why corn was offered often to Europeans as mentioned in the documents and why it is almost absent from the archaeological record.

Therefore, considering the argument presented above I conclude that the measurement of the carrying capacity for the valley can be based solely on caloric consumption, mainly in the form of manioc, which was the main subsistence staple of Caribbean groups. Nevertheless, in order to explore other possibilities, to establish some parameters for future studies, and to address some of the concerns stated by Keegan, the carrying capacity based on maize production and consumption is also estimated below.

Manioc and Carrying Capacity

Manioc is a tuber or root crop that in terms of composition is almost pure starch, giving a high caloric content (see Roosevelt 1980:119–139). Nevertheless, the roots are deficient in many other kinds of nutrients necessary for human survival, such as protein, fats, and some vitamins and minerals (see Table 6.1). It is believed that manioc and other tropical root crops may have been originally domesticated in seasonally arid environments, which explains why it is tolerant of dry conditions that adversely affect many other domestic plants (Roosevelt 1980:120; Sanoja 1981, 1989). On the one hand, manioc can be cropped satisfactorily in almost any kind of soil, can tolerate drought without injury, and requires little attention during the growth cycle (see Roosevelt 1980; Sanoja 1981). On the other hand, this tuber "is highly intolerant of waterlogging; when subjected to wet conditions for any amount of time, the root rots, and the plant dies" (Roosevelt 1980:121). It is possible that one of the reasons for using the technique of *montones* was to avoid extremely humid conditions. In this sense, the *montones* can be considered similar to raised fields. Manioc does not need to be cropped annually, and it can be left in the

Table 6.1. Contents of 100 g Edible Portion of Raw Manioc Roots and Dry Whole Kernel Yellow Maize (Roosevelt 1980, Tables 1, 2, and 5).

	Manioc	Zea mays
Food Energy	148 calories	361 calories
Average Yields	14.2×10^6 calories/ha	4.4×10^6 calories/ha
Protein	.8 gm	9.4 gm
Fat	.3 gm	4.3 gm
Carbohydrates	37.4 gm	74.4 mg
Calcium	36.0 mg	9.0 mg
Iron	1.1 mg	2.5 mg
Phosphorous	48.0 mg	290.0 mg
Vitamin A value	5 µg	70? µg
Thiamine	.06 mg	.43 mg
Riboflavin	.04 mg	.1 mg
Niacin	.7 mg	1.9 mg
Ascorbic Acid	40.0 mg	Traces

ground for several years after the roots have matured. Even after it is cropped, manioc can be processed into flour and bread (i.e., cassava), which, if protected from direct contact with moisture and insects, can be stored indefinitely.

So far we have only complied with the first step for measuring carrying capacity: determination of the least abundant critical resource (i.e., identifying the limiting factor: calories). In order to satisfy the next two considerations (i.e., technology, and viability of resources), and to avoid any source of overestimation of carrying capacity, the least intensive or productive situations are considered. In the case of the second step (i.e., technology), the only agricultural technique to be considered will be slash-and-burn, while other more intensive methods that could produce greater yields will be ignored. In terms of the viability of resources this approach will estimate the maximum population able to be supported by the valley under low conditions of food production. In practice, this is an "unrealistic" underestimation of the "real" carrying capacity.

To estimate the viability of the resources without degrading the environment, several factors concerning the quantity and quality of arable soils have to be considered. The study zone covers approximately 42.7 km², which includes the following soils of interest for agricultural production: Inceptisols (31.47 km² or 73.7 percent), Entisols (4.51 km² or 10.6 percent), Mollisols (2.41

km² or 5.6 percent), and Alfisols (.68 km² or 1.6 percent). Other classes of soils of low agricultural productivity are also present but in small amounts, most of them located on the mountains.

Although more than 90 percent of the valley consists of relatively good soils for growing manioc, a large part of them (in particular the Inceptisols) are located on steep mountain slopes. This does not mean that they are not good for manioc production since modern inhabitants of Maunabo and other mountainous areas of Puerto Rico still produce these and other products successfully on similar kinds of slopes. In some cases, erosion is controlled by keeping mostly fruit and lumber trees (e.g., guayacán, guava, orange, guanábana, avocado, etc.) in farm fields. Since there is no information on how much of the area is topographically possible to cultivate in practice, and to avoid any overestimation, it will be assumed that prehistoric groups used only soils on the valley bottom and piedmonts, which are defined here as the areas at elevations lower than 50 m above sea level. The total area covered by the valley bottom and piedmont is 15.75 km² or 36.9 percent of the study zone.

However, ethnographic studies among Amazonian groups document a lower proportion of land area under cultivation. Due to the low quality of the soils in the tropical forests in lowland South America, a maximum of 10 percent of the land available is actually exploited every year using the slash-and-burn technique (Roosevelt 1980:183) to allow enough time for old fields to regenerate their soils. Although the situation in the Valley of Maunabo (and for the rest of the Greater Antilles; see Guarch Delmonte 1989 for a more thorough statement of this argument) is different because the soils are deeper and of better quality, the carrying capacity will also be calculated for only 10 percent of the total area of the valley or 4.27 km², assuming that prehistoric groups maintained a similar proportion in their agricultural tradition inherited from their South American origin. It is worth mentioning here that early European chronicles present a different view, where descriptions of whole valleys and mountains being cultivated at one time are common (e.g., Colón 1965:74, 82). Thus, the assumption of only 10 percent of the valley being under cultivation is an unrealistic underestimation of the productive potential of the valley. Nevertheless, the carrying capacity is calculated using this area to obtain the most conservative values under reasonable circumstances. Notice that I have decided to use the 10 percent of the whole valley and not of the valley bottom. The reason for this is that this figure for the valley bottom would have been only 1.6 km², a figure that in my opinion is extremely low and unrealistic considering the information we have available on Amerindian

Table 6.2. Estimates Used for Calculating the Carrying Capacity.

Source	Manioc Annual Yield (kg/ha) (Ym)	Manioc Calories per Kg (Cm)	Manioc Calories per Person per Year (Tc)	Maize Annual Yield (kg/ha) (Yc)	Maize Grams of Protein per Kg (Pc)	Protein (KG) per Person per Year (Tp)
Carneiro 1957	16,450	938	1,095,000			
Goldman 1963	13,478					
Smole 1976		1,091	850,000			
Roosevelt 1980	5,000	1,500	1,000,000	1,000	90	18.25
Hassan 1981			859,200			18.25

agricultural practices. While my intention is to maintain a conservative, and perhaps underestimated, value for carrying capacity, it is necessary to keep a certain level of reality in order to maintain a certain level of validity in the analysis.

To calculate the carrying capacity based on the production of manioc the following formula was used:

$$P_{max} = (Y_m C_m) A / T_c$$

where Y_m is the annual yield of manioc (kg/ha), C_m is the amount of calories per kg of manioc, A is the area under cultivation in hectares, T_c is the annual caloric requirement per person, and P_{max} the maximum number of people sustainable (i.e., carrying capacity).

Estimates of the annual yield of manioc per unit of land (Table 6.2) reported by Goldman (1963, cited in Smole 1976:150), Carneiro (1957:158–159), and Roosevelt (1980:185) were used in the estimation of the carrying capacity based on calories. As can be observed from Table 6.2, there is a wide variability in the estimates, ranging from about 5,000 to 16,450 kg/ha. Since the reasons for this variation are unknown, three estimates will be used here to calculate the carrying capacity, in order to determine and explore the range of possible estimates. In terms of caloric content of edible manioc, Smole (1976) and Roosevelt (1980) present relatively similar values of about 1,100 and 1,500 cal/kg, respectively, while Carneiro's (1961) estimate is slightly lower.

Smole (1976:151), Roosevelt (1980:183), and Hassan (1981:18, 80) have published varied, although similar, estimates for the caloric requirements for a balanced diet. With the exception of Roosevelt's estimate, the rest of them were based on estimates published either by the Food and Agriculture Organization (FAO), the World Health Organization (WHO), or both. According to Roosevelt (1980:183), these estimates tend to be low since "Many of these estimates assume, on the basis of evidence of Third World populations, that per capita consumption of nutrients would be low and that the population would be a relatively young one. However, these assumptions are not necessarily valid for prehistoric populations." For this reason, she decided to increase the estimates reported by these organizations to an arbitrary value of one million calories. However, Clark and Haswell (1970:16) present a contrasting argument based on cross-cultural comparisons: "While our estimate of the calorie [*sic*] requirements of an able-bodied man under African conditions comes out somewhat higher than the result based on the FAO scale, we have to conclude that the FAO scale requirements for children, and in consequence their estimates for the whole population, have been placed considerably high." Although it is difficult to determine the actual requirements for prehistoric population, I tend to agree with Clark's and Haswell's argument on FAO's scale. Nevertheless, the use of either one of these high values for caloric requirements will tend to lower the carrying capacity of the valley, avoiding any possible overestimation. One further problem with FAO's and WHO's figures is that they are based on observations of actual caloric intake by populations from different parts of the world. Differences in the caloric intake between populations do not necessarily reflect biological needs, but perhaps their social, economic, and/or political conditions.

In summary, and as can be seen in Table 6.2, the values to estimate the carrying capacity based on manioc exhibit great variability. Thus, in order to explore the range of possibilities several estimates for the carrying capacity were calculated using the different values. The results of the application of the carrying capacity formula based on calories are presented in Table 6.3, where a 10 percent loss of the manioc crop was assumed following Roosevelt's suggestions (1980:183). Carneiro's and Roosevelt's estimates were calculated using the values they reported, while the estimate based on Goldman's manioc yield (Y_m) was combined with Smole's estimates for caloric content (C_m) and requirements (T_c). Since Hassan's value for caloric requirements is similar to Smole's, it was not used in the estimates.

In general, the carrying capacities calculated by using Carneiro's and Goldman's values produced similar results, while Roosevelt's values are considerably lower. This disagreement can be explained partly by differences in the nature of each ethnographic case (i.e., soil fertility, social group, ecological

Table 6.3. Estimates of Maximum Number of People That Could Have Been Supported in the Two Areas under Cultivation Based on Manioc Production in the Valley of Maunabo, Assuming a 10% Loss of the Annual Crop.*

Source of Production Estimate	Estimated Maximum Population	
	15.75 km^2	4.27 km^2
Carneiro 1957	19,975	5,415
Goldman 1963	24,469	6,642
Roosevelt 1980	10,631	2,882

* Smole's estimate of annual caloric requirement = 850,000 cal/yr.
Roosevelt's estimates of annual caloric requirement = 1,000,000 cal/yr.
Hassan's estimate of annual caloric requirement = 859,210 cal/yr.
In the case Goldman's estimates the value of 1091 cal/kg of manioc reported by Smole was used.

variables, etc.). However, another source of difference is that while Carneiro's and Goldman's values for manioc annual yield were obtained from primary data, Roosevelt's value was gathered from government reports or secondary sources, which might have been less accurate. And finally, Roosevelt overestimated the value for caloric requirements to compensate for what she believes is an underestimation present in FAO's and WHO's scales. Despite these differences and possible sources of errors, and for the sake of argument, the whole range of estimates is used in this study. Particularly of interest is the carrying capacity estimate of 2,882 people, which is the first threshold value that could have been exceeded by prehistoric populations. Thus, based on caloric consumption and depending on the manioc yields, caloric content, and land area under cultivation, the carrying capacity of the Valley of Maunabo can be estimated at between 2,900 and 24,500 people.

It is important to point out here that at least two major stated and unstated assumptions were made in calculating these estimates. The first one is that prehistoric Caribbean groups were exploiting the same varieties of staples as modern ethnographic groups. This factor can affect the estimates of staple yield per unit of area and the nutrient content. And second, it was assumed that prehistoric populations had available all the labor necessary to produce the amounts of staple needed to sustain the number of people estimated by the carrying capacity (i.e., that the workforce's productivity was enough to produce resources to feed themselves plus the nonproductive sector of the population, including children, elders, and ill people or dependency ratio; see Feinman 1991).

In general, the carrying capacity estimates were obtained under extremely conservative assumptions and without considering other factors such as (1) agricultural intensification (e.g., terracing and the well-known ridge fields or *montones* of the Chican period), (2) the higher quality of Caribbean soils compared to those from lowland South America (Guarch Delmonte 1989), from where most of the estimates used in the calculations were obtained, (3) other sources of calories (e.g., other tubers, wild vegetables, marine resources, terrestrial animals), (4) larger areas under cultivation, as suggested by the chronicles, and (5) the possibility that varieties of manioc cropped in the Caribbean were different from those utilized by South American groups. The inclusion of at least the first four factors in our analysis would dramatically raise the estimates of the carrying capacity presented here.

Based on these results we can present some expectations about the population estimates. If indigenous populations felt population pressure at any particular time, then it is expected that prehistoric population estimates for that particular period should at least approach the lowest (conservative and underestimated) value for the carrying capacity based on manioc, or 2,900 people. If there was no population pressure then the population estimates should be far below the threshold of the carrying capacity.

Maize

Although it has been determined that the limiting resource for Caribbean prehistoric groups were the calories in the form of manioc, for comparative purposes in this section I present estimates of the carrying capacity for the Valley of Maunabo based on maize production. However, here maize is mainly seen as a source of protein.

Maize is a cereal, which contains large amounts of protein, and, for this reason, requires high amounts of soil nutrients, which restricts its production to few types of soils. Although maize alone does not fulfill all human requirements in terms of protein (since it lacks two essential amino acids: lysine and tryptophan), it is a good agricultural source of most of the amino acids needed by human populations. In addition, maize has a relatively high quantity of calories in the form of oils, and contains higher quantities of several vitamins and minerals than manioc (see Table 6.1), but has lower yields per hectare.

Contrary to manioc, maize needs more attention to assure a successful crop. For example, to produce good yields of maize it is necessary to keep the ground clear of weeds early in the cycle of cultivation, a task that may require a large amount of labor in tropical environments. Furthermore, high rainfall and humidity can affect maize maturation and storage, since molds can attack the crop before and after cropping. This may be the reason why native groups in tropical areas tend to consume maize when it is still green, a practice also reported for Caribbean indigenous groups in early European chronicles (Newsom 1993). In short, contrary to manioc, maize is a good source of both protein and calories but provides lower yields per hectare. Maize is included in this study mostly as a source of protein rather than calories since manioc is a better supplier of this latter nutrient and needs less attention or labor. However, considering the lower production yield of maize due to its high soil requirement it is expected that the carrying capacity estimate based on protein consumption will be smaller than the one based solely on manioc. It is for this reason that a second carrying capacity is calculated below based not on the protein content of maize but on the total amount of corn needed per person per year to be able to survive (see Kowalewski 1980, 1982).

For estimating the carrying capacity based on the production of corn a formula similar to the one applied to manioc was used:

$$P_{max} = (Y_c P_c) A / T_p$$

where Y_c is the annual yield of maize (kg/ha), P_c is the amount of protein per kg of maize, A is the area under cultivation in hectare, T_p is the annual protein requirement per person, and P_{max} the maximum number of people sustainable (i.e., carrying capacity).

For the yield of corn per unit of land and protein content the estimates reported by Roosevelt (1980:186–187) are the only ones used here (see Table 6.1) since these are the only ones available for South American groups (see Cancian [1972:Table 6.3], Kirkby [1973], Kowalewski [1980, 1982] and Marcus [1982:256] for examples from Mesoamerica). Roosevelt (1980:185, 186) and Hassan (1981:18, 80) have published exactly the same estimates for the protein requirements for a balanced diet. Another estimate presented in the literature used to calculate the carrying capacity based on corn is the total consumption of corn per person per year instead of the amount of a specific nutrient. For Mesoamerica, Kowalewski (1980:156) has reported that ethnographically consumption needs may vary from 160 to 290 kg per person per year. While these amounts are not based on caloric or protein needs, they represent the total

Table 6.4. Estimates of Maximum Number of People That Could Have Been Supported in the Valley of Maunabo on Maize, Assuming a 20% Loss of the Annual Crop.

Area under Cultivation	Based on Protein Content (Roosevelt 1980)	Based on Total Consumption (Kowalewski 1980)
15.75 km2	6,214	7,875
4.27 km2	1,685	2,135

amount of maize necessary for a person to survive in a year. Tolstoy (1982:8) has considered the lowest of these amounts (i.e., 160 kg) as sufficient to provide the calories needed each day by a person whose diet consists of 80 percent maize. (However, he considers that a person needs about two million calories every year, a figure that is somewhat exaggerated when compared with other estimates presented in Table 6.2. This difference would not invalidate his argument completely, on the contrary, it means that more than one person could be sustained with 160 kg of maize.) Thus, the carrying capacity based on maize is estimated here by using both its protein content and the lowest amount needed per person (i.e., 160 kg) as suggested by Kowalewski (1980).

The estimates of the carrying capacity based on the protein content and total consumption of maize are presented in Table 6.4. For all of these estimates the maize annual yield (Y_c) reported by Roosevelt (1980) was used. In addition, it was assumed that maize was the only source of protein and that the total annual crop loss of 20 percent (Roosevelt 1980:186). Using maize as a protein source, a total of 6,214 people could have been supported if 15.75 km^2 were available for cultivation (the valley bottom and piedmont), and 1,685 if only 10 percent of the whole valley (i.e., 4.27 km^2) was cultivated. In the case of the carrying capacity based on the total consumption of maize, the estimates are higher (ranging from 2,135 to 7,875) and slightly lower than some of the estimates based on manioc production (see Table 6.3). However, it has to be mentioned that both of these estimates will rise sharply and dramatically if even small amounts of terrestrial and marine protein sources are considered.

As Keegan (personal communication, 2004) has correctly pointed out, these estimates assume that people allow the corn to mature so kernels could be stored for use in seasons when corn is not producing. In other words, an underlying premise of these values for the carrying capacity is that corn was available throughout the annual cycle in order to provide the protein necessary for the population. This normally requires the storage of mature corn, but evidence for facilities of this type have not been reported archaeologically or ethnohistorically. Nevertheless, the heuristic exercise being conducted here is to estimate the capacity of the environment to support a population assuming the knowledge of at least the most basic productive and storage technology, not the actual values. This is being done to compare the "reality," as defined using the archaeological record, to hypothetical, underestimated values for carrying capacity. Thus, what is being emphasized here is the potential of the region to support a population and not the actual population and subsistence practices of that population.

Summarizing, the carrying capacity based on the maize content of protein is relatively low as it was expected, while the figure based on total consumption allows a higher population level. Nevertheless, whether under population pressure or not, it is not expected that prehistoric populations were lower than the carrying capacity based on maize since protein was in abundance in the form of terrestrial and marine animals. In contrast, expectations similar to the ones presented for manioc should also be true for the carrying capacity based on the total consumption of maize since in both cases the lowest values are similar (i.e., 2,882 people in the case of manioc and 2,135 in the case of maize total consumption). However, of these figures the one based on manioc is the more useful for several reasons, including: (1) manioc produces higher yields and is a better source of calories than corn; (2) manioc was produced in larger quantities than maize in late prehispanic times as evidenced by the chronicles and the archaeological record; (3) manioc needs less attention or labor; and (4) while manioc is one of the best sources of calories, there are other alternate sources of protein besides maize.

Estimates of Archaeological Populations for the Valley of Maunabo

Prehistoric populations of the Valley of Maunabo were estimated by using the total area of the archaeological sites. Several works (Curet 1998; Hassan 1981; Howells 1986; Kolb 1985; Schacht 1981; Schreiber and Kintigh 1996) have already reviewed many of the methods used to estimate archaeological populations and their problems, and I am not repeating them here. I particularly use the logarithmic formulae developed by Curet (1998) where the total areas of the archaeological sites are correlated with data taken from ethnographic reports. Specifically, I make use of the formulae developed separately for small (i.e., < 9,000 m^2) and large sites (i.e., > 9,000 m^2). The equation for larger settlements was applied to all the habitation sites from the Valley of Maunabo, with two exceptions, Mu-15 and Mu-16, which are smaller than 9,000 m^2 and probably represent isolated houses similar to other sites found in Puerto Rico (e.g., Rivera and Rodríguez 1991).

Since almost all sites have been plowed in the past, the site sizes used in these calculations were modified versions of the areas measured in the field to compensate for this effect. Roper (1976:Table 1) has determined that the amount of lateral displacement induced by plowing averaged less than 5 m. However, other studies have also demonstrated that dispersion produced by plowing depends on the size and form of the artifacts, as well as on the conditions of the plowing process (see Lewarch and O'Brien 1981:308–310). In the case of the Valley of Maunabo, I decided to modify the site sizes by arbitrarily subtracting 10 percent of the total area to compensate for the spread effect of plowing. The figure of 10 percent subtracts a smaller area of the total size of most of the sites than reducing the total lateral dispersion by 5 m as is suggested by Roper's study (1976). Site Mu-7 is the only site where the reduction of 10 percent is not smaller, but has exactly the same effect as reducing the dispersion by 5 m (i.e., the population estimate was the same under both reductions of the total area). The decision of using the smaller 10 percent value instead of reducing the dispersion by 5 m was made to avoid any possibility of underestimating prehistoric populations, which could invalidate the test of the demographic models.

The population estimates for all habitation sites from the Valley of Maunabo obtained from the application of the regression formulae are presented in Table 6.5. It is important to stress that three basic assumptions were made in calculating these estimates and which are not necessarily true. The first is that each one of the sites lasted for the entire period to which they were assigned. This might not be true, since intra- and interregional migration during any of the periods is a possibility that has not been ruled out (e.g., Meggers 1992). Old sites might have been abandoned, and others formed sometime within a phase or style. The second assumption is that none of the sites changed in size or number of people while it was inhabited. Again this is likely not to be true since settlements are dynamic entities whose size is modified according to changes in their populations and particular histories (Rodman 1985; Sumner 1989). And, third, all multicomponent sites in the sample are assumed to have had the same size during all periods. Although any or all of these assumptions can be false, their rejection will tend to lower the population estimates and not to increase them. This is so because the estimates are the maximum possible number of people living in each site based on the total area of the deposits. Therefore, for the comparison with carrying capacity it should be kept

Table 6.5. Surface Area and Estimated Population for All Sites and Strata from the Valley of Maunabo.

SITE	ACTUAL AREA (sq. m)	MODIFIED* AREA (sq. m)	HACIENDA GRANDE	CUEVAS	MONSERRATE	SANTA ELENA	ESPERANZA
Mu-3	15,200	13,700		199	199	199	199
Mu-5	16,300	14,700	219				
Mu-7	27,800	25,000					374
Mu-9	N/A	N/A				10	10
Mu-15	3,341	3,007				80	
Mu-16	3,900	3,510		90	90	297	
Mu-18	21,300	19,200				269	
Mu-19	19,400	17,400		269	269		
TOTAL IN SURVEYED AREA IN STRATUM 1†			219	558	558	845	573
TOTAL IN SURVEYED AREA IN STRATUM 2††			0	0	10	10	10
EXTRAPOLATED POPUL. FOR STRATUM 1			413	1,048	1,048	1,589	1,078
EXTRAPOLATED POPUL. FOR STRATUM 2			0	0	0	569	569
TOTAL ESTIMATED POPULATION			413	1,048	1,048	2,158	1,647

* Calculated by subtracting 10% of the actual site area.
† Stratum 1 refers to the valley bottom and piedmont.
†† Stratum 2 refers to the mountainous area.

in mind that there is a tendency to severely overestimate the prehistoric populations.

The total population during each period for the surveyed area is also included at the bottom of Table 6.5. However, the surveyed area consisted of a sample or a fraction of the valley bottom, piedmont, and mountainous area. Therefore, the population for the survey area was extrapolated separately for the valley bottom and piedmont versus the mountainous region (Table 6.5), assuming that the population density was homogeneous within each one of these topographic subareas, but not at the level of the valley.

In terms of the mountainous region it was assumed that site Mu-9 represented a single house structure, probably housing a nuclear family. Similar sites have been reported for other areas of Puerto Rico (e.g., Rivera and Rodríguez 1991). Although it was impossible to measure the site area and, therefore, estimate the prehistoric population, due to its destruction by the construction of a road, it is assumed that no more than 10 people lived at one time in this site. This estimate is likely to be somewhat high since it is possible that prehistoric nuclear families averaged five people (Siegel 1989:195; Roosevelt 1991:342).

Another source of overestimation of population in the highlands is related to a bias in the survey sampling procedure. The surveyed area in the mountains was not chosen randomly; instead, relatively flat areas were selected. I assumed that these areas presented better physiographic conditions for habitation sites than the steep and dangerous slopes that characterize the Cuchilla de Panduras and Sierra de Guardarraya. Consequently, the prehistoric population density in the surveyed areas of the highlands should be higher than other nonsurveyed areas. Therefore, the extrapolation of this density to the rest of the mountain ranges should, once more, overestimate the real prehistoric population. Nevertheless, these figures were retained in the analysis to rule out any possibility of bias that would favor the rejection of the demographic models and in the absence of an alternative measure that would correct the bias.

Population Trends

A summary of the population estimates, growth rates (Yaukey 1990:41; see next chapter for a short explanation on calculating growth rates), and the carrying capacity based on caloric consumption for the Valley of Maunabo are presented in Figure 6.3. The carrying capacity used here is the lowest es-

Ancient Demography of the Valley of Maunabo / 177

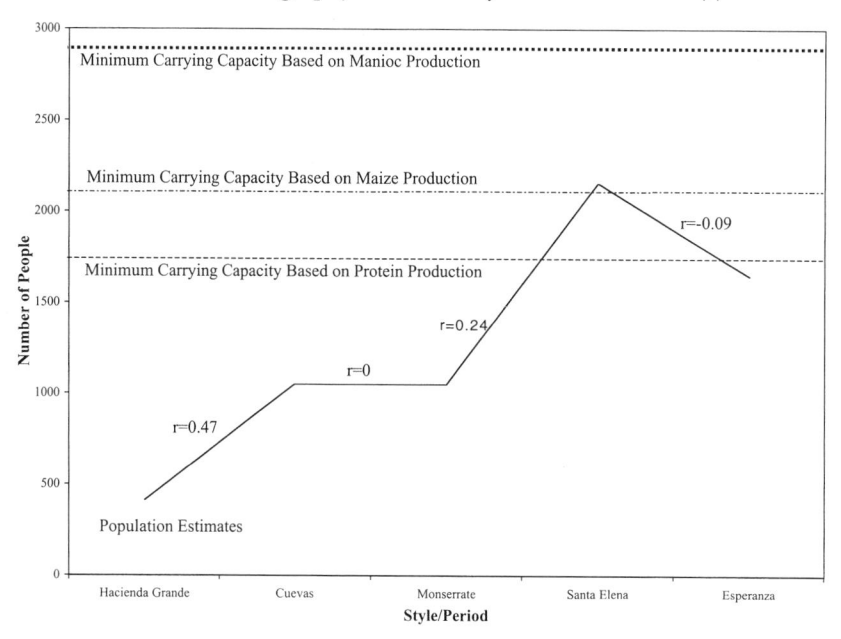

Figure 6.3. Population and carrying capacity estimates through time for the Valley of Maunabo.

timate based on the production of manioc presented in Table 6.3 since this was the main staple produced by prehistoric groups as evidenced by both the early chronicles and the archaeological record. In addition, as discussed before, of all the agricultural products this is one of the best sources of calories that was selected as the limiting nutrient for Caribbean prehistoric groups. It should be remembered that each population estimate represents the maximum possible population that could have existed, presumably by the end of each period, while the value for the carrying capacity is the smallest estimate calculated for the valley. As can be appreciated from the graph, prehistoric populations never reached or exceeded the carrying capacity of the valley based on calories.

In terms of the values obtained for the minimum carrying capacity based on protein consumption, the population estimates for the Santa Elena style are the only ones to exceed the lowest estimate of the carrying capacity (Figure 6.3), although the population estimate for the Esperanza style is very close. Nevertheless, as mentioned before, this carrying capacity value is the lowest estimate obtained, and it was estimated ignoring many other protein sources, particularly marine resources, which, according to early chronicles were exploited extensively and intensively by using a wide variety of methods (e.g., Fernández Méndez 1976; Keegan 1982; Mercado 1990; Vega 1980). If other protein sources are included in the analysis the minimum value of carrying capacity will assuredly rise dramatically. Therefore, this result should not be considered reliable, and future research should try to include these other alternative sources of protein.

When the carrying capacity is calculated using instead the total amount of corn needed annually by one person (assuming that they had the ability to store the corn for the whole year), the figures approach the lower estimates based on manioc production. In this case, the Santa Elena population estimate is the only figure to barely exceed the values of the carrying capacity. Although these estimates are not based specifically on the caloric or protein content of maize, they represent empirical figures made from ethnographic observations that can be generalized for any person. These estimates have been accepted and used, for example, in population studies in Mesoamerica (Kowalewski 1980; Sanders 1976:144–145; Tolstoy 1982:8).

In general, population grew during the Cuevas style (A.D. 400–600) or the Santa Elena (A.D. 900–1200) times, while the Monserrate style (A.D. 600–900) did not show any change. During the Esperanza style (A.D. 1200–1500) the population seems to have declined. None of the population growth rates for any of these periods appears to have been abnormally high, and they all are biologically feasible. However, the population trend seems to suggest that population grew at a faster pace during the Cuevas and Santa Elena times, while the Monserrate and Esperanza periods had slower and negative growth rates, respectively. These patterns are similar to the one discussed in the previous chapter for the Loíza and Salinas River Basin.

The Cuevas style has the largest population growth rate for all prehistoric times ($r = .47$ percent). This relatively large increase in population seems to be related to the initial population of the island, where migration combined with natural population growth (i.e., by birth within the region) are responsible for the large growth rate. Island demographic models predict similar results, where the initial colonizing population tends to grow at faster paces than later populations (Goodwin 1979, 1980; Keegan 1995; Kirch 1980). However, this argument does not take into consideration the possible contribution of Archaic populations to the general population trend. In other words, possible Archaic populations are not considered in the estimation of early populations (i.e., Hacienda Grande style) or in their biological input to later population growths (i.e., the Cuevas, Monserrate, and Esperanza styles).

An increase in population during the Santa Elena period is common for many regions of eastern Puerto Rico as it was suggested in the previous chapter based on total number of sites. The null growth rate for the Monserrate style might have been a product of our inability to distinguish the ceramics of the early forms of this style from those of late Cuevas. It is possible that sites belonging to only one of these styles were dated to both of them since in many occasions they were assigned to intermediate periods (Curet 1992a). Although I have reasons to believe that some of these sites belonged to only one period, I have decided to include them in both periods to avoid any personal bias. However, even if they were assigned to only one style, the growth rate would not have been more than .05 percent (Curet 1992c), which is still a relatively low value compared to the Cuevas and Santa Elena periods. Thus, based on the available data, it is certain that the Monserrate period saw a decrease in the growth rate in comparison to that of the Cuevas style. But, the reasons for this demographic stagnation are not clear (i.e., emigration, high mortality rates, or low fertility rates; see next chapter).

Discussion and Conclusions

The results presented above show that the Valley of Maunabo experienced a population increase between the Saladoid and the Elenan periods, while a decrease is registered in the Chican subseries, a pattern that has been found in other areas of Puerto Rico in terms of number of sites. Particularly, population increase was registered during the times of the Cuevas and Santa Elena styles. Although somewhat overestimated, the population estimates for both the "formative" periods of the Santa Elena and Esperanza style are comparable to estimates of hierarchical societies from other parts of the New World, including the Valley of Oaxaca (e.g., Feinman 1991:10.2) and the Southeast of the United States (e.g., Barker 1992:Table 6.1).

In Puerto Rico and other parts of the Caribbean, demographic models have been used to explain the development of social inequality during the Ostionan and Elenan Ostionoid, particularly during Santa Elena times. A major premise of these models is that population grew to a point that the local environment was unable to produce enough resources, making dramatic changes in the subsistence system necessary. This increase in population is indicated in the archaeological record by a large number of sites during the Santa Elena style. However, if social hierarchy developed as a response to population pressure, then we should expect population pressure to be present everywhere previous to the development of complexity; in other words, during the Monserrate or, at the latest, with the early Santa Elena styles.

When population estimates for each of the chronological periods are compared to the minimum carrying capacities calculated (underestimated) for the Valley of Maunabo based on manioc consumption (Figure 6.3), it can be seen that none of the ancient populations exceeded or even approached the lowest estimate. Population increase was experienced mostly during the Cuevas and Santa Elena times, the former presenting a larger population growth rate than the latter. Nevertheless, none of them seemed to have enough population to approach the carrying capacity of the valley. Surprisingly, the Monserrate and Esperanza times present low and negative population growth rates respectively, suggesting that some kind of cultural population control method was being used either consciously or unconsciously. Although several alternative reasons can be considered, I suggest here that most of the archaeological evidence from Puerto Rico and neighboring islands indicates that migration, either to other areas of Puerto Rico or other islands, is responsible for these low growth rates.

Although population was growing faster during Cuevas times compared with the Monserrate and the Esperanza periods, the total number of people was about one-third of the minimum carrying capacity of the valley. Moreover, the population also grew during the times of the Santa Elena style, when chiefdoms probably were already present. Still, the estimated population for this period was not a threat to the subsistence of prehistoric groups. Therefore, it can be concluded that the Valley of Maunabo was not overpopulated in relation to the resources available. Furthermore, the highest population level was not reached prior to the development of chiefdoms, but during the Santa Elena times when social complexity seemed to have been present already in other areas of Puerto Rico, and possibly in Maunabo, as well. Thus, the population increase during the times of the Santa Elena style might be related to social factors, such as the elite's need for labor (see discussion below).

The estimates for Santa Elena styles surpass the minimum carrying capacities estimated based on protein obtained from maize and the total consumption of maize. Nevertheless, it has to be considered that (1) other sources of protein that are abundant in the region were not considered, and (2) the estimates are the lowest value obtained from a wide range of estimates. Once these factors are taken into consideration, the estimate for the carrying capacity of the region based on protein for sure will increase immensely and most probably it will be several magnitudes larger than the population estimates. Even if the minimum carrying capacity obtained from the consumption of proteins is taken as given, it is only surpassed by the population of Santa Elena style, when supposedly the process of social hierarchization was already in an advanced stage (i.e., social hierarchization is already present). Thus, even if population pressure was present, it happened after the development of social inequality and not before as predicted by the models.

In conclusion, the results presented here reject the premises of demographic models on the development of complex society in Puerto Rico and in the Greater Antilles, since population levels are under the minimum carrying capacity based on manioc consumption or were not high enough before the development of social hierarchies. Furthermore, the low number of people estimated for prehistoric times in comparison to the carrying capacity does not give any reason to suspect an over-exploitation of the environment in order to simply satisfy the dietary needs of the population. It should be recalled that the carrying capacity was calculated taking into consideration the regeneration of the soils (i.e., only 10 percent of the valley was being cultivated at one time).

It is not argued here that the Valley of Maunabo was one of the pristine areas where chiefdoms developed, or that it was a major political center. However, it is believed by some researchers that chiefdoms developed for the first time in the southern coast (e.g., Veloz Maggiolo 1987:80, 1991:170) or eastern region (Rouse 1992:126 and Figure 8) of Puerto Rico. If this is the case, then it has to be explained why prehistoric groups did not move to other nearby areas, such as the Valley of Maunabo, where space and resources were still available. Migration seemed to have been an option during the early stages of prehistoric colonization of the Caribbean islands, and probably in the late Ceramic Age as well. People could have migrated to other islands such as Hispaniola and Cuba in earlier times, before experiencing sociopolitical changes. At this time, these islands were inhabited primarily by noncultivating groups. Furthermore, if population pressure was the prime mover for the development of sociopolitical organizations such as chiefdoms, then the increase in population should have happened before such a development occurred. Although more refinement of the chronology is needed, the results presented here suggest that population increase occurred at the same time that or most probably after social complexity arose. If true, then population growth might have occurred as a response to the development of institutionalized social stratification (e.g., a higher demand for commoner's labor or demographic support) (Friedman and Rowlands 1977).

It is true that one possible reason for this relatively low population in the valley might have been the preference for more advantageous zones than Maunabo, such as the area of Salinas (Rodríguez 1985; Torres 2001). This area, located on the south coast and about 65 km west of the Valley of Maunabo, seems to have been heavily populated since Archaic times (Rodríguez 1985; Veloz Maggiolo et al. 1975). The reasons for this are the highly fertile soils and the presence of one of the largest estuaries of the island. Nevertheless, this still does not explain why migration to areas where higher populations could have been supported was not used as an escape valve, if over-population existed in these preferred regions.

It will be interesting to see if similar population levels are obtained by future research in other areas of the Caribbean, in particular other regions in Puerto Rico. If the results of these studies support the conclusions obtained here, factors other than ecological and demographic variables, such as social factors, which could have motivated or forced the development of stratification, should be considered. Traditionally social factors are ignored in archaeological studies due to the difficulty of measuring them in the archaeological record. However, recent models have been suggested concerning the development of chiefdoms where more weight is given to social institutions and processes (Friedman and Rowlands 1977; see various papers in Barker and Pauketat 1992; Blanton et al. 1996; Clark and Blake 1994; Earle 1991; McGuire and Saitta 1996; Saitta 1997), and which should be considered in future research designs.

As mentioned in the introduction to this chapter, another of the purposes of this chapter was to demonstrate that demographic issues are more intricate, difficult, and complicated than many scholars of the ancient Caribbean have recognized in their modeling of past human behavior. In part this was demonstrated when variables as simple as population and population pressure are tested against a more rigorous evaluation where both of them were quantified and many related aspects and factors considered. Many of the complexities of the processes related to these variables had to be simplified in this analysis in order to overcome many of the epistemological and methodological limitations. Even so, it is expected that this example fulfilled the purpose of demonstrating that demographic variables should not be taken to lightly in the modeling of human behavior.

Nevertheless, it has to be admitted that ancient population dynamics were much more complex than most of the discussion presented in this chapter and by the demographic models. Variables other than carrying capacity, environmental resources, and population estimates not considered in this analysis may have played a role in several social, political, economic, demographic, and historic processes that are not readily visible with the data at hand. For example, even though the analysis presented here does not show the presence of over-exploitation of environmental resources, this conclusion was reached considering the use of those resources only for dietary purposes. It did not consider the possibility of the over-use of these resources for other purposes such as feasting and financing of elite projects, and that could have led to activities detrimental to the environment (e.g., deforestation, soil erosion, over-exploitation of faunal resources, etc.). These practices combined with a possible demand for labor and higher populations by the hierarchical and stratified political organization may have led to other forms of population/resource imbalances. Therefore, population and the availability of resources should not always be considered as independent variables that can affect human behavior, but they can actually be independent variables that can be shaped by social and political issues. But, in order to determine the relationship between all these factors or variables more refined studies are needed where fine-grain data on population estimates, chronology, and social, political, and economic contexts are collected. It is not until then that we will be able to reach a more realistic perspective of the complexity of the issues that we are studying.

Before ending this chapter I believe that a point of clarification and warning is necessary. I have received comments from several colleagues about using my estimates of carrying capacity and population trends to support aspects of, or as an example of carrying capacity models such as the one proposed by Keegan (1995) discussed in this chapter. I have not, however, used the concept of carrying capacity as a model of population growth as used in many ecological or biological studies. Here this concept was used to come up with an estimate of the population that could potentially be supported by the region under very *conservative* conditions. To calculate the true carrying capacity of a region one has to consider the great variety of resources available. Since I used only one resource (either manioc or corn), the results underestimate the carrying capacity. Certainly, if other sources of protein and calories are considered, the estimates will increase dramatically.

Furthermore, most of the criteria used in calculating these *conservative* estimates were low to the point that the final output may be markedly unrealistic. This was done in order to have a strong argument to reject the demographic models; in other words, even under these unrealistic conditions, no evidence for population pressure could be found. A similar but converse strategy was followed for the population estimates, in this case by overestimating them. The assumptions of the estimates were selected in all instances to obtain the highest population possible. Needless to say, these assumptions are not always true and, therefore, the true population values most probably are much lower than the ones obtained here. Thus, the estimates obtained and compared in this chapter are not quite realistic in the sense of representing true values. They were purposefully exaggerated in the expressed manner to demonstrate that even under such exaggerated conditions the evidence does not support the demographic models. For these reasons the estimates obtained should not be used for any application or as proof of the applicability or strength of carrying capacity models. In fact, since the true value for carrying capacity is much higher than the one used here, and the populations most probably were smaller, these results may not support, but contradict some of the models applied for human populations such as Keegan's (1995).

7 / Paleodemography at the Local Level

Up to this point, demographic issues in ancient Puerto Rico have been dealt with superficially by considering only number of people and their spatial distribution. This approach has produced trends in population distributions and estimates through space and time that have allowed us to propose possible relationships between the number of people and cultural and social changes. However, while useful for a number of purposes, these levels of study tend to obscure considerable variability, especially within the structure of local populations. The details of the internal structure and nature of local populations play a major role in shaping the economic, social, and in some instances, political organization and dynamics of human societies. In other words, it is not only how many people compose a society but also who is included in that population that is important. For example, a relatively young or old population (i.e., with a large number of "unproductive" members) can cause economic problems because of the low number of young or middle-aged adults who normally compose the labor force of society. The same is true if one gender is disproportionately represented, since males and females tend to have different social, not to mention biological, roles in society. Thus, in studying the role of population variables in our modeling of human behavior, it is necessary to take into consideration the number of people, the age and sex distribution, and issues such as fertility and mortality rates. This chapter attempts to present some of the demographic issues related to the internal structure of local populations. It also demonstrates the usefulness of paleodemographic studies to evaluate the representativeness of or bias in skeletal samples, two issues that are critical to understand since they can affect our final results and interpretation of the data.

In archaeology, issues of population structure are studied by a relatively young, multidisciplinary branch called paleodemography. As Meindl and Russell (1998:376) have stated: "Paleodemography is more than the study of mortality and fertility of archaeological populations. It also includes the estimation of the distribution, density, and age composition of prehistoric peoples. It considers intrinsic rates of growth or decline, and it may include migration and the age and sex structure of migration as well." Paleodemography also attempts to study issues related to paleopathology and paleoepidemiology such as diseases, frailty, and morbidity. Here I focus almost exclusively on issues of population trends and structure, and not so much with these last aspects of the paleodemography.

Paleodemographic studies based on osteological remains in Puerto Rico, and in the Caribbean in general, are especially difficult due to the nature of the samples and the osteological studies. As Crespo Torres (2000) argues, in the Caribbean, most samples of human remains were the product of accidental discoveries, and few studies, if any at all, have been designed a priori to recover appropriate skeletal samples. For this reason, assemblages of archaeological, human remains tend to be too small to reach significant results or conclusions. Further, even in the cases where samples are large enough, many of them have not been studied appropriately from an osteological or pathological perspective, or the results of the studies are not published, at least not in a format that can be used by other researchers. These difficulties in obtaining the appropriate data have hindered significantly the furthering of paleodemographic goals in the study of the ancient history of Puerto Rico and the Caribbean.

Nonetheless, there are some recent exceptions to these general problematic trends in the study of skeletal populations for Puerto Rico (e.g., Budinoff 1991; Crespo Torres 1994, 1998, 2000; Siegel 1992) and the rest of the region (Baetsen 1999; Hoogland 1996; Rivero de la Calle 1990; Versteeg et al. 1997; Versteeg et al. 1990; Versteeg and Schinkel 1992). In this chapter, I make use of information provided for skeletal collections from three sites in Puerto Rico to conduct a comparative study of specific variables of the population structure. The three collections are from the sites of Punta Candelero (Crespo Torres 2000), Paso del Indio (Crespo Torres 2000), and Tibes (Crespo Torres 1998) (Figure 7.1). The primary goal of the study is not so much to test alternative hypotheses or inferences but instead to conduct an exploratory study

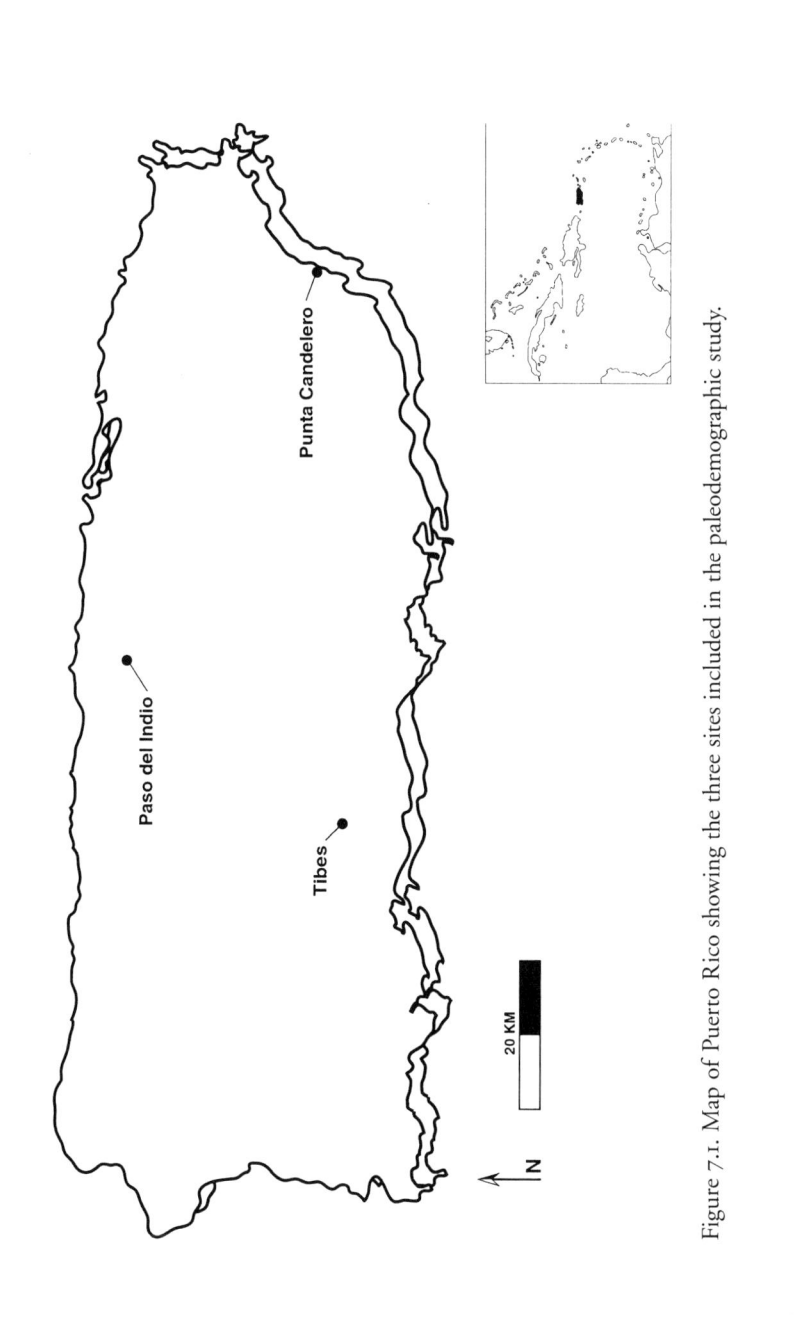

Figure 7.1. Map of Puerto Rico showing the three sites included in the paleodemographic study.

of ancient population structures in order to generate independently testable hypotheses. Another goal is to begin building a paleodemographic data set that can be used by future researchers for comparative purposes. Until we build a number of regional data sets on population structures at the local level we will not be able to test many of our models or understand many of the factors involved in the decision-making process at the community level. Another aim is to show the importance of considering population sex and age structure, in addition to aspects of fertility and mortality, in studying their material remains. A population that is experiencing marked negative growth rates tends to behave differently from populations that are growing. Also, populations dominated numerically by one of the sexes or few age categories can produce variability in the social and cultural behavior. This information is also used to evaluate the integrity of skeletal samples.

This chapter begins with a short discussion of paleodemography as a field of study emphasizing at the end the variables used in the study. A description of the skeletal samples, the sites where they come from, and the history of the excavation projects that unearthed them is included in the next section. This is followed by the calculation and analysis of several paleodemographic variables and indexes for the three populations, a comparison of the results, and a final conclusion section.

PALEODEMOGRAPHIC ASSUMPTIONS AND PRINCIPLES

Paleodemography is a relatively young, multidisciplinary line of study that mixes techniques, methods, and theories from archaeology, biological anthropology, osteology, pathology, demography, and epidemiology. It focuses on ancient populations mainly through the study of skeletal remains. On some occasions, researchers make use of other sources of information such as demographic models obtained from ethnographic reports or demographic information from historical documents. In general, paleodemography can be divided into two areas of interest. The first one deals with more pure demographic variables such as population growth, fertility, and mortality rates, sex distributions, life expectancy, and others. The second focuses more on pathological issues such as frailty and morbidity, and the role and/or impact of diseases on populations and cultural and social processes. Due to the focus of this study, the discussion that follows concentrates solely on the first area of interest of paleodemography, population issues. This discussion is not intended to be a thorough review of the state of the art of this branch of study, nor will osteological aspects related to methods for sexing and aging skeletons be discussed, but some biases would be mentioned. Even though these are important issues in paleodemography, they are not relevant to the present discussion and analysis of the Puerto Rican samples. A number of reviews (Civera Cerecedo and Márquez Morfín 1998; Jackes 1992; Larsen 2002; Meindl and Russell 1998; Milner et al. 2000; Paine 1997a; Wright and Yoder 2003) of many of these issues have been recently published, and there is no need to repeat them here. For sake of simplicity, I have divided this section in three parts: the uniformitarian principle and other assumptions, sample biases, and the demographic variables.

The Uniformitarian Principle and Other Assumptions

The main assumption in paleodemographic studies is the uniformitarian assumption, which states that modern regularities of human biology are also true for ancient human populations. These regularities include demographic aspects such as age patterns of birth, death, or sexual maturation. As Howells (1986:26) has summarized it:

> A uniformitarian position in paleodemography implies that the human animal has not basically changed in its direct biological response to the environment in processes of ovulation, spermatogenesis, length of pregnancy, degree of helplessness of the young and rates of maturation and senility over time. This does not imply that humans have not changed in the rates of performance of these processes, but only that the processes still respond in the same way to variations in environment, including the cultural and technological aspects of human society as part of the external environment.

The critical point of this premise is not that factors affecting human demography are constant across human populations and time, but that the variability in these factors is limited and predictable. Human demographic factors are constrained by a number of biological factors producing regularities, "We should not expect to see demographic patterns in prehistory that deviate wildly from what is known about modern human populations, for example, modal ages at death in the fourth or fifth decade of life as opposed to later ages" (Milner et al. 2000:468). This premise is used in almost every stage of research in paleodemography, from methodological aspects of studying the osteological samples in the laboratory to the calculation of demographic variables such as fertility, mortality, and life tables. It also allows the use of ethnographic analogy to understand ancient demographic processes. Using this premise, several researchers have created uniformitarian models (e.g., Coale and Demeny 1983; Weiss 1973) and simulation studies that serve to "provide baseline expectations that may be used to help us describe and evaluate the patterns that we observe in the archaeological/skeletal record" (Paine 1997b: 192). Empirical data is then compared to the models, and deviations from the expectations are seen as the result of biological or cultural processes, differential preservation, or problems with the recovery and/or analysis of the osteological samples.

Many paleodemographic studies also include other assumptions, two of the most used being stability and stationarity in the populations under study. These are assumptions that are used even by modern demographers to facilitate the analysis, measurement, calculation, and modeling of population variables and trends. Stable population theory assumes a hypothetical population with no migration and with a constant growth rate based on constant fertility and mortality rates. By assuming these conditions, it is easier for demographers (and paleodemographers) to calculate indexes such as life expectancy and fertility since all changes in the population can be ascribed solely to shifts in birth and death rates.

A stationary population is a special case of a stable population where the constant population growth is zero and, therefore, there is no growth or decrease of the total population. In this case, migration is still not included. Contrary to other stable populations with positive or negative population growth rates, stationary populations do not suffer changes in the age-at-death distribution. Due to the nature of the archaeological data where we can only account for the dead people and not the survivors, this last assumption facilitates the measurement of many demographic variables. For example, under this assumption the average age-at-death equals the life expectancy (mortality) of the osteological population.

A final assumption made by most traditional paleodemographic studies is that the skeletal population is a direct reflection of the living population that produced it. Age and sex distribution, prevalence of pathologies and traumas, and measurements of mortality and fertility rates obtained from the archaeological samples are proportionally related to the ancient living populations.

Needless to say, many of these premises and assumptions are not true in all situations, and, at least in the case of the assumption of stationary population, are rarely valid. Despite the strong arguments pointing out these problems, many paleodemographic studies have decided to ignore or discard criticisms as of minimal importance for their research. Of course, this has inspired strong criticisms from inside (Bocquet-Appel and Masset 1982; Wood et al. 1992) and outside the discipline (Petersen 1975). The problems pointed out by these criticisms were so strong and seemingly unavoidable that some critics suggested the abolition of paleodemography and classified it as a dead science due to its inability to measure true demographic variables. The conceptual issues most criticized are the assumption of stationarity and the premise that the ancient living population is reflected in the skeletal sample. Important issues pointed out are how selective mortality and heterogeneity risks can invalidate the demographic and epidemiological measurements obtained from the dead populations (Wood et al. 1992). There are two basic arguments in this criticism. The first one is that paleodemographic samples are biased mainly because we are dealing with the dead, a group that includes a larger number of sick, weak, and frail individuals than the surviving, living population. Since we do not know the demographic characteristic of the surviving population, it is "impossible" to determine many aspects of the structure of the population. Second, not everyone has the same probability of dying nor is at the same level of risk. Thus, skeletal samples do not necessarily reflect the population structure or age and sex distribution of the living population. These two problems have been called the "Osteological Paradox" by Wood et al. (1992).

Another critical comment made by Wood et al. (1992) is the possibility that many weak and frail individuals may have died of some diseases in such a fast rate that did not allow for the illness to affect the bones. Hence, the person died before the disease could leave a mark in the bones. Contrarily, healthy and strong individuals may have suffered from the same illness, but being capable to resist it and survive it, there was ample time for the disease to show some signs on the bones. Osteologically, therefore, these two types of individuals may look different from what they were in reality. The strong, surviving individuals will show signs of diseases (or pathologies), and the weak, frail, and fast-dying individuals may seem relatively healthy. This problem has been called by some the "Osteological Counter-Paradox," and it will distort any epidemiological study of the ancient population.

However, instead of these criticisms being a requiem for paleodemography, they became the standard or "yardstick" used to measure the quality of research and advancements in the discipline. For example, in many instances recent studies do not take many of the assumptions discussed above as givens, but actually test their applicability. Further, researchers are making use of more realistic models, complex statistical analyses, and computer simulations to evaluate the cases of ancient populations. There is a broader recognition of the limitations of the discipline and a larger acceptance of using the results of paleodemographic studies for hypothesis building rather than for testing hypotheses or inferences. Also, it has inspired the development and use of new analytical methods tailored to skeletal population, instead of uncritically applying methods used by modern demographers. More importantly, it has made paleodemographers more realistic in terms of which questions they can actually answer instead of which ones they would like to answer (Milner et al. 2000). Instead of burying it, this painful and long process of auto-evaluation has strengthened paleodemography as a scientific field of study of ancient human populations.

Sample Biases

As is the case with the great majority of archaeologically recovered collections, skeletal samples tend to be biased in many ways. In most instances, some age- or sex-based groups tend to be underrepresented or overrepresented, according to the source of the bias. Further, some biases directly or indirectly invalidate almost completely one or more of the assumptions discussed above (i.e., uniformanitarianism, stability, and/or stationarity). Although factors producing this skewness in the data can be many and diverse, most paleodemographers divide them in four basic categories (Jackes 1992; Milner et al. 2000; Paine and Harpending 1998).

The first type of biasing factors are those produced by cultural traditions of the deposition of the dead or other related practices that can affect the composition of the sample. For example, dead people from different strata or sectors of hierarchical, segmentary, or differentiated societies can be buried in different locations or cemeteries. Thus, a sample of only one location may provide a skewed view of the total population of the group. Other social groups do not bury preinitialized infants or children in the same place as people that have gone through a rite of passage that "officially" made them part of the social group, producing a sample where infants are underrepresented. The practice of infanticide can also produce a similar effect, since in many instances the victims are disposed of in nondistinct areas. Furthermore, in cases where female infanticide is more prevalent, this practice produces a sex bias in the sample as well. Also, practices such as chronic warfare, raiding, and migration can lead to a sample with greater numbers of young and middle-aged adult males than expected.

The second type of factor is taphonomic processes, a problem present in all archaeological studies. This type of factor includes differential preservation of the osteological remains due to the physical properties of the skeletons. For example, it has been argued by many that children's and elderly's bones tend to be less dense and thinner than young and middle-aged adults, resulting in a higher probability of survival among the latter and an underrepresentation of the former. The impact of natural and cultural transformational processes is going to be more pronounced in the skeletal remains of the young and old, but lesser on the bones of intermediate ages. However, the effect of this problem is more pronounced among the old than the young due to the span of the ages represented in these two categories. For example, many times the badly preserved skeletal remain of a child can be placed in an age range of 5–10 years (e.g., anywhere between 5 and 15 years old). However, the true age of badly preserved bones of an older adult could be placed in a wider age range (e.g., anywhere between 40 and 60 years old).

The third type of biasing factor is differential archaeological recovery. This factor is related to both the archaeological strategies and methods employed, and the skills of the excavators. Here also, the losers are the young, not only because of the low density and thinness of their bones but also because of the small size of their remains. This problem is of great concern when dealing with old collections in museums but is also a problem with more recently excavated collections. Another bias introduced by this factor is related to the sampling procedure. As mentioned previously, the great majority of skeletal collections are obtained by fortuitous discoveries and not as part of a conscious effort to sample human remains in a systematic and representative manner. In many cases the large size of the samples is used to compensate for the presence of this bias or to ignore any sampling problem. However, even large-sized samples can be skewed in favor of or against individuals with certain social or economic status, gender, age. Moreover, this problem generally tends to be discussed more often in the context of stratified societies but ignored in many cases of the so-called egalitarian societies. This is unfortunate, since this last type of society can also have differential treatments of the dead (e.g., in segmentary societies) based on sex, age, social status, or kinship affiliation that will require a strict and disciplined sampling procedure.

The final biasing factor is related to age estimation methods. This bias, introduced by osteological methods, has received a considerable amount of attention in recent years (e.g., Lovejoy et al. 1997). The basic issue here is the accuracy of many of the age markers used by osteologists to determine age-at-death of individual skeletons. Contrary to some of the previous factors, this one tends to misrepresent the elderly (i.e., ages above 45 years) by assigning them to younger age categories.

These biases should not be taken lightly since they can affect many of the demographic measurements that are of interest in the study of ancient populations. Unless they are taken into consideration they can produce sizeable errors in our calculations and, therefore, in our final conclusions on trends in population structure, distribution, and constitution.

Demographic Variables

For decades, paleodemographers have attempted to develop analytical methods to obtain various important demographic statistics from skeletal collections. In this section I discuss the variables that are more relevant to this chapter; specifically, I concentrate on four main areas: fertility, mortality, migration, and life-tables of a population. In the early days of paleodemography, when biases in the collections were ignored and it was assumed that the skeletal sample was a reflection of the living population, researchers tended to uncritically use standard demographic techniques and life tables to measure these variables. However, for the past 10 to 15 years, and after recognizing the limitations and true nature of the data, paleodemographers have been developing new analytical methods to circumvent some of these problems. Some of these new approaches, used later in this chapter, are also discussed in this section.

The definitions and discussion of the terms and concepts that follow are based on the books by Hassan (1981) and Yaukey (1990). *Fertility* is the number of live births that occur in a population, and it is normally presented as the *crude birth rate*. Crude birth rates are calculated by dividing the number of births in one year by the total population and are normally represented by the number of births per 100 or 1,000 people. In some cases, it is divided instead by the number of fertile women (i.e., more or less from 15 to 50 years old), and this is called the *age-sex specific fertility rate*. This rate is also exhibited as the total number of births per 100 or 1,000 fertile women. *Mortality* refers to the frequency with which death occurs in a population and is normally illustrated as the *crude death rate* or, in other words, the number of deaths per 1,000 people. The distribution of mortality changes according to age. In most populations, mortality is moderate during infancy, tends to decline to minimal mortality during youth, and then climbs again gradually through the middle years, rising rapidly in senescent years. Another measurement that is normally related to the degree of mortality in a population is *life expectancy*, which can be defined as the average (mean) number of years yet to be lived by people attaining a given age.

To measure aspects of mortality, especially life expectancy, demographers make use of *life tables*. Life tables are used for tracing the cumulative effect of a specified series of age-sex-specific death rates over a life cycle for a hypothetical cohort. To construct these tables, demographers use the number of people at different ages that have died compared to the ones that still live in a population. Assuming that the age distribution of a population represents individuals of the same cohort through time, then variables such as estimated life expectancy could be calculated. Among paleodemographers the same assumption is made, that is, that all individuals from a skeletal population belong to the same cohort. Life tables can include a variety of variables and indices, the following being the most used in demographic studies:

- x: age category
- D_x number of deaths between age x and $x + 1$
- d_x proportion of the dead between age x and $x + 1$
- l_x proportion of survivors of exact age x
- q_x probability of dying between age x and $x + 1$
- L_x total number of years lived by survivors between ages x and $x + 1$
- T_x total years (for the cohort) lived after exact age x
- E_x life expectancy, or average number of years lived after exact age x

These variables are normally measured for each year of life, but due to incomplete or imprecise data, demographers can also use abridged tables where ranges of age categories are used (e.g., 0–5 years, 5–10 years, etc.). Examples of life tables are included below for the skeletal population studied in this chapter. Abridged life tables used to be popular in paleodemographic studies because of the information related to the age-sex specific mortality rate that can be obtained from them by simply using the age-at-death distribution, a type of information that can be easily acquired from skeletal collections.

Many paleodemographers have cautioned against the use of life tables because they feel that due to several unfounded assumptions (i.e., that skeletal populations represent one cohort, death rates are even for all ages, and stable population) the tables falsify biological facts. Because of the unrealistic biological expectations, most researchers have discouraged the use of life tables in their analysis and have suggested other ways of investigating mortality among skeletal populations (Johansson and Horowitz 1986). In the study below, life tables are used for comparative purposes in conjunction with other archaeological and osteological evidence. While, admittedly, this comparison may be invalid, the results are used to define some trends in order to develop realistic working hypotheses for future studies.

Population growth rate is the change in population size, in either a positive or negative manner, through time. In theory the population growth rate can be calculated for a year as:

$$r = b + d + m \qquad (1)$$

where b is the birth rate, d the death rate, and m the addition or subtraction of individuals due to migration. However, in many cases the birth and death rates are not available and the population growth rate has to be calculated by considering changes in the total population and using the following formula:

$$r = [\ln(N_t/N_0)]/t \qquad (2)$$

where N_t is the number of people at time t and N_0 at $t = 0$. In most instances, population growth rates are not easily obtained from osteological collections due to the lack of chronological information. However, they can be calculated using information gathered by settlement archaeology such as population estimates from site size and the number of rooms or structures (Curet 1998; Kolb 1985; Schacht 1981; Schreiber and Kintigh 1996). This is the strategy used for estimating growth rates for the Valley of Maunabo in the previous chapter.

Originally, issues of *fertility* and *mortality rates* in paleodemography were obtained from life tables calculated from the skeletal remains as mentioned above. For example, mortality was estimated from the mean age-at-death, since under conditions of stationary population mean age-at-death is equal to life expectancy at birth. Also, under the assumption of zero growth rate, and still assuming that no migration was occurring, mortality and fertility are always equal. In some cases, when population growth rate was not assumed to be zero, fertility was estimated by using the number of infants in the sample and comparing it to the total number of individuals. Thus, by using the assumptions spelled out above and by using standard demographic techniques, fertility, mortality, and other variables (e.g., sex distributions) supposedly could be calculated from life tables in a more or less accurate fashion.

Of course, due to unfounded assumptions, in most cases these estimates tend to be erroneous and inaccurate. For example, it has been demonstrated that mean age-at-death and "life expectancy" estimated from life tables assuming stationary populations are more a measure of fertility than of mortality (Johansson and Horowitz 1986; Sattenspiel and Harpending 1983). Life expectancy is more sensitive to changes in crude birth rates than in crude death rates, and therefore is not a measure of mortality. However, exceptions exist about this relationship between fertility and age-at-death distribution, as for example the effects of catastrophic deaths and massive migrations (Keckler 1997; Paine 2000) among other influential processes (Dumond 1997). Another problem is how the biases in the sample, especially the under- or overrepresentation of certain ages, can affect these measurements since the main piece of information used to calculate them is mean death-at-age (Dumond 1997:181).

For these reasons, many paleodemographers have argued in favor of not using life tables or the statistics obtained from them in the study of skeletal populations (e.g., Sattenspiel and Harpending 1983). Instead, many of them have suggested the use of the distribution of age-at-death data (e.g., Buikstra et al. 1986; Johansson and Horowitz 1986; Konigsberg et al. 1989; Milner et al. 1989), comparisons with ideal models (Dumond 1997; Storey and Hirth 1997), computerized simulations (Keckler 1997; Paine 1997b, 2000), and more sophisticated statistical and quantitative methods (Buikstra 1997; Konigsberg et al. 1997).

The analysis presented below specifically examines the following four aspects of the demographic structure and characteristics of the three populations under study:

Sex distribution: frequency of females and males among the adults represented in the sample. This will be obtained from the raw data provided by the osteological analysis.

Age-at-death distribution: the graphic representation of the distribution of each sample is examined visually and compared to ideal models and the other collections.

Fertility rates: fertility is measured using four different procedures. The first one is the ratio of the number of individuals over 30 years old to the number of individuals over 5 years or D30+/D5+ as proposed by Buikstra et al. (1986; see also Konigsberg et al. 1989). According to these authors this ratio has a high negative correlation with fertility in the form of crude birth rates. The advantage of the D30+/D5+ is that it eliminates the effects of undernumeration of infants younger than 5 years old and to a certain point it reduces the impact of mis-aging individuals in senescent ages. Using simulation procedures, Paine and Harpending (1996) have demonstrated that this index is a representative measurement of fertility for various populations under a variety of conditions, but it tends to be accompanied by large variability. Thus, it is a good estimate of fertility, but it fails to differentiate populations under different conditions of both fertility and growth rates. The second one is the ratio D45+/D5− suggested by Milner et al. (1989), who argued that it would be a more sensitive measurement than the one mentioned above. Paine and Harpending (1996) found that this ratio is a proportionally good estimate of fertility in ideal models, and that it can clearly distinguish between populations under different conditions. However, due to its reliance on age-categories that are more susceptible to be underrepresented, it is significantly affected by infant undernumeration and age estimation errors among older individuals. Further, this estimate is extremely sensitive to stochastic processes in small populations. In addition to this ratio, Milner et al. (1989) recommended the use of visual comparison of the age-at-death distribution of the sample with four ideal models generated based on the extreme cases of the !Kung (low fertility and mortality rates) and the Yanomamo (high fertility and mortality rates). This method is the third one used here. However, at least in theory, it seems to be highly susceptible to underrepresentation of infants and underaging of senescent individuals, a problem present in most analyses in one way or another. Finally, the ratio of D20+/D5+ suggested by Konigsberg et al. (1989:628) is also used since it is more reliable in many situations where D30+/D5+ is unsuitable, such as when adult age determinations are uncertain. Basically, this ratio considers all adults independently of their ages, at the same time that it controls for the possible underrepresentation of infants.

Mortality rates are probably the index most difficult (if not impossible) to estimate due to the big unknown of skeletal samples: the survival rate for each age category (i.e., we need to know how many people survived to have an idea of the proportion of deaths). Due to the inaccuracy of our methods to calculate it at this time, I have decided not to include this index in the discussion that follows.

POPULATION STRUCTURE AND DEMOGRAPHIC STATISTICS AT THE LOCAL LEVEL

As mentioned before, three skeletal collections are used here for the paleodemographic study. They were obtained from different parts of the island and, in general, they belong to different periods. One advantage of using these collections is that all of them were analyzed by the same osteologist (Crespo Torres 1994, 1998, 2000), reducing in some ways errors and variability produced by idiosyncrasies and differences in methods and criteria during the analysis.

Punta Candelero

The first sample used in the study is from the site of Punta Candelero, a site located in the eastern coastal plain of Puerto Rico, less than 300 meters from the shore. The site occupies a good portion of a sandy peninsula that extends about one kilometer into the ocean (Crespo Torres 2000). Its average altitude is 2 m above sea level.

The site of Punta Candelero was excavated in the late 1980s by a cultural resource management project and is one of the earliest ceramic settlements in the island (Rodríguez 1989a, 1991). The archaeological deposits are composed of two main assemblages or occupations. The first one belongs to the controversial La Hueca complex mentioned in Chapter 2, while the second one belongs to the Cuevas style (A.D. 400–600) (Rodríguez 1989, 1991). The La Hueca complex deposits are located toward the western side of the settlement and form an east-west lineal arrangement. The Cuevas deposits are located toward the eastern boundaries of the site and form a circular or semicircular arrangement around an area of low artifact concentration. Both deposits overlap around the center of the site where the Cuevas materials are always located stratigraphically above the La Hueca deposits. The different pieces of chronological evidence for both occupations are contradictory, possibly the result of the complexity of multiple cultural- and natural-formation processes that have impacted the site in ancient and modern times. Nonetheless, based on stratigraphic and stylistic evidence, the excavator of the site (Miguel Rodríguez personal communication, 2003) believes that the assemblages do not represent continuous or contemporaneous occupations, but a process of occupation, abandonment, and re-occupation centuries later.

Altogether 85 skeletal samples were obtained from the excavations at the

Table 7.1. Abridged Life-Table for the Punta Candelero Population (Both Sexes).

x	D_x	d_x	l_x	q_x	L_x	T_x	E_x
0–4	6	7.059	100.000	.071	482.353	3291.176	32.912
5–9	5	5.882	92.941	.063	450.000	2808.824	30.222
10–14	0	.000	87.059	.000	435.294	2358.824	27.095
15–19	1	1.176	87.059	.014	432.353	1923.529	22.095
20–24	9	10.588	85.882	.123	402.941	1491.176	17.363
25–29	14	16.471	75.294	.219	335.294	1088.235	14.453
30–34	9	10.588	58.824	.180	267.647	752.941	12.800
35–39	11	12.941	48.235	.268	208.824	485.294	10.061
40–44	7	8.235	35.294	.233	155.882	276.471	7.833
45–49	14	16.471	27.059	.609	94.118	120.588	4.457
50–54	9	10.588	10.588	1.000	26.471	26.471	2.500
55–59	0	.000	.000		.000	.000	
60+	0	.000	.000		.000	.000	
Total	85	100.000	–	–	3291.176	–	–

site, all of them belonging to the Cuevas occupation. No human burial has been discovered for the La Hueca assemblage, although several canine interments were found. Crespo Torres (1994, 2000) conducted a thorough osteological sample of this collection, and his results are used in the analysis below.

Of the 85 individuals, 40 were identified as adult males, 27 as adult females, 11 as subadults, and 7 as indeterminates. As can be seen, this sample is heavily tilted in favor of adults, particularly males (59.7 percent of all sexed individuals). The differences in age-at-death are also visible in its distribution shown in Table 7.1 and Figure 7.2. This distribution is not common for preindustrial populations where infant mortality rates tend to be much higher.

One or more of the following processes could have produced this supposedly "abnormal" age and sex distribution. First, the observed pattern could have been produced by differential preservation, where the remains of infants, children, and adult females were at a disadvantage over older adult male skeletal remains. Although this option may explain the low number of infants and children in the sample, it does not completely explain the low frequency of women represented in the collection, since in general adult bones are stronger and denser than subadults. A second process involved in the creation of this pattern may be that the archaeological methodology favored older and male individuals over younger and female individuals. This could have been produced by the sampling process as well as by the field methodology used. Con-

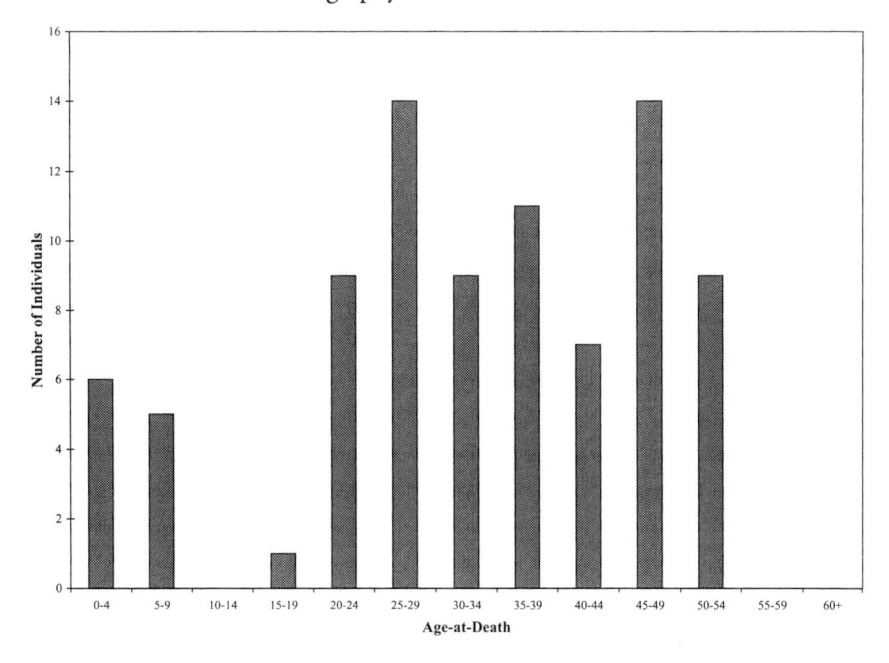

Figure 7.2. Distribution of age-at-death for the site of Punta Candelero.

sidering that more than 65 percent of the site was excavated, the probability of sampling bias is relatively low. While some field methodology and the skill of the field personnel could have been a factor in the omission of infants and children from the sample, it is difficult to visualize a field practice that could explain the low number of females compared to males.

A third process could have been mis-aging and mis-sexing errors due to the limitations of the osteological techniques. While this is a problem that could be present in the work of even the most experienced osteologist, it is difficult to believe that this bias could have produced the different aspects of the observed pattern (i.e., skewness in terms of both age and sex). For example, while mistakes could be made in the aging of adults, chances of this occurring with infants are considerably lower. This last problem is compounded even more in the case of skeletal remains that are poorly preserved.

The fourth possibility is that this pattern is a true reflection of the ancient living population of Punta Candelero. To evaluate this, it is necessary to understand the cultural context of the skeletal sample. As mentioned before, the Cuevas occupation of Punta Candelero represents a new occupation of the site and not an in situ development where this culture evolved from a previous one in the same location. That means that the original Cuevas occupation of the site was an immigrant, colonizing population. As discussed in Chapter 3, cross-culturally, migrant populations are normally characterized by higher proportions of young- and middle-aged adults, most of them males. If true, then the age and sex distribution for the Punta Candelero sample may be reflecting the migrant nature of the population, instead of the demographic dynamics of the population, especially if this population was unable to reproduce successfully.

Using simulation studies, Paine (1997b) has demonstrated that immigration in already established populations does not create the young adult bulge seen in the age-at-death distribution similar to the one found in Candelero and in many archaeological samples throughout the world. He argues instead that in-migration tends to increase the proportion of infant deaths, a decrease in the proportion of senescent deaths, and an overall decrease in the mean age-at-death. This is explained by the fact that most immigrants tend to be in their prime reproductive years, and their addition to the already established population increases fertility or crude birth rates, which at the same time increases the number of infants dying due to the high infant mortality in pre-industrial societies. However, his study is not applicable for the case of Punta Candelero since its population is not only an immigrant group but also a colonizing population. The Cuevas people that settled in Punta Candelero were not being incorporated into an already established population as in the studies conducted by Paine.

Another possible explanation for this young-adult bulge is widespread warfare that may have produced a higher number of dead males at relatively younger ages. However, this option is not supported by the paleopathological evidence that indicates that only one individual (an adult male) or 2.7 percent of all males, show any kind of antemortem trauma (Crespo Torres 2000).

Table 7.2 shows the values D_{30+}/D_{5+}, D_{20+}/D_{5+}, D_{45+}/D_{5-}, and the crude birth rate (in number of births per 1,000 persons in the population) calculated using the regression formula obtained by Buikstra et al. (1986). It is important to remember that the values of the different ratios are inversely or negatively correlated with crude birth rates. Thus, the higher the values, the lower the fertility of a population and vice versa. In general, the fertility estimates tend to suggest that the population of Punta Candelero had relatively low fertility (see comparison to other sites below), which to a certain point is consistent with a recent migrant population where there are more men than women. Further, the graphic distribution of age-at-death of Punta Candelero

Table 7.2. Fertility Values for the Skeletal Samples from All Sites. (High values are shown in bold and low values in italics.)

Site	D30+/D5+	Crude Birth Rates	D20+/D5+	D45+/D5−
Punta Candelero	**.633**	**54.379**	.924	3.833
Tibes Propor. Adj.	*.423*	*78.498*	**.946**	.763
Tibes Equally Adj.	.540	65.071	**.946**	**5.093**
Paso del Indio	.489	70.961	*.693*	*.195*

does not match any of the extreme patterns used by Milner et al. (1989) to evaluate fertility and mortality visually. However, this was expected since none of the examples used by these researchers included recently colonizing or migrant groups.

In conclusion, considering that Punta Candelero was already abandoned before the next period, possibly in less than 200 years, the low values for fertility are not surprising. Demographically speaking, this settlement seems to represent a failed attempt to populate this location.

Tibes

Tibes is located in the south-central coast of Puerto Rico, just north of the urban area of Ponce, and 10 km from the coast. The site is situated in a terrace of the Portugués River, at the beginning of the foothills of the Central Mountain Range of the island, a location that is intermediate between the coastal plains and fast-rising mountains. The soils are mostly river silt with moderate content of clay.

A resident of the area discovered the site, and it was eventually investigated by a local advocacy archaeological group named Sociedad Guaynía (Alvarado Zayas 1980; Curet and Rodríguez Gracia 1999; González Colón 1984). The Sociedad surveyed the site and began excavations in the second half of the 1970s. The site seems to have been occupied mostly between Saladoid and Elenan Ostionoid times. Evidence for occupation is extremely scant for later periods and seems that it was practically abandoned by Chican Ostionoid times (Alvarado Zayas 1981; Curet et al. 2003; Curet and Rodríguez Gracia 1999; González Colón 1984). During the first occupation, the site appears to have been an average Saladoid village with middens, and possibly houses, forming a semicircle around a central artifact-devoided clearing. Researchers of the Sociedad Guaynía discovered two concentrations of burials belonging to this period. The first and largest one was found under the middle part of the central clearing, while the second was in the western part of the clearing close to the river. Later on, some time during the Elenan Ostionoid subseries, a major rearrangement of the use of space took place in the site, and ball courts and plazas were built. Interestingly, the main plaza located in the central portion of the arrangement of monumental structures was built over the first cluster of Saladoid burials, possibly indicating continuity in the ritual use of space (Curet 1992a; Curet and Oliver 1998). A large ball court was built over the second cluster of burials.

After analyzing the skeletal collections deposited in the museum at the site, Crespo Torres (1998) was able to find 126 skeletons among the collections from the original excavations. Crespo Torres (1998) also reported that a great number of the remains were in a poor state of preservation, a factor that affected the aging, sexing, and determining the presence of pathologies. Although contextual data for these collections are not available at the moment, Pedro Alvarado (personal communication, 2003) pointed out which of them belong to the central Saladoid cluster. Therefore, this study includes 95 burials found under the main plaza of the site, many of which apparently were accompanied by Cuevas style (A.D. 100–600) vessels (González Colón 1984). However, it is difficult to determine if all burials belong to this period since not all of them had offerings, and C-14 dates for the skeletons are not available. Thus, a more precise chronological assignment is not possible with the information available, and the possibility exists that some of the burials belong to Hacienda Grande times.

The sample from the site of Tibes was composed of 14 adult males, 23 adult females, 8 subadults, and 50 indeterminates, for a total 95 individuals. Contrary to the previous case study, the sample from Tibes tends to be heavily skewed in favor of adult females. However, the sample size of aged and sexed individuals is too small to determine if this is a real pattern or the result of sampling problems. Only about 43 percent (n = 37) of all adults (n = 87) were in conditions good enough to be sexed, and no evidence is available to suggest any cultural practice (e.g., warfare) that could explain the deficiency of adult males. A similar problem is present in the distribution of age-at-death since less than half of the individuals (n = 46) were preserved enough to be aged properly.

In order to enhance the sample size of the distribution of age-at-death the indeterminate adults were assigned to age categories using two different adjustments that are commonly applied in paleodemography (Jackes 1992; Milner et al. 2000). The first one consists of adding the indeterminate adults to

Table 7.3. Abridged Life-Table for the Tibes Population Adjusting Age-at-Death Distribution by Distributing Indeterminate Adults Proportionally among All Adult Age Categories (Both Sexes).

x	D_x	d_x	l_x	q_x	L_x	T_x	E_x
0–4	3.000	3.158	100.000	.032	492.105	2845.152	28.452
5–9	2.000	2.105	96.842	.022	478.947	2353.047	24.298
10–14	1.000	1.053	94.737	.011	471.053	1874.100	19.782
15–19	2.000	2.105	93.684	.022	463.158	1403.047	14.976
20–24	32.053	33.740	91.579	.368	373.546	939.889	10.263
25–29	16.026	16.870	57.839	.292	247.022	566.343	9.792
30–34	9.158	9.640	40.970	.235	180.748	319.321	7.794
35–39	20.605	21.690	31.330	.692	102.424	138.573	4.423
40–44	6.868	7.230	9.640	.750	30.125	36.150	3.750
45–49	2.289	2.410	2.410	1.000	6.025	6.025	2.500
50–54	.000	.000	.000	.000	.000	.000	.000
55–59	.000	.000	.000		.000	.000	
60+	.000	.000	.000		.000	.000	
Total	95.000	100.000	–	–	2845.152	–	–

each adult-age category proportionally to the frequency of aged individuals in that category compared to the total number of aged adults. The second adjustment consisted of distributing the indeterminate adults equally over all adult-age categories with the exception of ages older than 55 years. The decision of omitting the age categories older than 55 years was made because none of the three ancient populations included in this study show any individual in that age range. Although this may be a by-product of the under-aging of older adults and the poor preservation of the material, this decision was made to maintain some consistency of the sources of errors in the comparison between the three samples. As a result of these adjustments, two different age-at-death distributions and life-tables were generated (see Tables 7.3 and 7.4 and Figures 7.3 and 7.4).

As can be observed from the tables and the figures, as in the case of Punta Candelero, the age-at-death distribution of the Tibes population shows a larger proportion of adults than infants and children. Interestingly, of the 37 individuals that were sexed and aged more females (n = 14) are represented between ages 20 and 40 than males (n = 9). The opposite is true for older ages with only 1 woman older than 40 years versus 3 men. This is not surprising since in preindustrialized societies, more women tend to die younger than

Table 7.4. Abridged Life-Table for the Tibes Population Adjusting Age-at-Death Distribution by Distributing Indeterminate Adults Equally among All Adult Age Categories under 50 Years Old (Both Sexes).

x	D_x	d_x	l_x	q_x	L_x	T_x	E_x
0–4	3.000	3.158	100.000	.032	492.105	3089.105	30.891
5–9	2.000	2.105	96.842	.022	478.947	2597.000	26.817
10–14	1.000	1.053	94.737	.011	471.053	2118.053	22.357
15–19	2.000	2.105	93.684	.022	463.158	1647.000	17.580
20–24	21.140	23.337	91.579	.255	399.553	1183.842	12.927
25–29	14.140	15.968	68.242	.234	301.289	784.289	11.493
30–34	11.140	12.811	52.274	.245	229.342	483.000	9.240
35–39	16.140	18.074	39.463	.458	152.132	253.658	6.428
40–44	10.140	11.758	21.389	.550	77.553	101.526	4.747
45–49	8.140	9.653	9.632	1.002	24.026	23.974	2.489
50–54	7.140	.000	−.021	.000	−0.053	−0.053	2.500
55–59	.000	.000	.000		.000	.000	
60+	.000	.000	.000		.000	.000	
Total	95.020	100.021	–	–	3089.105	–	–

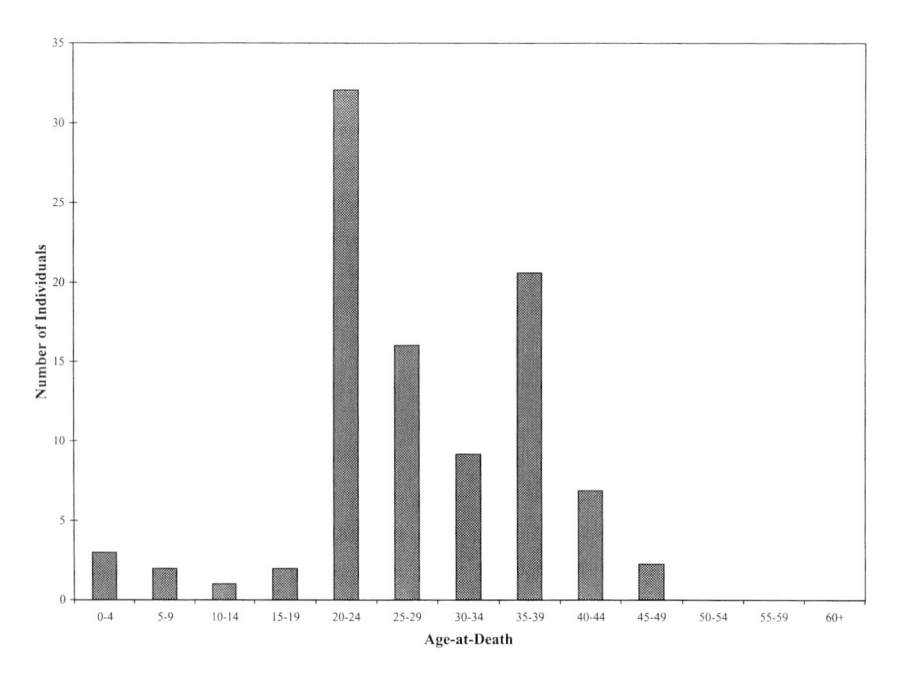

Figure 7.3. Distribution of age-at-death for the site of Tibes, adjusted proportionally.

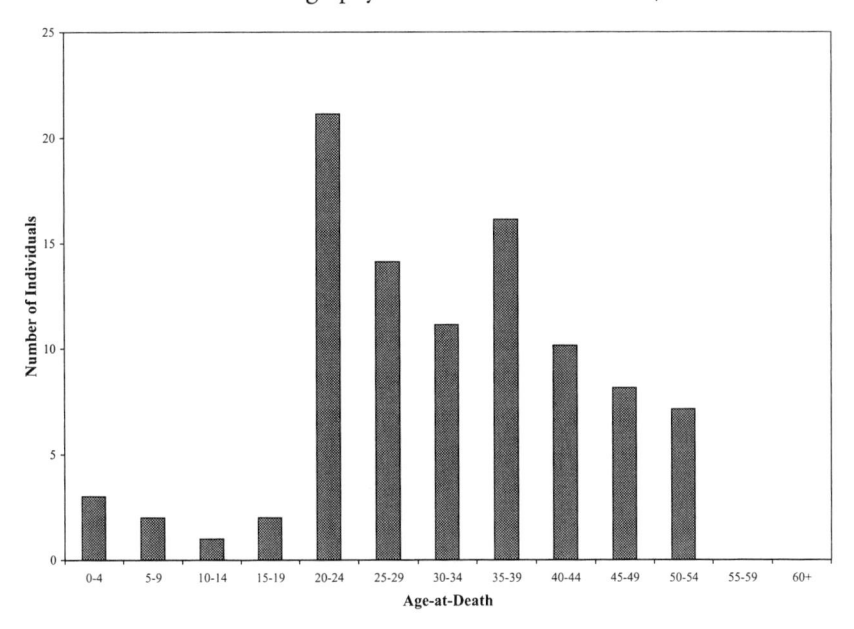

Figure 7.4. Distribution of age-at-death for the site of Tibes, adjusted equally.

men as a result of the nutritional demands of the fertile years and the health risks related to childbearing. Nonetheless, it is important to mention again that the number of sexed individuals is too small to make any definite conclusive remarks. Both the sex and age-at-death distribution in this sample are suspicious. Although they could have been produced by real cultural behavior, the poor preservation of most of the skeletal remains as described by Crespo Torres (1998) strongly suggests that infants, children, and possibly elderly individuals are underrepresented in the sample. This is exactly what is observed as an unusually small number of individuals younger than 20 years old, and no skeletal remain of individuals older than 50 years are present among the aged individuals. The distribution of the adjusted sample using the second method has seven individuals in the 50- to 54-year category due to the procedure used to distribute the indeterminate adults, not because they were empirically assigned to that age range. The poor preservation of subadults and elderly individuals may be related to the natural formation processes active in the site. The site is located in a terrace of the Portugués River that tends to get flooded frequently. The constant process of alternating wet and dry conditions is not the best circumstance for the preservation of skeletal remains, especially ones with lesser density such as those from infants and elderly people. This lack of preservation of the most fragile bones may explain also the lower number of males present in the sample, since in preindustrialized societies more men tend to be represented among the elderly. However, the possibility still exists that this pattern could have been produced by cultural practices such as disposing of the remains of subadult individuals in different locations from the adults.

The fertility indexes for both of the Tibes samples are presented in Table 7.2. As can be observed, all but one of the indexes suggest that the samples have low fertility rates. Even the values of the D_{45+}/D_{5-} ratio for both samples, ranging from .763 to 5.093, tend to be very high indicating low fertility. The only exception is the D_{30+}/D_{5+} ratio, which has a moderate value indicating a moderate fertility rate. I tend to favor the low fertility rate values obtained for the $D_{20+}/5+$ ratio over the other moderate ones because this estimate considers children 5 years or older to avoid the underrepresentation of infants, at the same time as taking into consideration all mature individuals in order to compensate for errors related to under-aging of adults. Both of these problems (underestimation of infants and under-aging of older adults) seem to be present in the Tibes sample, making this estimate the most appropriate one. Unsurprisingly, a visual comparison of the age-at-death distribution graphs did not match any of the cases suggested by Milner et al. (1989). Therefore, tentatively, the skeletal sample from the Saladoid occupation at Tibes is characterized here as representing a population with low fertility rates. However, we cannot ignore the possibility of strong biases being present in the sample and the poor preservation of the skeletal materials, and this conclusion should be taken simply as a suggestion for further studies (see below).

Summarizing, the sample obtained from the site of Tibes seems to represent a population with low fertility rates. This is a pattern similar to the one observed for the Punta Candelero population. However, these results are plagued with inconsistencies that strongly suggest that the sample is biased in more than one way, including underrepresentation of young and old individuals and the presence of more female than male adults. Thus, this sample (1) may not be a proportional reflection of the original ancient population and (2) seems to be far from representing a stable or stationary population.

Paso del Indio

The site of Paso del Indio is located in the north-central coast of Puerto Rico on the floodplain of the Cibuco River in the boundary between the north coastal plain and the karst zone of the island, at approximately 6.6 km from

Table 7.5. Abridged Life-Table for the Paso del Indio Population (Both Sexes).

x	D_x	d_x	l_x	q_x	L_x	T_x	E_x
0–4	41	31.783	100.000	.318	420.543	1970.930	19.709
5–9	20	15.504	68.217	.227	302.326	1550.388	22.727
10–14	5	3.876	52.713	.074	253.876	1248.062	23.676
15–19	2	1.550	48.837	.032	240.310	994.186	20.357
20–24	7	5.426	47.287	.115	222.868	753.876	15.943
25–29	11	8.527	41.860	.204	187.985	531.008	12.685
30–34	9	6.977	33.333	.209	149.225	343.023	10.291
35–39	13	10.077	26.357	.382	106.589	193.798	7.353
40–44	13	10.077	16.279	.619	56.202	87.209	5.357
45–49	4	3.101	6.202	.500	23.256	31.008	5.000
50–54	4	3.101	3.101	1.000	7.752	7.752	2.500
55–59	0	0	0		0	0	
60+	0	0	0		0	0	
Total	129	100	–	–	1970.93	–	–

the shore. The soil matrix is composed of river silt and clay with good drainage and moderate permeability.

The site was excavated in the first half of the 1990s by a cultural resource management project. Although the final reports are not finished, the site seems to have been occupied from Archaic to Chican Ostionoid (A.D. 1200–1500) times. The Archaic and Saladoid occupations, however, seem to have been relatively small compared to those belonging to the Ostionan and Chican Ostionoid subseries. Although Crespo Torres reports the discovery of 149 individuals, only 129 were reported in his death-at-age distribution table (Crespo Torres 2000:Cuadro 33), and these are the individuals included in this analysis. Because of the lack of published chronological information available for the burials, it is difficult to assign them to a particular period or cultural tradition. However, it is clear that the great majority of them belong to the Ostionan Ostionoid subseries or (A.D. 600–1200), particularly to the second half or the Modified Ostiones style (i.e., A.D. 900–1200) (Crespo Torres 2000). Thus, considering the data at hand, and for the sake of framing this population chronologically, this collection is going to be considered as representative of the Ostionan Ostionoid subseries.

The skeletal sample from the site of Paso del Indio shows the most balanced distribution between the sexes. Of 129 individuals, 29 represent adult males, 29 adult females, 67 subadults, and 4 indeterminates. Table 7.5 and

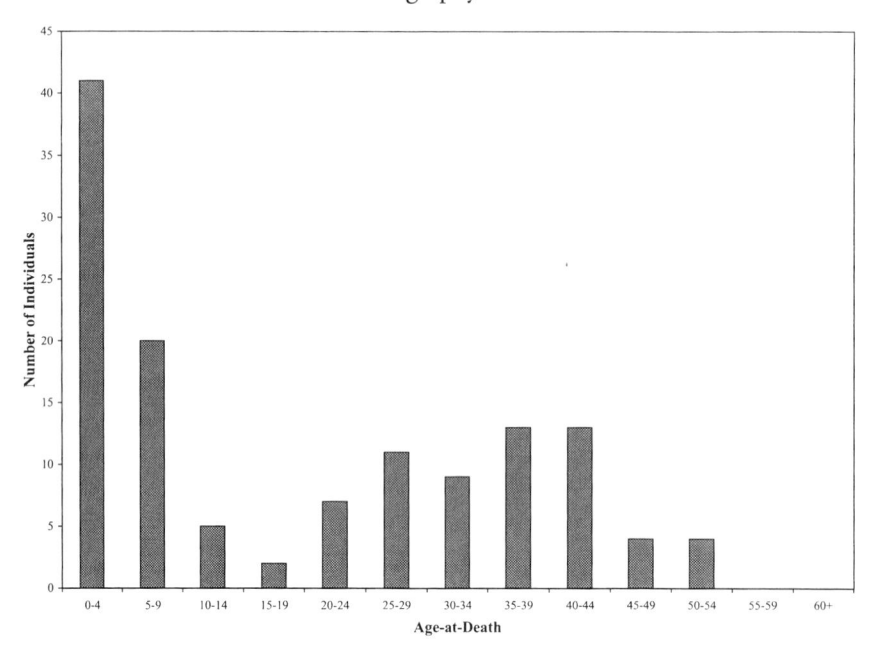

Figure 7.5. Distribution of age-at-death for the site of Paso del Indio

Figure 7.5 also show a relatively balanced distribution of age-at-death for preindustrial populations, with a relatively high number of infants younger than 5 years. One major difference, however, is that a rise in the number of individuals in senescent ages normally present in preindustrialized societies is missing from this sample. The low representation of old-aged individuals may represent some form of bias in the sample or a true reflection of the age distribution of the ancient living population. If some source of bias is present, the main suspect, on the one hand, is the under-aging of old adults due to the methodological difficulties involved in the analytical process (Jackes 1992; Lovejoy et al. 1997; Milner et al. 2000; Wood et al. 1992). On the other hand, high mortality among middle-aged adults due to malnutrition, diseases, or even warfare can also produce a similar pattern, as it has been observed in other archaeological populations (e.g., Lovejoy et al. 1977; see below). Another cultural behavior that may have produced this pattern is the emigration of a significant number of people. As mentioned above, migrant populations tend to be dominated by young and middle-aged adult males. When these individuals, who normally are healthy, are removed from the living population, they would not be added eventually to the skeletal population once they die at an older age. Thus, younger age individuals will be present in the sample and their proportion in the age distribution will decrease at the same time that the proportion of other categories increases. This trend partially explains some of the observed patterns but not all of them. For example, the sex distribution does not support the idea of people emigrating out of the population, since men are more likely to migrate than women, having the effect of reducing the number of men in the whole population, a discrepancy that is not observed in the sex distribution. Despite these issues and the possibility that older adults were under-aged, the sex and young age distributions in Paso del Indio suggest that this sample may represent a more stable population, and/or that it does not contain as many biases than the preceding two.

Fertility rate values for the Paso del Indio population are presented in Table 7.2. All of these values but one show moderate fertility rates for the Paso del Indio population. The only exception is the D_{45+}/D_{5+}, which shows an extremely low value. This is not surprising since this ratio is highly dependent on the number of older adults, an age category that seems to be underrepresented in this skeletal sample. In conclusion, and considering all the indexes for fertility rates, it is suggested that the ancient living population from Paso del Indio had moderate fertility rates.

The age-at-death distribution from Paso del Indio was also visually compared to the four extreme cases suggested by Milner et al. (1989): (1) low fertility and low mortality; (2) high fertility and low mortality; (3) low fertility, high mortality; and (4) high fertility, high mortality. As can be seen from comparing Figure 7.5 to Milner et al.'s (1989) graph for extreme cases of fertility and/or mortality, the distribution observed in the sample from Paso del Indio does not match perfectly any of the patterns. The main difference is that the bimodal pattern of concentration of deaths early and late in life found in Milner et al.'s examples is not found in the age distribution at Paso del Indio. While the high death concentration is present for ages 0–15, most adult deaths are distributed between ages 25 and 45, and decreases in ages above 45. This distribution pattern is not unique since it has been observed in other archaeological samples from the New World (e.g., Storey and Hirth 1997). Based on this observation, Storey and Hirth (1997:140) have suggested that these are real patterns from the living populations, and that they probably represent age-at-death distributions in ancient times not present among modern ethnographic cases or in ideal model tables generated from these cases.

In conclusion, the Paso del Indio skeletal sample seems to indicate that the ancient population had moderate fertility rates. These fertility rates are reflected in the relatively high proportion of infants and children. Based on the age-at-death distribution, this population seems to be the closest one to ideal models.

SUMMARY AND COMPARATIVE ANALYSIS OF THE THREE SAMPLES

The three samples included in this study have produced results that seem to be considerably far from most ideal model tables used by paleodemographers. This is not uncommon in archaeology, since there are many examples where skeletal populations deviate markedly from modern populations (e.g., Lovejoy et al. 1977; Paine 1997b; Storey and Hirth 1997). In many instances, it is difficult to determine if these patterns are true reflections of the ancient living populations or if they were the result of taphonomical or methodological biases imposed on the sample. The effects of some of these biases can be detected by carefully investigating every population individually, paying close attention to contradictions in the results, and the conditions of the recovery and analysis of the skeletal remains. It is because of the acknowledgment of the presence of and weeding out of these biases and problems that paleodemographic studies can provide strong results and information to build working hypotheses for future studies and detect demographic trends in the structure of archaeological populations that can help us understand past cultural and social processes.

This section consists of a brief comparison of the three samples included in this study. The intention is to show how through the study of paleodemographic variables or indices, combined with other biological and archaeological evidence, information can be obtained not only about the structure of the population but also about the nature and integrity of the sample. This is true for even biased samples, populations that deviate considerably from patterns in modern samples, or samples that do not comply with the assumption of stable and stationary population.

Sex Distribution

The three samples differ in their sex distribution. The population from Punta Candelero tended to have a higher number of adult males, while the one from Tibes was the opposite. The Paso del Indio sample was the only one that had a "normal" distribution, with all sexed adults equally divided between both sexes. These differences seem to have been produced by multiple processes and no single explanation can account for all of the differences. In Punta Candelero, the abundance of adult males seems to have been related to the migrant nature of the population. It is suggested here that in this case the sex distribution is a true reflection of the ancient living population, the colonizers of a previously abandoned location.

The distribution in Tibes is more difficult to explain. Since to date, however, there is no strong evidence that cultural behaviors could have been important factors in creating this distribution, the presence of some form of bias in the sample, such as those induced by natural formation processes (frequent floods) were responsible for the destruction and/or poor preservation of the skeletal remains as reported by Crespo Torres (1998). Also, these biases are responsible for the general poor conditions of the skeletal remains, which allowed only 37 out of 87 adults to be sexed, a small sample to reach any conclusion about the larger population. The sex distribution in the collections from Paso del Indio suggests that, at least in terms of this variable, the sample seems to be representative of the ancient living population, and, perhaps, of a stable population. It also indicates that no selectivity or bias in favor of one of the sexes over the other is present.

Age-at-Death Distribution

Interestingly, none of the age-at-death distributions for the three samples actually matches any of the ideal models. Age-at-death distributions in ideal models for preindustrialized populations are characterized by a large number of individuals between ages 0 and 5 years, then dropping rapidly after that. A second rise is, then, observed at older ages of 50+ years. The distribution from the sample of Paso del Indio is the only one that gets close to this ideal pattern by showing a sharp peak of individuals in early ages between 0 and 10 years old, but without the final rise at old age. The highest deaths among adults concentrate in ages between 20 and 45 years, possibly indicating a higher mortality around these age categories than for later ages. Because of the good preservation of infants, the probability of this pattern being the product of the disintegration of the bones of the elderly is very low. A possibility that cannot be discarded, though, is the under-aging of senescent individuals related to the methodological problems with the indexes used for aging older individuals.

The other two samples also show deviations from modern models by having lower numbers of deaths between ages 0 and 5 and 50+ years. These collections present substantially higher numbers of individuals around the young and middle-aged adults (i.e., between 20 and 45 years) than among infants or children. In the case of Punta Candelero, this distribution may be related to the nature of the ancient population, which may have been composed of migrant colonizers. As mentioned before, cross-culturally migrant populations tend to be dominated by young and middle-aged adult males with fewer numbers of subadults and adult females. In fact, it is interesting to notice the significance of the lower number of individuals between ages 10 and 20 years old. It can be speculated that people in these age categories tend to have parents older than the parents of younger children. Since the probability of migrating during adulthood decreases with age (see Chapter 3), then there should be fewer individuals in these categories because their parents had lower probability of migrating. Put in another way, there are more young children than older ones because there are better chances of their parents being in the prime age to migrate.

The interpretation of the sample from Punta Candelero originating from a migrant population is supported also by the settlement archaeology. This site has been assigned to the Cuevas style, which in Puerto Rico is dated from A.D. 400 to A.D. 600. Assuming that these dates are also applicable to this site, that means the site was occupied for 200 years or less. If, in addition, it is considered that no significant evidence for later occupations was found at the site, it can be said that Punta Candelero was a failed effort of a Cuevas group to colonize this location (see Moore 2001).

In general, the age-at-death distribution for the Tibes population is very similar to the one observed for Punta Candelero. The only discrepancy is the considerable lower number of individuals in ages between 0 and 10 and between 40 and 55 years. Again, the undernumeration of these ages is expectable if the conditions for preservation were poor. The underrepresentation of these ages supports the conclusion reached about sex distribution that this collection is biased in favor of older children and young to middle-aged adults. Nevertheless, even if the numbers of individuals in ages between 0 to 10 and 50+ are tripled, the high concentration of young and middle-aged adults is still considered elevated compared to other populations. Thus, the possibility exists that notwithstanding the poor preservation of skeletal remains from these ages, the distribution of age-at-death of the population from Tibes does not conform to the ideal models based on preindustrialized modern populations. If true, then the similarity of this distribution to the one obtained for Punta Candelero may be more real than biased, a conclusion that may mean that this sample may also represent a colonizing population. Considering that many of the burials seem to belong to the Cuevas style, and that the site shows evidence of being inhabited since the early Saladoid, this suggestion seems to be improbable, however. Furthermore, contrary to Punta Candelero, the founding of Tibes seems to have been a successful endeavor. The site was inhabited for approximately 800–1,000 years, lasting until the Santa Elena style, when the site became a civic-ceremonial center and was eventually abandoned around A.D. 1200. Still, at the present, the skeletal sample from Tibes seems to be too biased to differentiate which systemic processes were present in the living population.

Fertility Rates

Fertility rate is an important factor in all populations. In fact, populations tend to be more susceptible to changes in fertility rates than mortality rates. It is for this reason that fertility rates are considered critical determinants of population growth rates. As mentioned earlier in this chapter, several "indexes" to estimate fertility rates of archaeological populations have been suggested, and in this study we used three of them. Each index or ratio has its advantages and disadvantages (Paine and Harpending [1996] have compared the efficiency of several of them). The D_{30+}/D_{5+} (Buikstra et al. 1986) eliminates the effects of undernumeration of infants younger than 5 years old and it reduces the impact of mis-aging individuals in senescent ages. The D_{20+}/D_{5+} (Konigsberg et al. 1989; see also Jackes 1992) has been suggested for cases where aging of the adult population is problematic. The third ratio, D_{45+}/D_{5-} (Milner et al. 1989), is highly susceptible to underrepresentation of infants and under-aging of senescent individuals. All ratios correlate negatively with fertility rates.

Table 7.2 presents the estimates of the three indexes and the estimate of the crude birth rates (based on the D_{30+}/D_{5+} ratio) for all the samples used in the study. While included in this chart, I have decided not to discuss the D_{45+}/D_{5-} ratio because it tended to behave somewhat erratic. In general, the results obtained from this analysis indicate that, with the exception of the D_{45+}/D_{5-}, the Punta Candelero population tended to have low fertility rates, while the ones from Tibes and Paso del Indio produced intermediate values. The results from Punta Candelero are in agreement with the suggestion that it represents a migrant, colonizing community that could not flourish. In fact, low fertility would explain partially why this population failed in settling this area since it shows that they were not able to reproduce biologically or socially.

The values obtained for the sample from Tibes show that, in general, this population had moderate fertility rates. However, sample biases have to be considered here. As already mentioned above, for multiple reasons, the sample from Tibes tends to underestimate the number of infants and under-age adults over the age of 45. This being the case, theoretically speaking, the ratio $D20+/D5+$ is the most accurate, since it reduces the effects of both biases by ignoring infants under the age of 5 and lumping all adults in one category independently of their specific ages. When this is taken into consideration, the two adjusted samples from Tibes produce high values for the ratio $D20+/D5+$ suggesting low fertility rates for this population. Yet, this result is not in agreement with the archaeological data that indicate that the site was continuously occupied for a long period of time, suggesting a higher fertility rate. Several possibilities can explain this discrepancy. The first one is that the bias in this sample is so strong that it cannot be avoided even by using the $D20+/D5+$ ratio. A second possibility is that these estimates are accurate and that the population continued existing because of relatively smaller mortality rates. However, mortality rates are difficult to measure in the archaeological record and this cannot be tested. A third possibility is that this sample does not represent a stable stationary population, but, instead, a population whose structure is rapidly changing (either positively or negatively). A last possibility is that the site was not actually occupied continuously as the archaeological data suggest. It is possible that the site was occupied and abandoned intermittently, but it is difficult to detect archaeologically due to the low precision of our chronometric techniques. Independently of the reasons, the evidence at hand for the population from Tibes lacks some consistency, and it should not be taken at face value without complementary, independent evidence.

The Paso del Indio population produced relatively low values for the ratios, in some cases the lowest numbers. This suggests that this population had the highest fertility rates of all the samples. Taking into consideration that the population from Paso del Indio showed a balance distribution of sexes and an age-at-death distribution closer to ideal models, this sample may represent the most stable population of the three case studies. If true, the estimates of fertility rates may be more applicable in this case than in the other examples. Therefore, it can be concluded that the Paso del Indio population had a relatively moderate fertility rate, higher than the estimates for Punta Candelero and Tibes.

In conclusion, the low fertility rate values for Punta Candelero are in accordance with the interpretation that this sample represents a migrant population that most probably never reached stability or stationarity. The estimates for Tibes are somewhat contradictory and require more information. The fertility rates for Paso del Indio are higher than the first two samples, suggesting that this was a thriving community at least in terms of fertility rates.

CONCLUSIONS

The aim of the paleodemographic analysis presented here is not to come up with definite answers to questions dealing with demographic aspects about the indigenous groups from Puerto Rico. On the contrary, it is to provide archaeologists and biological anthropologists with more questions (i.e., hypotheses) to be answered in their research. But also, another goal is to show the importance and implications of considering populations' sex and age structures, and fertility rates for the process of studying past human societies. In this final conclusive section, both of these issues are discussed.

First of all, the analysis reported in this chapter has shown the importance of evaluating each population individually, even in the cases where two or more of them seem to be affected by the same biases or produced by similar processes. This is the case of the samples from Punta Candelero and Tibes that show similar distributions of age-at-death, and both present some skewness in their sex distribution. However, after considering the condition of the skeletal remains and the archaeological evidence, it seems that the similarities may be more coincidental than once thought. In fact, the distribution in one case seems to be a true pattern present in the original living population, while the other is the product of poor preservation. This is not to say that they are free of other biases (e.g., under-aging of senescent individuals), but that there are some pieces of data that can be salvaged from seemingly hopeless cases.

Another point is the contributions that paleodemographic evidence can make to basic archaeological research. Most archaeological studies in the Caribbean (Baetsen 1999; Budinoff 1991; Crespo Torres 1994, 1998, 2000; Hoogland 1996; La Rosa Corzo and Robaina 1994, 1995; Rivero de la Calle 1990; Siegel 1992; Versteeg et al. 1997; Versteeg et al. 1990; Versteeg and Schinkel 1992), and the rest of the world, tend to assume, consciously or unconsciously, that the settlement under investigation was inhabited by a stable population, with normal sex and age distribution, and with fertility and mortality rates at levels that would allow a positive growth rate. Some of the results presented above put this assumption into question. First, the fact that none of the distributions from the samples studied here matched any of the ideal (stable) model tables published by Coale and Demeny (1983) strongly suggests that none of them represent stable populations (at least as we know them today). The implications of this evidence have to be taken into consideration when evaluating the rest of the archaeological data.

For example, the conclusion about the migrant nature of the population from Punta Candelero is a good example of the consequences that paleodemographic evidence can have for the archaeology of Puerto Rico, the Caribbean, and worldwide. It is a common practice among archaeologists to choose "pure," or single-component, sites to characterize archaeological cultures by identifying the "normal" traits in this settlement and applying them to multicomponent sites and even whole regions. However, more often than not, these sites may represent colonizing populations that went through great demographic, genetic, and nutritional stress, factors that can and do affect peoples' behavior in many ways. More important is the fact that many of them may have failed in reproducing biologically and socially, as is being suggested for Punta Candelero. Thus, the rubric of these sites being "pure" and representative of a particular culture or period may be a mistaken premise that affects further studies, research, and conclusions. A similar problem is present in paleopathological studies that do not take into consideration the nature of the population, and use the frequency of diseases, traumas, and nutritional factors at one site as representative of other populations with similar cultural backgrounds.

Paleodemographic studies can also contribute to the history of human population dynamics by identifying possible demographic trends that have not been identified among modern groups. The pattern observed in the skeletal sample from Paso del Indio is one of many archaeological human collections from other parts of the world that do not follow the distributions of ideal model tables. Many of these populations show the high infant mortality rates, but not the one at older ages (50+ years). Instead, adult mortality tends to be distributed variably between young and middle age categories. Although sometimes these patterns are discarded as the product of biases in osteological samples or analyses, several researchers have posed the possibility of them representing true distributions of ancient populations (e.g., Lovejoy et al. 1977; Storey and Hirth 1997). By identifying and interpreting the demographic distributions from particular populations and comparing them to other samples, paleodemography can contribute by determining the range of demographic patterns possible in human populations and what social, biological, and cultural behavior could have produced them.

Finally, by considering the paleodemographic data, archaeologists can be in a better position to interpret the basic osteological data, as is traditionally done. Paleodemographic evidence can provide hints of the integrity of the sample and possible biases that can affect the conclusions obtained, for example, by paleopathological studies. The skeletal remains from Tibes are a case in point. Based on Crespo Torres's analysis (1998) one could easily determine that the Tibes population enjoyed good health and nutrition since little evidence was found of pathological or nutritional disorder. However, when the age and sex distributions are combined with information on the preservation of the sample and other archaeological data, the integrity of the evidence and the conclusions are put into question. Furthermore, it is possible that the poor preservation of the skeletal remains may have obscured the presence of these disorders (Edwin Crespo Torres, personal communication).

Many paleodemographers may consider the analyses conducted in this chapter as basic and simple compared to more elaborate techniques developed in recent years. The discussion does not include other complex issues related more directly to economic and social conditions, such as dependency ratio. Despite this simplicity, these analyses show the advantage and necessity of incorporating paleodemographic analysis into standard archaeological research. Without it, even the most basic analysis of archaeological and osteological evidence can be plagued with biases and unfounded assumptions that could invalidate our conclusions. This type of analysis can help archaeologists to learn more about the nature and integrity of the population they are studying, critical information that can affect the interpretation of the rest of the archaeological data. In Caribbean archaeology, more often than not, osteological analyses are relegated to an appendix in project reports without giving any thought to (1) the wealth of information that they can provide beyond the simple sex, age, and pathological evidence, and (2) the potential of paleodemographic studies to contribute to the array of multidisciplinary strategies that archaeologists use in their research.

8 / Conclusions

Paleodemography and Caribbean Archaeology

Archaeology is the only social science that studies past and present human societies through their material culture. Using patterns and variability in the archaeological record, archaeologists reconstruct culture history and lifeways and attempt to trace, understand, and explain the processes and meanings of social and cultural behavior. In order to make the difficult connection between material culture and the intangibles of society, archaeology has emphasized the study of objects and their distribution by developing or borrowing from other disciplines a plethora of models, methods, and techniques. However, because of the very nature of the discipline, archaeology has a tendency to emphasize objects, social organizations, and cultural traditions, and not to consider the actual people who created the objects, lived in the society, and practiced the traditions. This is not saying that we have been excluding the human group that created the archaeological record, but that we have been ignoring the very essence of those groups, the people who lived, ate, cohabited, interrelated, and reproduced within those groups. Most of our work tends to visualize these faceless people as an amalgamated group and assume that it represents an ideal population. By doing this, we overlook some of the basic and fundamental types of human behavior and interaction and their impact on the history of those groups. Behavior at lower levels of society, such as mating patterns, household decision-making, intragroup relationships, and the exploitation of natural resources by individuals, households, or communities, has an effect on the global behavior of the group that, when compounded, can influence large-scale processes at higher levels.

One way of addressing these types of fundamental behavior is by considering demographic issues in our research. Demographic processes and their social correlates and consequences can provide a window to past human populations not provided by many other approaches. Although this does not mean that we are able to get to the individual, household, or even the kinship group, in many instances the behaviors at these lower or even higher levels of society are reflected in the demographic characteristics, processes, and trends of the population. More important, demographic traits and dynamics and their effects are not constrained to a single level of society but tend to cut across multiple levels. Decisions made at a lower level can affect higher levels and larger scales, and large-scale processes affect the demography of smaller units. Thus, a good sense of the human and social side of history can be obtained by studying demographic processes at various levels and how they interrelate with each other.

In order to accomplish this, however, there are two things that have to be considered. The first one is to recognize that demographic processes by their own nature are social processes. In other words, population issues are social behavior and not necessarily cultural. Social groups such as the household, the community, the kinship group, or the polity are the main actors in all demographic dynamics. Cultures do not reproduce, migrate, or die in a biological sense; people, individually or in a group, do. The second issue is that in order to study demography and populations of a group in an efficient manner, we have to be constantly aware of the proper unit(s) and scale(s) of analysis for the problem of interest. This does not only mean selecting the immediate unit of analysis in which the process occurred but also including in our analysis other units and scales that may be affected by the process. In fact, in many instances the process under study may have been produced by dynamics that operated at higher or lower levels. For example, migration of households or communities may be caused by a macroregional factor such as a generalized, long-lasting drought or endemic warfare. At the same time, the response of these smaller groups can affect processes at higher levels or on a larger scale, as in the case of the compounded migration of communities resulting in the abandonment of a region, or the removal of the demographic base of a polity at war. Moreover, despite their social nature, population processes and dynamics may be responsible for many of the changes, traits, and structures present in the archaeological record and that traditionally archaeologists have depicted as cultural. Therefore, paleodemographic studies can shed light on both social and cultural processes operating at multiple levels.

When seen from this perspective, demographic studies can help researchers understand and explain the ancient histories of past societies, including groups identified as island societies. Since the early 1970s, island societies have been seen as a special and, to a certain point, a unique case of human society. This led to the development of a new branch of study within the discipline called Island Archaeology, and to the application of new models, many of them borrowed from island ecology, such as island biogeography (Keegan and Diamond 1987; Kirch 1986). The great contribution of this perspective was to switch the emphasis in archaeology from cultures to some basic, geographically defined populations that lived in islands. Moreover, it promoted the use of demographic variables as a way to reach a better understanding of past human behavior. However, because of the cultural ecological emphasis of many of its practitioners, island archaeology tended to use island populations, not social groups, as the main unit of analysis to explain and understand past societies, and, by emphasizing ecological models, tended to treat human populations as if they were animal and plant populations. This approach has been criticized recently on many grounds (e.g., Rainbird 1999; Terrell 1999; see also Curet 2004) but particularly for the assumption that island groups behave differently than continental groups (see several papers cited in Rainbird 1999). One particular point of criticism is that island populations, as opposed to cultures, may still not be the appropriate unit of analysis for examining issues of interest to archaeologists. Further, human populations do not always behave the same way as ecological models predict for animals and plants, since humans are capable of intentional behavior and advance planning, as a result of which they have the option of return migration, migrating to other islands, introducing new plant and animal species, exploiting the resources of some islands without inhabiting those locales, or developing alternative subsistence strategies. Thus, while it is true that island populations have some different experiences from many continental groups, they are still human populations that behave similarly within certain parameters. Island societies are only another example of the wide and immense variety of human populations present even within continental groups.

This book is a contribution to both of these aspects of the study of human populations, the use of paleodemography to study island societies. The case study is the Caribbean archipelago, and, more particularly Puerto Rico. Island societies are not treated here as a unique case of human populations but as another example of human variability. Neither is their behavior treated as a modified form of ecological models developed to explain animal and plant populations in islands, although it is recognized that some aspects of these models are still applicable to some human cases. The book also considers the various demographic issues not merely as cultural or whole island population factors but as social circumstances in which people or groups of people had an active role in the decision-making process.

The Caribbean islands had a very dynamic ancient history that saw many social and cultural developments. Since early times, the Caribbean experienced great population movements that populated the archipelago for the first time and that led eventually to the peopling of almost every inhabitable island. In the process, the indigenous people left the first strong and robust traces of their presence in the archaeological record. Little is known about Archaic peoples, the first inhabitants of the archipelago, because they did not leave much in the way of cultural artifacts, and they have been poorly studied. But we do know that groups moving north from the South American continent on oceanic voyages eventually landed and had contact with these Archaic groups. The great panorama presented in this book begins with their contact. The ages after this contact saw the rise, flourishing, and sometimes disappearance of cultures, and the settlement, population growth, and abandonment of sites and regions. There is ample evidence during this long history for different kinds of social organizations (including stratified societies), monumental architecture, and religious practices, and of different groups adopting a variety of economic strategies in different ways. Throughout this history many and diverse demographic processes were involved that made important contributions to the formation of the Caribbean groups encountered by Europeans.

The various demographic analyses conducted at different levels in this book were framed within this dynamic history. Particularly, this book concentrated on topics that both traditional and island archaeology have considered important in understanding island societies. However, the latter has tended to approach it from the perspective of culture and the former from the view of whole island populations. Here they were emphasized from the perspective of the social units involved, and it is hoped that this approach will contribute to the long tradition of studies of population and island societies. These topics include long-distance migration between islands and between islands and the continent; population trends and short-distance migration; elements of the relationship between population and resources; and population structure and processes, including age and sex distribution, fertility, and mortality. In this final chapter I discuss each one of these analyses, how they relate to the other analyses, and some of the implications for archaeological modeling and interpretations.

MIGRATION

The traditional perspective on migration that is used not only in the Caribbean but also in archaeology in general was founded on the theoretical framework developed in the first half of the 1900s (Willey et al. 1956) and was based on the normative view of culture and a colonial approach to culture contact that was commonly accepted at that time. The normative view is an approach promulgated by culture-historical archaeologists that "regarded cultures as collections of ideas held in common and transmitted over generations by members of particular social groups" (Trigger 1989:297). Accordingly, these ideas or norms are shared and followed by everyone in the culture. Two corollaries of this view are (1) that cultures, or at least their norms, are internally uniform or homogeneous, and therefore (2) the norms of the culture can be obtained from the study of a segment or sample of that group. The normative view and these two corollaries are strongly present in Caribbean archaeology (Rouse 1986, 1992), in this case in the methods used for detecting and studying migrations. A consequence of this approach is the use of culture, or supracultural units, as the basic unit of migration. This premise has limited in a great manner our potential to explain not only migration per se but also the social dynamics involved in such a complicated and multifactorial endeavor.

In the case of the Caribbean, the analyses conducted in Chapters 3 and 4, based on modern anthropological theory and cross-cultural generalizations, resulted in several suggestions that in many respects differ from either Rouse's expectations or the traditional beliefs in the Caribbean about migrations (e.g., Alegría 1955; Chanlatte Baik 1981; Chanlatte Baik and Narganes Storde 1983, 1985; Goodwin 1979, 1980). First, it is suggested that many of the early Saladoid–La Hueca people that migrated from either the continent or Trinidad targeted Puerto Rico and/or the northern Lesser Antilles as their point of destination. Therefore, questions normally made by Caribbeanists, such as why they stopped in Puerto Rico and did not continue to the rest of the Greater Antilles, make little sense when this migration is seen from this perspective. Second, these groups most probably knew where they were going and had some, but not necessarily perfect, knowledge about their destinations. Third, it is likely that the Saladoid–La Hueca groups had some previous contact with the Archaic groups that already inhabited these islands, as suggested by Rouse (1992) and others (e.g., Rodríguez Ramos 2002a). And fourth, at present there is no evidence in Puerto Rico or the Lesser Antilles of a conflictive or bellicose relationship between the Archaic groups and the Saladoid–La Hueca migrants. If anything, the little data available tend to indicate that some kind of relationship was present, as evidenced by the possible presence of raw materials from Hispaniola and western Puerto Rico in some of the earliest Saladoid–La Hueca sites in eastern Puerto Rico and Vieques.

Despite the intensity of Saladoid–La Hueca studies in Puerto Rico and the Caribbean, there are still many issues related to the process of the migration of these groups that need to be studied. For example, it is highly probable that the initial migrant groups maintained some form of contact with their parent community, but the intensity of the contact and whether reverse migration occurred is difficult to discern from the archaeological evidence. However, considering that Saladoid groups seem to have been relatively conservative and shared many cultural traits for a long period of time over an area that ranged from Venezuela to the Greater Antilles, it can be suggested that the interaction was constant and often. Other elements that have to be investigated with more empirical data are the reasons for migrating, the size and composition of the migrant groups, the precise stages of the migration process (e.g., exploration, scouting, special task groups, colonization, etc.), and what type of relationship the Saladoid and La Hueca people had with each other and with the Archaic groups before, during, and after migration. Moreover, we would be interested in trying to identify successful versus failed attempts at colonization. These are elements that are intimately related to the suggestions made before and are needed to complete the narrative of this important aspect of Caribbean archaeology.

Another apparent migration that was discussed in Chapter 4 was the Ostionoid expansion. Here the possibility of migration was evaluated against other possible social processes that could have produced the dispersal of the diagnostic markers for these groups. Specifically, the possibility of diffusion and transculturation through the constant and extensive interaction between groups was considered. After reviewing the evidence, especially the chronological data, I believe that these various factors cannot be discarded to explain the expansion of the Ostionoid ceramic series. If anything, considering the contemporaneity of the appearance of this series in many islands, the information at hand does not support the idea of a major migration as suggested by Rouse and others. If confirmed in the future, then the development of this series seems to have been produced more by the relations among Archaic societies and between Archaic and Saladoid groups. This would imply that the interaction of these groups, which possibly started early on, on the coast of

South America, may have had major consequences for later social, historical, and cultural developments in the indigenous societies of the Greater Antilles, as suggested by Chanlatte Baik and Keegan. However, it is still necessary to determine the nature and dynamics of these interactions and how they varied through time and from one region to another.

REGIONAL POPULATION TRENDS

The normative perspective that has haunted Caribbean archaeology since its beginning has had other consequences for the understanding of human behavior in ancient history. Because of its emphasis on culture and the migration of cultures instead of social groups, the normative approach has tended to concentrate on long-distance population movements and has practically ignored short-distance migrations. Moreover, the basic assumption of the methods of this approach is that cultures (or higher levels of human grouping) are uniform enough that one can go from the specific to the general (deductive reasoning) without any difficulty, an aspect heavily criticized during the heydays of the New Archaeology. The use of this approach becomes problematic when it is applied in a variety of studies without recognizing that in reality it was tailored for the particular and unique goals of reconstructing culture history. Although treating culture as an analytical unit is useful for comparative purposes, the approach tends to hide a great amount of variability. This practice basically assumes that every group of people within these units behaved the same way for the simple reason that they all belonged to the same cultural categories (i.e., style, subseries, series). Obviously, this blanket categorization obscures regional and local variability, especially in respect to local decision-making, where different people, families, households, communities, or regional polities could have followed different strategies. But it is exactly this variability that is necessary in order to understand the social, political, and economic processes that are of interest to many of the traditional studies that keep using cultural categories as their main unit and level of analysis.

This view of the uniformity of social behavior through time and space is questioned by the comparisons discussed in Chapter 5. Here we saw that four different regions experienced different population growth rates, trends, and settlement patterns despite several of them being assigned to the same cultural/chronological category (i.e., style, subseries, and series). If it is considered that population structure and spatial distribution are determined by many historical factors including social and political organization and a population's interaction with the physical environment, then it should not be surprising for different regional groups to show different trends. This finding, however, goes against the premises of the normative view already mentioned, and any generalization produced from this perspective on past human behavior has to be tested, not assumed. The bottom line of this argument is that different local and regional populations belonging to the same cultural group can develop diverse political, social, cultural, and economic strategies that can vary according to a population's needs, immediate environment, and historical processes. Thus, we cannot assume any universal population trend between different regional populations merely because they belong to the same cultural category.

The normative approach is also present in the view that many archaeologists have on island populations, in this case in the Caribbean islands. Local population trends, including short-distance migration, and settlement patterns in many instances are generalized to the rest of the culture and its chronological and spatial extension. For example, the Saladoid settlement pattern is still described uniformly for most of the eastern Caribbean as nucleated villages located in coastal areas near water streams (Rouse 1992), despite the evidence indicating that in some instances early Saladoid settlements seem to be located inland (e.g., Hernández Colón in Puerto Rico [Maíz López 2002], Golden Rock in St. Eustatius [Versteeg and Schinkel 1992], and Hope Estate in St. Martin [Hofman and Hoogland 1999]).

Another example is the general view of what happened to populations once they settled on an island. Following either "common sense" or ecological models for animal and plant populations, many archaeologists assume that once settled, regional populations increase relatively fast, creating new settlements farther from the coast (wave-of-advancement model), and eventually reaching the carrying capacity of the region. This view, common among several prominent early island archaeologists (e.g., see various papers in Kirch [editor, 1986]) , has several limitations. First, it assumes that all colonization attempts were successful and that populations increased immediately after landing. Not all migration and colonization attempts were fully established, many times resulting in a population that was unable to reproduce and eventually died out or returned to the parent group in a reverse migration. The early sites of La Hueca and Punta Candelero, for example, seem to represent examples of failed colonization processes. In the case of the Cuevas component from Punta Candelero, this is a result that is supported by the age and sex distribution of its skeletal sample, which is dominated by middle-aged adult men, as presented in Chapter 7. Second, it is based on the unfounded assumption that human populations have a natural tendency to increase. There are many historical, social, and environmental factors that can affect the population growth of a group, ranging from external factors such as availability of resources and the presence of diseases to cultural practices such as the need for labor, female infanticide, marriage patterns, and personal preferences.

The evidence presented in Chapters 5 and 6 does not support these premises. The study of population estimates based on site number and size suggests that a rapid population growth (or an increase in population density) did not occur in Puerto Rico for several centuries after the colonization by the Saladoid–La Hueca people. This increase is not visible until much later (about 1,200 years later), when major social and cultural changes became apparent in the archaeological record. The case of Vieques appears to be different, where population increase occurred considerably earlier, but still centuries after the earliest dates.

The lesson to be learned from the study on short-distance migrations and changes in settlement patterns is that these processes are normally determined by a number of factors, including biological, social, political, economic, and cultural. Although some generalizations can be made as to how, when, and under what circumstances populations increase, decrease, and move, a great variability exists in the range of possible demographic responses, and these responses can be heavily influenced by the particular history of the local or regional group independently of the rest of the culture.

POPULATION/RESOURCE RELATIONSHIP

The relationship between environmental resources and population needs more attention. There are two main traditional views on the relationship between human populations and their immediate environment in the Caribbean and in archaeology in general. The first one is the traditional perspective, which holds that the indigenous groups lived in a balanced relationship with their surroundings, in an ecological equilibrium. This view is part of the idea that Caribbean societies lived in a tropical paradise where most of their needs were fulfilled with little effort on their part. A corollary of this view is that, due to the richness of the environment and the balanced relationship, there was little need from the indigenous groups to alter the landscape and, therefore they lived in a quasi-pristine ecology. The second view is the complete opposite of the first. It assumes that human populations have a natural tendency to grow unchecked, and the increase in consumers must put a stress on the economic system and the local environment, leading to the overexploitation of resources or population/resource imbalance.

In Caribbean studies, both of these views have been put forth with different levels of rigor to explain various aspects of migration, sociopolitical change, and violent conflict, among others. Independently of which of these views is adopted, however, the population/resource relationship is normally treated in an informal manner, most of the time based on untested assumptions or "common sense" about the capacity of the environment or population size and growth rates. Very few studies have actually measured empirically some of the variables at issue (e.g., Curet 1992a; Keegan 1985, 1992) to evaluate the relationship between these two factors and their impact on social and cultural traits and changes.

As Chapter 6 demonstrates, it is imperative that hypotheses and models in which population and natural resources are used as dependent or independent variables be tested in a rigorous and disciplined way. These tests are critical to understanding the relationship between demographic variables, society, and natural resources. A specific issue that needs to be determined by testing these models is the actual role that each variable has in the phenomenon under study. Is population increase, for example, a causal factor that triggers social and political changes, or is it a result of those changes? Also, are changes to the landscape and in economic strategies the result of detrimental conditions of the environment, or are these conditions produced by changes in the landscape or in economic behavior? How are populations integrated into the local and regional environment? What is the relationship between availability of resources, economic strategies, and populations? And how do these relate to other cultural values, traditions, and behavior? Recently Wood (1998) has proposed a preliminary model for the study of populations in preindustrialized societies, where he takes into consideration the availability of resources, number of people, and well-being of individuals, among other factors, to determine patterns in population trends in these societies. Suggestions like this one can be used as a starting point to develop more realistic models that take into consideration other cultural practices, social and political situations, and the particular historical events.

The results presented in Chapter 6 on comparing population estimates with carrying capacity strongly suggest that the relationship between population density, resources, and social change is extremely intricate. These factors are normally treated as either independent (causal) or dependent variables, but most probably their function was different at different times. For example, the development of a centralized leadership may have promoted an increase in population in order to increase the demographic support necessary to maintain such a political system. However, it is possible for a population to increase to a point that it becomes problematic promoting some changes in the economic, social, or even political organization. Thus, the relationship between demographic, social, economic, and political factors should not be envisioned as a simple action/reaction process, but more as a dialectic process in which even individuals and the decision-making process can have an effect on the final outcome.

POPULATION STRUCTURE AND DEMOGRAPHIC VARIABLES

The structure and the age and sex distribution of populations at the local level have rarely been considered in many Caribbean archaeological studies. Although studies mention the number of burials and in some instances the distribution of the sex and age-at-death, they regularly overlook the meanings and consequences of population structures and other demographic variables. At best, skeletal collections are used to determine prevalence of pathologies and traumas among certain populations, although more recent studies have included their structure for the study of mortuary practices and diets (e.g., Crespo Torres 2000).

Two common assumptions present in most studies in archaeology are that we are dealing with stable and ideally distributed populations and that the skeletal collections are a true reflection of the original living, ancient population. As was discussed in Chapter 7, these are premises that more often than not are untrue and, if unnoticed, could lead to misinterpretations and erroneous conclusions. In this same chapter it was also shown that a careful paleodemographic study and analysis can help in evaluating these premises by determining three things. First, a paleodemographic study can determine the internal structure of the skeletal collection and certain demographic variables such as fertility and dependency ratios. These are important factors that can affect archaeological interpretations. For example, populations that are under some form of demographic stress and struggling to reproduce may not necessarily behave in the same way as populations that are not experiencing the same duress. Interestingly, archaeologists have traditionally sought explanations for low fertility rates or high mortality rates in nutritional and health stress. However, healthy and well-fed populations can experience low fertility or high mortality for other reasons, including simple demographic changes. This may be the case for Punta Candelero, where, as suggested in Chapter 7, the low fertility rate may have resulted from the low representation of female adults in the migrant population. Other cultural and social practices may produce similar results.

Second, a paleodemographic analysis can help evaluate such issues as the stability and stationarity of a population. Examples of this are the analyses of the samples from Punta Candelero, Paso del Indio, and Tibes. By comparing these three populations with ideal models of age-at-death distribution, it was determined that the one from Paso del Indio population appeared to be the most stable. The two other samples did not seem to represent stable, much less stationary, populations, and, so, cannot be treated by most models developed for paleodemographic analysis. Nevertheless, the rejection of stability in and of itself may suggest that other social, economic, cultural, or demographic processes were operating in this population, as in the case of the sample from Punta Candelero, which seems to represent a migrant, unstable population.

And third, paleodemographic methods can help determine the integrity of the sample. An aspect that has to be considered from this type of analysis is sample bias. Biases due to differences in cultural practices, cultural and natural formation processes, sampling problems in field methods, and innate error in the ability to determine the sex and age of skeletons may be present in any skeletal sample. A detailed analysis of the distribution of sex and age-at-death, combined with careful observation from the time the remains are discovered to the final laboratory analysis, can also help in determining whether the sample is biased. This is the case of the sample from Tibes, which does not seem to represent a stable population. However, the reduced number of children and older adults, combined with the poor preservation of the osteological remains, strongly suggests that the sample is biased due to poor preservation as mentioned by Crespo Torres (1998). Such a finding should serve as a cautionary note for future research on these collections.

Of all of the analyses presented in this book, the paleodemographic study of skeletal populations is probably the one that brings us closest to the individuals, not only because osteological analysis of the bones uses individual skeletons but also because by studying issues such as sex-and-age distributions, fertility, and mortality, we can observe the compounded effect of the behavioral decisions made by individuals, couples, families, households, kinship groups, or communities. For example, by determining the possible composition of a migrant community and comparing it to modern generalizations about migration, we can begin reconstructing the process of the migration and the structure of the migrant groups. If it is true that the sample from Punta Candelero represents a migrant community, then it seems that the structure of migration was not much different from the structures observed ethnographically. From this it can be speculated that the migration may have been caused by factors that especially affected the young and middle-aged adult men. Other issues have also to be resolved to complete the narrative, including the place of origin and whether it was a short- or long-distance migration. Nevertheless, paleodemographic study of the skeletal population is a good starting point, at a lower level of society, that can help in understanding processes that are observed at higher levels.

CONCLUSIONS

During the climax of cultural ecology, demographic variables were used, misused, and abused in many anthropological and archaeological investigations. Later studies showed that many of these variables were used in loose, uncritical, and nonrigorous ways, and, therefore, many of the conclusions could not be accepted until further appropriate testing was undertaken. Unfortunately, since then, demographic variables fell into disuse and are not considered in many studies. Recent studies in paleodemography, however, are promoting the re-use of demography as an important social, biological, and cultural factor in the study of past human groups.

However, in many parts of the world, including the Caribbean, demography is still poorly studied or hardly considered by archaeologists. I believe this reluctance to include demography in modeling past human behavior is in part an overreaction to the prominence assigned to certain population/resource imbalance models, and in part reflects a lack of the interest necessary to deal with demographic variables. Although it is true that population and population pressure were over-used in previous decades, it is unfortunate that demographic variables are being ignored in a great number of research studies where it is clear that they may have been important factors in historical trends. Population, as an independent, dependent, or "dialectic" variable, is a vital aspect of all human societies. Issues related to sex and age distribution, fertility, mortality, and other demographic variables affect many social, cultural, economic, and political factors. Unfortunately, their influence has been underestimated, when not outright overlooked. If factors like these are critical in large modern nations, such as Japan, Malaysia, the United States, or Nicaragua (just think of the problem in the United States with Social Security and the baby boomers), imagine what their effects could have been for comparatively small, ancient populations: even the smallest stochastic demographic variation could have strongly affected such a population. These are aspects of social and cultural groups that are as relevant as any other topic traditionally treated by archaeologists and bioarchaeologists, such as technology, diet, and other economic and subsistence issues.

One major difference between recent and past uses of demography in archaeology is how population factors relate to people. In the past, cultural ecology models often tended to consider population as an independent variable out of the control of people, to the point that it was considered an external factor placing pressure on human societies. In other words, humans had little to say on their population trends. Contrarily, today it is recognized that human decision-making has a role in the population dynamics of societies. Demographic factors are intrinsic to populations; they are the substance of what a population group is. They are not extrinsic factors. This is not to say that they have complete control over it, but that within the complicated formulae that describe the relationship between populations, economy, society, culture, and the environment, people have options that can affect positively or negatively their population trends and structures. This is an issue that was present in all the analyses included in this book, from the decision to migrate to aspects of fertility and mortality.

In our search to gain a better understanding of the differences and similarities of past human behavior, archaeologists study these societies at various levels of human organization and interaction, such as the household, the community, or the region. This involves gathering as much information as possible about a number of variables at each level. One of many commonalities at each level that ties them in a congruent system is population, and the assortment of other demographic variables that go along with population. It is critical to have a better understanding of the role of demography in society in order to have a more complete picture of past social and cultural processes. Demographic analysis has as much a role in modern archaeological research as the more traditional faunal, botanical, ceramic, and lithic analyses, and is essential to developing a clearer understanding of ancient societies.

References Cited

Alegría, R. E.
 1955 On Puerto Rican Archaeology. *American Antiquity* 21:113–31.
 1983 *Ballcourts and Ceremonial Plazas in the West Indies.* Yale University Publications in Anthropology, No. 79. New Haven.
Alegría, R. E., H. B. Nicholson, and G. R. Willey
 1955 The Archaic Tradition in Puerto Rico. *American Antiquity* 21:113–21.
Allaire, L.
 1997 The Lesser Antilles before Columbus. In *The Indigenous People of the Caribbean,* edited by S. M. Wilson, pp. 20–28. University Press of Florida, Gainesville.
Alvarado Zayas, P. A.
 1981 *La cerámica del centro ceremonial de Tibes: Estudio descriptivo.* Unpublished master's thesis, Centro de Estudios Avanzados de Puerto Rico y el Caribe, San Juan, Puerto Rico.
Ammerman, A. J., and L. L. Cavalli-Sforza
 1973 A Population Model for the Diffusion of Early Farming in Europe. In *The Explanation of Culture Change,* edited by C. Renfrew, pp. 343–357. Duckworth, London.
 1979 The Wave of Advance Model for the Spread of Agriculture in Europe. In *Transformations: Mathematical Approaches to Culture Change,* edited by C. Renfrew and K. L. Cooke, pp. 275–294. Academic Press, New York.
 1984 *The Neolithic Transition and Genetics of Populations in Europe.* Princeton University Press, Princeton.
Anderson Córdova, K. F.
 1990 *Hispaniola and Puerto Rico: Indian Acculturation and Heterogeneity, 1492–*

1550. Ph.D. dissertation, Yale University, New Haven. University Microfilms International, Ann Arbor.

1995 Aspectos demográficos de los cacicazgos taínos. In *Proceedings of the Fifteenth International Congress for Caribbean Archaeology,* edited by R. E. Alegría and M. Rodríguez, pp. 351–365. Centro de Estudios Avanzados de Puerto Rico y el Caribe, San Juan, Puerto Rico.

Anthony, D. W.

1990 Migration in Archaeology: The Baby and the Bathwater. *American Anthropologist* 92:895–914.

Ayes Suárez, C.

1989 Angostura: Un campamento arcaico temprano del Valle de Manataubón. *Revista Universidad de América* 1:24–37.

Baetsen, S.

1999 Human Remains. In *Archaeological Investigations on St. Martin (Lesser Antilles),* edited by C. L. Hofman and M. L. P. Hoogland, pp. 249–250. Faculty of Archaeology, Leiden University, Netherlands.

Barker, A. W.

1992 Powhatan's Pursestrings: On the Meaning of Surplus in a Seventeenth Century Algonkian Chiefdom. In *Lords of the Southeast: Social Inequality and the Native Elites of Southeastern North America,* edited by A. W. Barker and T. R. Pauketat, pp. 61–80. Archaeological Papers of the American Anthropological Association, No. 3. American Anthropological Association, Washington, D.C.

Barker, A. W., and T. R. Pauketat (editors)

1992 *Lords of the Southeast: Social Inequality and the Native Elites of Southeastern North America.* Archaeological Papers of the American Anthropological Association, No. 3. American Anthropological Association, Washington, D.C.

Bartholomew, G. A., and J. B. Birdsell

1953 Ecology and the Protohominids. *American Anthropologist* 55:481–498.

Beckerman, S.

1994 Hunting and Fishing in Amazonia: Hold the Answers, What are the Questions? In *Amazonian Indians from Prehistory to the Present: Anthropological Perspectives,* edited by A. Roosevelt, pp. 177–200. University of Arizona Press, Tucson.

Beeker, C. D., G. W. Conrad, and J. W. Foster

2002 Taíno Use of Flooded Caverns in the East National Park Region, Dominican Republic. *Journal of Caribbean Archaeology* 3:1–26.

Berman, M. J., and P. L. Gnivecki

1993 The Colonization of Bahamas. In *Proceedings of the Fourteenth International Congress for Caribbean Archaeology,* edited by A. Cummins and P. King,

pp. 170–186. International Association for Caribbean Archaeology, Barbados.
- 1995 The Colonization of the Bahama Archipelago: A Reappraisal. *World Archaeology* 26:421–441.

Billman, B. R.
- 1997 Population Pressure and the Origins of Warfare in the Moche Valley, Peru. In *Integrating Archaeological Demography: Multidisciplinary Approaches to Prehistoric Population,* edited by R. R. Paine, pp. 285–310. Center for Archaeological Investigations, Occasional Paper No. 24. Southern Illinois University, Carbondale.

Birdsell, G. A.
- 1953 Some Environmental and Cultural Factors Influencing the Structuring of Australian Aboriginal Population. *American Naturalist* 87:171–207.

Blanton, R. E., G. M. Feinman, S. A. Kowalewski, and P. M. Peregrine
- 1996 A Dual-Processual Theory for the Evolution of Mesoamerican Civilization. *Current Anthropology* 37:1–14.

Bocquet-Appel, J. P., and C. Masset
- 1982 Farewell to Paleodemography. *Journal of Human Evolution* 11:321–333.

Boomert, A.
- 2000 *Trinidad, Tobago, and the Lower Orinoco Interaction Sphere: An Archaeological/Ethnohistorical Study.* Cairi Publications, Alkmaar, Netherlands.
- 2001 Saladoid Sociopolitical Organization. In *Proceedings of the Eighteenth International Congress for Caribbean Archaeology,* Vol. 2, edited by G. Richard, pp. 55–77. International Association for Caribbean Archaeology, Guadeloupe.

Brumfiel, E. N., and T. K. Earle
- 1987 Specialization, Exchange, and Complex Societies: An Introduction. In *Specialization, Exchange, and Complex Societies,* edited by E. M. Brumfiel and T. K. Earle, pp. 1–9. Cambridge University Press, New York.

Brush, S.
- 1975 The Concept of Carrying Capacity for System of Shifting Cultivation. *American Anthropologist* 77:799–811.

Budinoff, L. C.
- 1991 An Osteological Analysis of the Human Burials Recovered from an Early Ceramic Site Located on the North Coast of Puerto Rico. In *Proceedings of the Twelfth International Congress for Caribbean Archaeology,* edited by L. S. Robinson, pp. 117–133. International Association for Caribbean Archaeology, Martinique.

Buikstra, J. E.
- 1997 Paleodemography: Context and Promise. In *Integrating Archaeological Demography: Multidisciplinary Approaches to Prehistoric Population,* edited by

R. R. Paine, pp. 367–380. Center for Archaeological Investigations, Occasional Paper No. 24. Southern Illinois University, Carbondale.

Buikstra, J. E., L. W. Konigsberg, and J. Bullington
1986 Fertility and the Development of Agriculture in the Prehistoric Midwest. *American Antiquity* 51:528–246.

Burney, D. A.
1997 Tropical Islands as Paleoecological Laboratories: Gauging the Consequences of Human Arrival. *Human Ecology* 25:437–457.

Burney, D. A., L. P. Burney, and R. D. E. MacPhee
1994 Holocene Charcoal Stratigraphy from Laguna Tortuguero, Puerto Rico, and the Timing of Human Arrival on the Island. *Journal of Archaeological Science* 21:273–281.

Callaghan, R. T.
1993 Passages to the Greater Antilles: An Analysis of Watercraft and the Marine Environment. In *Proceedings of the Fourteenth International Congress for Caribbean Archaeology*, edited by A. Cummins and P. King, pp. 64–72. International Association for Caribbean Archaeology, Barbados.
1995 Antillean Cultural Contacts with Mainland Regions as a Navigation Problem. In *Proceedings of the Fifteenth International Congress for Caribbean Archaeology*, edited by R. E. Alegría and M. Rodríguez, pp. 181–190. Centro de Estudios Avanzados de Puerto Rico y el Caribe, San Juan, Puerto Rico.
1999 Computer Simulations of Ancient Voyaging. *The Northern Mariner/Le Marin du Nord* 1:24–33.
2001 Ceramic Age Seafaring and Interaction Potential in the Antilles: A Computer Simulation. *Current Anthropology* 42:308–313.
2003 Comments on the Mainland Origin of the Preceramic Cultures of the Greater Antilles. *Latin American Antiquity* 14:323–338.

Calvera, J., E. Serrano, M. Rey, Irán Perdomo, and Y. Yparraguirre
1996 El sitio arqueológico Los Buchillones. *El Caribe Arqueológico* 1:59–67.

Cameron, C.
1995 Migration and Movement of Southwestern Peoples. *Journal of Anthropological Archaeology* 14:104–124.

Cameron, C. M., and S. A. Tomka (editors)
1993 *Abandonment of Settlements and Regions: Ethnoarchaeological and Archaeological Approaches.* Cambridge University Press, Cambridge.

Cancian, F.
1972 *Change and Uncertainty in a Peasant Economy: The Maya Corn Farmers of Zinacatan.* Stanford University Press, Stanford.

Carlson, B.
1999 *Aftermath of a Feast: Human Colonization of the Southern Bahamian Archi-*

pelago and Its Effects on the Indigenous Fauna. Ph.D. dissertation, University of Florida, Gainesville. University Microfilms, Ann Arbor.

Carneiro, R. L.
- 1957   *Subsistence and Social Structure: An Ecological Study of the Kuikuru.* Ph.D. dissertation, University of Michigan, Ann Arbor. University Microfilms, Ann Arbor.
- 1960   Slash-and-Burn Agriculture: A Closer Look at Its Implications for Settlement Patterns. In *Men and Cultures: Selected Papers of the Fifth International Congress of Anthropological and Ethnological Sciences,* edited by A. F. C. Wallace, pp. 229–234. University of Pennsylvania Press: Philadelphia.
- 1961   Slash-and-Burn Cultivation among the Kuikuru and Its Implications for Cultural Development in the Amazon Basin. In *The Evolution of Horticultural Systems in Native South America: Causes and Consequences,* edited by J. Wilbert, pp. 47–67. Sociedad de Ciencias Naturales La Salle, Caracas, Venezuela.
- 1970   A Theory of the Origin of the State. *Science* 169:733–738.

Caro Alvarez, J. A.
- 1977a   *Cemíes y trigonolitos.* Museo del Hombre Dominicano, Santo Domingo, Dominican Republic.
- 1977b   *La cohoba.* Museo del Hombre Dominicano, Santo Domingo, Dominican Republic.

Carr, C.
- 1995a   Building a Unified Middle-Range Theory of Artifact Design: Historical Perspectives. In *Style, Society, and Person: Archaeological and Ethnological Perspectives,* edited by C. Carr and J. E. Neitzel, pp. 105–170. Plenum Press, New York.
- 1995b   A Unified Middle-Range Theory of Artifact Design. In *Style, Society, and Person: Archaeological and Ethnological Perspectives,* edited by C. Carr and J. E. Neitzel, pp. 171–258. Plenum Press, New York.

Cassá, R.
- 1974   *Los Taínos de la Española.* Editora Alfa y Omega, Santo Domingo, Dominican Republic.
- 1995   *Los indios de las Antillas.* Fundación MAPFRE AMERICA, Madrid.

Casteel, R. W.
- 1972   Two Static Models for Hunter-Gatherers: A First Approximation. *World Archaeology* 3:19–40.

Chanlatte Baik, L. A.
- 1976   *Investigaciones arqueológicas en Guayanilla, Puerto Rico.* Museo del Hombre Dominicano, Santo Domingo, Dominican Republic.
- 1977   *Primer adorno corporal de oro (nariguera) en la arqueología antillana.* Museo del Hombre Dominicano, Santo Domingo, Dominican Republic.

1981 *La Hueca y Sorcé (Vieques, Puerto Rico): Primeras migraciones agroalfareras antillanas.* Published by the author, Santo Domingo, Dominican Republic.

1986 Cultura Ostionoide: Un desarrollo agroalfarero antillano. *Homines* 10:1–40.

1995 La presencia huecoide en Hacienda Grande, Loíza. In *Proceedings of the Fifteenth International Congress for Caribbean Archaeology,* edited by R. E. Alegría and M. Rodríguez, pp. 501–510. Centro de Estudios Avanzados de Puerto Rico y el Caribe, San Juan.

2000 Los arcaicos y el formativo antillano (6000 AC–1492 DC). *Boletín del Museo del Hombre Dominicano* 28: 29–42.

Chanlatte Baik, L. A., and Y. M. Narganes Storde

1983 *Vieques-Puerto Rico: Asiento de una nueva cultura aborigen antillana.* Published by the authors, Santo Domingo, Dominican Republic.

1985 Asentamiento poblacional Agro-I, complejo cultural La Hueca, Vieques, Puerto Rico. In *Proceedings of the Tenth International Congress for the Study of the Pre-Columbian Cultures of the Lesser Antilles,* edited by L. Allaire, pp. 225–250. Centre de Reserches Caraïbes, Université de Montréal, Montreal.

1986 *Proceso y desarrollo de los primeros pobladores de Puerto Rico y las Antillas.* Published by the authors, Santo Domingo, Dominican Republic.

Civera Cerecedo, M., and L. Márquez Morfín

1998 Paleodemografía: Sus alcances y limitaciones. In *Perfiles demográficos de poblaciones antiguas de México,* edited by L. Márquez Morfín and J. Gómez de León, pp. 15–29. Instituto Nacional de Antropología e Historia, Mexico City.

Clark, C., and M. Haswell

1970 *The Economics of Subsistence Agriculture.* Macmillan/St. Martin's Press, London.

Clark, J. J.

2001 *Tracking Prehistoric Migrations: Pueblo Settlers among the Tonto Basin Hohokam.* University of Arizona Press, Tucson.

Clark, J., and M. Blake

1989 El origen de la civilización en Mesoamerica: Los Olmecas y Mokaya del Soconusco de Chiapas, México. In *El preclásico o formativo: Avances y perspectivas,* edited by M. Carmona Macías, pp. 385–403. Instituto Nacional de Antropología e Historia and Museo Nacional de Antropología, Mexico City.

1994 The Power of Prestige: Competitive Generosity and the Emergence of Rank Societies in Lowland Mesoamerica. In *Factional Competition and Political Development in the New World,* edited by E. M. Brumfiel and J. W. Fox, pp. 17–30. Cambridge University Press, New York.

Clark, W. A. V.

1986 *Human Migration.* Scientific Geography Series, edited by G. I. Thrall. Sage, Beverly Hills.

Coale, A. J., and P. Demeny
    1983   *Regional Model Life Tables and Stable Populations,* 2nd ed. Academic Press, New York.
Cody, A.
    1991   From the Site of Pearls, Grenada: Exotic Lithics and Radiocarbon Dates. In *Proceedings of the Thirteenth International Congress for Caribbean Archaeology,* edited by E. N. Ayubi and J. B. Haviser, pp. 589–604. Reports of the Archaeological-Anthropological Institute of the Netherlands Antilles, No. 9. Curaçao.
    1993   Distribution of Exotic Stone Artifacts through the Lesser Antilles: Their Implications for Prehistoric Interaction and Exchange. In *Proceedings of the Fourteenth International Congress for Caribbean Archaeology,* edited by A. Cummins and P. King, pp. 204–226. International Association for Caribbean Archaeology, Barbados.
Cohen, M. N.
    1997   Does Paleopathology Measure Community Health? A Rebuttal of "The Osteological Paradox" and Its Implication for World History. In *Integrating Archaeological Demography: Multidisciplinary Approaches to Prehistoric Population,* edited by R. R. Paine, pp. 242–260. Center for Archaeological Investigations, Occasional Paper No. 24. Southern Illinois University, Carbondale.
Colón, C.
    1965   *Diario del primer viaje de Colón.* Ediciones Nauta, Barcelona.
Conklin, H.
    1959   Population-Land Balance under Systems of Tropical Forest Agriculture. *Proceedings of the Ninth Pacific Congress of the Pacific Science Association, 1957* 7:63.
Conrad, G. W., J. W. Foster, and C. D. Beeker
    2001   Organic Artifacts from the Manantial de la Aleta, Dominican Republic: Preliminary Observations and Interpretations. *Journal of Caribbean Archaeology* 2:1–20.
Cook, S. F., and W. Borah
    1971– The Aboriginal Population of Hispaniola. In *Essays in Population History,*
    1974   Vol. 1, edited by S. F. Cooke and W. Borah, pp. 376–410. University of California Press, Berkeley.
Córdova Armenteros, P. L.
    1995   *Pesca indocubana, de guaicanes, guacanes, bubacanes y de corrales se trata.* Editorial Académica, Havana.
Cornejo B., L. E., and L. Sanhueza R.
    2003   Coexistencia de cazadores recolectores y horticultores tempranos en la cordillera andina de Chile central. *American Antiquity* 14:389–407.

Cowgill, G. L.
1975   On Causes and Consequences of Ancient and Modern Population Changes. *American Anthropologist* 77:505–525.

Cowgill, G. L., and G. E. Hutchinson
1963   Ecological and Geochemical Archaeology in the Southern Maya Lowlands. *Southwestern Journal of Anthropology* 19:267–286.

Crespo Torres, E. F.
1994   *Dental Analysis of Human Burials Recovered from Punta Candelero: A Prehistoric Site on the Southeast Coast of Puerto Rico.* Unpublished master's thesis, Department of Anthropology, Arizona State University, Tempe.
1998   *Osteobiografía de los restos humanos procedentes del centro ceremonial indígena de Tibes, Ponce, Puerto Rico.* Submitted to the Municipio Autónomo de Ponce, Puerto Rico.
2000   *Estudio comparativo biocultural entre dos poblaciones prehistóricas en la isla de Puerto Rico: Punta Candelero y Paso del Indio.* Unpublished Ph.D. dissertation, Instituto de Investigaciones Arqueológicas, Universidad Nacional Autónoma de México, Mexico City.

Crock, J. G.
2000   *Interisland Interaction and the Development of Chiefdoms in the Eastern Caribbean.* Unpublished Ph.D. dissertation, Department of Anthropology, University of Pittsburgh, Pittsburgh.

Curet, L. A.
1987   *The Ceramics of the Vieques Naval Reservation: A Chronological and Spatial Analysis,* 2 Vols. University of Río Piedras, Puerto Rico. Submitted to the Department of the Navy, Norfolk.
1992a *The Development of Chiefdoms in the Greater Antilles: A Regional Study of the Valley of Maunabo, Puerto Rico.* Unpublished Ph.D. dissertation, Department of Anthropology, Arizona State University, Tempe.
1992b House Structure and Cultural Change in the Caribbean: Three Case Studies from Puerto Rico. *Latin American Antiquity* 3:160–174.
1992c Demographic and Sociopolitical Change in Prehistoric Puerto Rico. Paper presented at the 57th Annual Meeting of the Society for American Archaeology, Pittsburgh.
1993   Prehistoric Demographic Changes in the Valley of Maunabo: A Preliminary Report. In *Proceedings of the Fourteenth International Congress for Caribbean Archaeology,* edited by A. Cummins and P. King, pp. 11–24. International Association for Caribbean Archaeology, Barbados.
1996   Ideology, Chiefly Power and Material Culture: An Example from the Greater Antilles. *Latin American Antiquity* 7:114–131.
1998   New Formulae for Estimating Prehistoric Populations for Lowland South America and the Caribbean. *Antiquity* 72:359–375.

2002   The Chief is Dead, Long Live . . . Who? Descent and Succession in the Protohistoric Chiefdoms of the Greater Antilles. *Ethnohistory* 49:259–280.

2003   Issues on the Diversity and Emergence of Middle-Range Societies of the Ancient Caribbean: A Critique. *Journal of Archaeological Research* 11:1–42.

2004   Island Archaeology and Units of Analysis in the Study of Ancient Caribbean Societies. In *Voyages of Discovery: The Archaeology of Islands,* edited by S. M. Fitzpatrick, pp. 187–201. Praeger, Westport, Connecticut.

Curet, L. A., L. A. Newsom, and D. Welch

2003   Space and Time in the Civic-Ceremonial Center of Tibes, Ponce, Puerto Rico. In *Proceedings of the Nineteenth Congress for Caribbean Archaeology, International Association for Caribbean Archaeology,* edited by L. Alof and R. A. C. F. Dijkhoff, pp.142–155. Publication of the Museo Arqueológico Aruba, Vol. 9, Aruba.

Curet, L. A., and J. R. Oliver

1998   Mortuary Practices, Social Developments, and Ideology in Precolumbian Puerto Rico. *Latin American Antiquity* 9:217–239.

Curet, L. A., and L. Rodríguez Gracia

1999   Informe preliminar del proyecto arqueológico del Centro Indígena de Tibes, Ponce, Puerto Rico. In *Proceedings of the Sixteenth International Congress for Caribbean Archaeology,* edited by G. Richard, pp. 113–116. International Association for Caribbean Archaeology, Martinique.

Curet, L. A., J. M. Torres, and M. Rodríguez

2004   Political and Social History of Eastern Puerto Rico: The Ceramic Age. In *The Late Ceramic Age in the Eastern Caribbean,* edited by A. Delpuech and C. Hofman, pp. 59–85. British Archaeological Reports, Oxford.

Cusick, J. G. (editor)

1998   *Studies in Culture Contact: Interaction, Culture Change, and Archaeology.* Center for Archaeological Investigations, Occasional Paper No. 25. Southern Illinois University, Carbondale.

Davis, D.

2000   *Jolly Beach and the Preceramic Occupation of Antigua, West Indies.* Yale University Publications in Anthropology, No. 84. New Haven.

Deagan, K.

1998   Transculturation and Spanish American Ethnogenesis: The Archaeological Legacy of the Quincentenary. In *Studies in Culture Change: Interaction, Culture Change, and Archaeology,* edited by J. G. Cusick, pp. 23–43. Center for Archaeological Investigations, Occasional Paper No. 25. Southern Illinois University, Carbondale.

deFrance, S. D.

1989   Saladoid and Ostionoid Subsistence Adaptations: Zooarchaeological Data from a Coastal Occupation on Puerto Rico. In *Early Ceramic Population,*

Lifeways, and Adaptive Strategies in the Caribbean, edited by P. E. Siegel, pp. 57–77. British Archaeological Reports, Oxford.

deFrance, S. D., W. F. Keegan, and L. A. Newsom.
  1996 The archaeobotanical, bone isotope, and zooarchaeological records from Caribbean sites in comparative perspective. In *Case Studies in Environmental Archaeology,* edited by E. J. Reitz, L. A. Newsom, and S. J. Scudder, pp. 289–304. Plenum Press, New York.

Dewar, R. E.
  1984 Environmental Productivity, Population Regulation, and Carrying Capacity. *American Anthropologist* 86:601–614.
  1995 Of Nets and Trees: Untangling the Reticulate and Dendritic in Madagascar's Prehistory. *World Archaeology* 26(23):301–318.

Domínguez, L. S.
  1991 *Arqueología del centro-sur de Cuba.* Editorial Academia, Havana.

Drennan, R. D. and C. A. Uribe
  1987 Introduction. In *Chiefdoms in the Americas,* edited by R. D. Drennan and C. A. Uribe, pp. xiii–xix. University of America Press, New York.

Duff, A. I.
  1998 The Process of Migration in the Late Prehistoric Southwest. In *Migration and Reorganization in the Pueblo IV Period in the American Southwest,* edited by K. A. Spielmann, pp. 31–52. Anthropological Research Papers, No. 51. Arizona State University, Tempe.

Dumond, D. E.
  1997 Seeking Demographic Causes for Changes in Population Growth Rates. In *Integrating Archaeological Demography: Multidisciplinary Approaches to Prehistoric Population,* edited by R. R. Paine, pp. 175–190. Center for Archaeological Investigations, Occasional Paper No. 24. Southern Illinois University, Carbondale.

Earle, T. K. (editor)
  1991 *Chiefdoms: Power, Economy, and Ideology.* School of American Research and Cambridge University Press, New York.

Ewel, J., and J. L. Whitmore
  1973 *Las sonas de vida de Puerto Rico y las Islas Vírgenes americanas, una sinópsis.* Instituto de Dasonomía Tropical, United States Department of Agriculture, Río Piedras.

Febles, J.
  1991 Estudio comparativo de las industrias de piedra tallada de Aguas Verdes (Baracoa) y Playitas (Matanzas): Probable relación de estas industrias con otras del S. E. de Estados Unidos. In *Archaeología de Cuba y otras áreas antillanas,* pp. 312–379. La Habana, Editorial Academia, Havana.

Febles, J., and J. González Colón
  1999 La industria de la concha del residuario Maruca, Ponce, Puerto Rico. *El Caribe arqueológico* 3:53–56.

Feinman, G. M.
  1991 Demography, Surplus, and Inequality: Early Political Formations in Highland Mesoamerica. In *Chiefdoms: Power, Economy, and Ideology,* edited by T. Earle, pp. 229–262. School of American Research and Cambridge University Press, New York.
  1995 The Emergence of Inequality: A Focus on Strategies and Processes. In *Foundations of Social Inequality,* edited by T. D. Price and G. M. Feinman, pp. 255–279. Plenum Press, New York.

Feinman, G. M., K. G. Lightfoot, and S. Upham
  2000 Political Hierarchies and Organizational Strategies in the Puebloan Southwest. *American Antiquity* 65:449–470.

Fernández Méndez, E.
  1976 Los corrales de pesca indígenas de Puerto Rico. *Boletín del Museo del Hombre Dominicano* 7:171–179.

Fernández de Oviedo y Valdez, G.
  1959 *Historia general y natural de las Indias.* In *Biblioteca de autores Españoles,* Vols. 117–122. Ediciones Atlas, Madrid.

Fewkes, J. W.
  1907 The Aborigines of Puerto Rico and the Neighboring Islands. In *Annual Report of the Bureau of American Ethnology for 1903–1904,* No. 25. Smithsonian Institution, Washington, D.C.

Figueredo, A. E.
  1976 Caño Hondo, un residuario precerámico en la isla de Vieques. In *Proceedings of the Sixth International Congress for the Study of Pre-Columbian Cultures of the Lesser Antilles,* edited by R. P. Bullen, pp. 247–252. Societé d'Histoire de la Guadeloupe, Guadeloupe.

Firth, R.
  1936 *We, the Tikopia: A Sociological Study of Kinship in Primitive Polynesia.* American Book Company, New York.
  1965 *Primitive Polynesian Economy.* Routledge and Kegan Paul, Hamden, Connecticut.

Fontánez, R.
  1991 Restos faunísticos y explotación del medioambiente en Punta Candelero, Puerto Rico, informe preliminar. In *Proceedings of the Thirteenth International Congress for Caribbean Archaeology,* edited by E. N. Ayubi and J. B. Haviser, pp. 251–263. Reports of the Archaeological-Anthropological Institute of the Netherlands Antilles, No. 9, Curaçao.

Friedman, J., and M. J. Rowlands
    1977   Notes towards an Epigenetic Model of the Evolution of "Civilization". In *The Evolution of Social Systems,* edited by F. Friedman and M. F. Rowlands, pp. 201–278. University of Pittsburgh Press, Pittsburgh.

Glassow, M. A.
    1978   The Concept of Carrying Capacity in the Study of Culture Process. In *Advances in Archaeological Method and Theory,* Vol. 1, edited by M. B. Schiffer, pp. 31–48. Academic Press, New York.

Godo, P. P.
    1997   El problema del protoagrícola de Cuba: Discusión y perspectivas. *El Caribe arqueológico* 2:19–30.
    2001   Contextos arqueológicos del protoagrícola en el centro-occidente de Cuba. *El Caribe arqueológico* 5:62–75.

Goldman, I.
    1963   *The Cubeo: Indians of the Northwest Amazon.* Illinois Studies in Anthropology, No. 2. University of Illinois Press, Urbana.

González Colón, J.
    1984   *Tibes: Un centro ceremonial indígena.* Unpublished master's thesis, Centro de Estudios Avanzados de Puerto Rico y el Caribe, San Juan.

Goodwin, C. R.
    1979   *The Prehistoric Cultural Ecology of St. Kitts, West Indies: A Case Study in Island Archaeology.* Unpublished Ph.D. dissertation, Arizona State University, Tempe.
    1980   Demographic Change and the Crab-Shell Dichotomy. In *Proceedings of the Eighth International Congress of the Lesser Antilles,* edited by S. M. Lewenstein, pp. 45–68. Archaeological Research Papers, No. 22, Department of Anthropology, Arizona State University, Tempe.

Graber, R. B.
    1997   A Rigorous Approach to Population Pressure's Contribution to Cultural Evolution. In *Integrating Archaeological Demography: Multidisciplinary Approaches to Prehistoric Population,* edited by R. R. Paine, pp. 263–284. Center for Archaeological Investigations, Occasional Paper No. 24. Southern Illinois University, Carbondale.

Graham, E., D. M. Pendergast, J. Calvera Roses, and J. Jardines
    2000   Excavations at Los Buchillones, Cuba. *Antiquity* 74:263–264.

Graves, M. W., and D. J. Addison
    1995   The Polynesian Settlement of the Hawaiian Archipelago: Integrating Models and Methods in Archaeological Interpretation. *World Archaeology* 26: 380–399.

Gross, D. R.
    1975   Protein Capture and Cultural Development in the Amazon Basin. *American Anthropologist* 77:526–549.

Guarch Delmonte, J. M.
- 1982 *Carta Informativa,* No. 29, Epoca II. Departamento de Arqueología, Instituto de Ciencias Sociales, Holguín, Cuba.
- 1989 Los suelos, el bosque y la agricultura de los aborígenes cubanos. In *Homenaje a José Luis Lorenzo,* edited by L. Mirambell, pp. 277–295. Colección Científica, Instituto Nacional de Antropología e Historia, Mexico City.
- 1990 *Estructura para las comunidades aborígenes de Cuba.* Ediciones Holguín, Holguín, Cuba.
- 2001 Crónica para el innominable. *El Caribe arqueológico* 5:29–33.

Hassan, F. A.
- 1981 *Demographic Archaeology.* Academic Press, New York.

Haury, E. W.
- 1958 Evidence at Point of Pines for a Prehistoric Migration from Northern Arizona. In *Migrations in New World Culture History,* edited by R. H. Thompson, pp. 1–6. Social Science Bulletin No. 27. University of Arizona Bulletin No. 29(2). University of Arizona, Tucson.

Haviser, J.
- 1991 Development of a Prehistoric Interaction Sphere in the Northern Lesser Antilles. *New West Indian Guide* 65:129–151.
- 1997 Settlement Strategies in the Early Ceramic Age. In *The Indigenous People of the Caribbean,* edited by S. M. Wilson, pp. 59–69. University Press of Florida, Gainesville.

Hayden, B.
- 1975 The Carrying Capacity Dilemma: An Alternate Approach. In *Population Studies in Archaeology and Biological Anthropology: A Symposium,* edited by A. C. Swedlund. SAA Memoirs 30:11–21. Society for American Archaeology, Washington, D.C.

Heckenberger, M. J.
- 2002 Rethinking the Arawakan Diaspora: Hierarchy, Regionality, and the Amazonian Formative. In *Comparative Arawakan Histories: Rethinking Language Family and Culture Area in Amazonia,* edited by J. D. Hill and F. Santos-Granero, pp. 99–122. University of Illinois Press, Urbana.

Heckenberger, M. J., A. Kuikuro, U. T. Kuikuro, J. C. Russell, M. Schmidt, C. Fausto, and B. Franchetto
- 2003 Amazonia 1492: Pristine Forest or Cultural Parkland? *Science* 301:1710–1714.

Hegmon, M.
- 1991 The Risk of Sharing and Sharing as Risk Reduction: Inter-Household Food Sharing in Egalitarian Societies. In *Between Bands and States,* edited by S. A. Gregg, pp. 309–329. Center for Archaeological Investigations, Occasional Paper No. 29. Southern Illinois University, Carbondale.

Helms, M. W.
  1979   *Ancient Panama: Chiefs in Search of Power.* University of Texas Press, Austin.
  1988   *Ulysses' Sail: An Ethnographic Odyssey of Power, Knowledge, and Geographic Distance.* Princeton University Press, Princeton.
  1993   *Craft and the Kingly Ideal: Art, Trade, and Power.* University of Texas Press, Austin.

Hofman, C. L.
  1993   *In Search of the Native Population of Pre-Columbian Saba (400–145 A.D.), Part One: Pottery Styles and Their Interpretations.* Leiden University, Netherlands.
  1995   Inferring Inter-Island Relationships from Ceramic Style: A View from the Leeward Islands. In *Proceedings of the Fifteenth International Congress for Caribbean Archaeology,* edited by R. E. Alegría and M. Rodríguez, pp. 233–241. Centro de Estudios Avanzados de Puerto Rico y el Caribe, San Juan, Puerto Rico.

Hofman, C. L., and M. L. P. Hoogland
  1991   The Later Prehistory of Saba, Netherlands Antilles, the Settlement Site of Kelbey's Ridge (1300–1450 A.D.). In *Proceedings of the Thirteenth International Congress for Caribbean Archaeology,* edited by E. N. Ayubi and J. B. Haviser, pp. 477–492. Reports of the Archaeological-Anthropological Institute of the Netherlands Antilles, No. 9. Curaçao.
  2003   Plum Piece: Evidence for Archaic Seasonal Occupation on Saba, Northern Lesser Antilles around 3300 BP. *Journal of Caribbean Archaeology* 4:12–27.

Hofman, C. L., and M. L. P. Hoogland (editors)
  1999   *Archaeological Investigations on St. Martin (Lesser Antilles).* Faculty of Archaeology, Leiden University, Netherlands.

Hoogland, M. L. P.
  1996   *In Search of the Native Population of Pre-Columbian Saba (400–145 A.D.), Part Two: Settlement Sites in their Natural and Social Environment.* Ph.D. dissertation, Leiden University, Leiden, Netherlands.

Hoogland, M. L. P., and C. L. Hofman
  1999   Expansion of the Taíno Cacicazgos towards the Lesser Antilles. *Journal de la Societé des Américanistes* 85:90–113.

Howells, N.
  1986   Demographic Anthropology. *Annual Review of Anthropology* 15:219–246.

Irwin, G.
  1992   *The Prehistoric Exploration and Colonisation of the Pacific.* Cambridge University Press, Cambridge.

Jackes, M.
  1992   Paleodemography: Problems and Techniques. In *Skeletal Biology of Past*

Peoples: Research Methods, edited by S. R. Saunders and M. A. Katzenberg, pp. 189–224. Wiley-Liss, New York.

Jardines Macía, J., and J. Calvera Roses
1999 Estructuras de viviendas aborígenes en Los Buchillones. *El Caribe arqueológico* 3:44–52.

Jochim, M. A.
1976 *Hunter-Gatherer Subsistence and Settlement, a Predictive Model.* Academic Press, New York.

Johansson, S. R., and S. Horowitz
1986 Estimating Mortality in Skeletal Populations: Influence of the Growth Rate on the Interpretation of Levels and Trends during the Transition to Agriculture. *American Journal of Physical Anthropology* 71:233–250.

Jones, A. R.
1985 Dietary Change and Human Population at Indian Creek, Antigua. *American Antiquity* 50:518–536.

Jouravleva, I., and N. González
2000 Las variaciones climáticas y la reutilización del espacio habitacional a través de la alfarería aborigen. *El Caribe arqueológico* 4:35–39.

Keckler, C. N. W.
1997 Catastrophic Mortality in Simulations of Forager Age-at-Death: Where Did All the Humans Go? In *Integrating Archaeological Demography: Multidisciplinary Approaches to Prehistoric Population,* edited by R. R. Paine, pp. 191–204. Center for Archaeological Investigations, Occasional Paper No. 24. Southern Illinois University, Carbondale.

Keegan, W. F.
1982 Lucayan Fishing Practices: An Experimental Approach. *The Florida Anthropologist* 35:146–161.

1985 *Dynamic Horticulturalists: Population Expansion in the Prehistoric Bahamas.* Ph.D. dissertation, University of California, Santa Barbara. University Microfilms International, Ann Arbor.

1986 The Optimal Foraging Analysis of Horticultural Production. *American Anthropologist* 88:92–107.

1991 An Anthropological Evaluation of Taíno Kinship. In *Proceedings of the Thirteenth International Congress for Caribbean Archaeology,* edited by E. N. Ayubi and J. B. Haviser, pp. 437–445. Reports of the Archaeological-Anthropological Institute of the Netherlands Antilles, Curaçao.

1992 *The People Who Discovered Columbus.* University Press of Florida, Gainesville.

1994 West Indian Archaeology, 1: Overview and Foragers. *Journal of Archaeological Research* 2:55–284.

1995 Modeling Dispersal in Prehistoric West Indies. *World Archaeology* 26:400–420.

1997 *Bahamian Archaeology.* Media Publishing, Nassau, Bahamas.
2000 West Indian Archaeology, 3: Ceramic Age. *Journal of Archaeological Research* 4:265–294.
2001 Archaeological Investigations on Ile á Rat, Haiti: Avoid the Oid. In *Proceedings of the Eighteenth International Congress for Caribbean Archaeology,* Vol. 2, edited by G. Richard, pp. 233–239. International Association for Caribbean Archaeology, Guadeloupe.

Keegan, W. F., and J. M. Diamond
1987 Colonization of Islands by Humans: A Biogeographical Perspective. In *Advances in Archaeological Method and Theory,* Vol. 10, edited by M. B. Schiffer, pp. 49–92. Academic Press, New York.

Keegan, W. F., A. Johnson, and T. Early
1985 Carrying Capacity and Population Regulation: A Comment on Dewar. *American Anthropologist* 87(3):659–663.

Keegan, W. F., and M. D. Maclachlan
1989 The Evolution of Avunculocal Chiefdoms. *American Anthropologist* 91:613–630.

Keegan, W. F., M. Maclachlan, and B. Byrne
1998 Social Foundations of Taíno Caciques. In *Chiefdoms and Chieftaincy in the Americas,* edited by E. M. Redmond, pp. 217–244. University Press of Florida, Gainesville.

Kirch, P. V.
1980 Polynesian Prehistory: Cultural Adaptation in Island Ecosystem. *American Scientist* 68:39–48.
1984 *The Evolution of Polynesian Chiefdoms.* Cambridge University Press, Cambridge.
1986 Introduction: The Archaeology of Island Societies. In *Island Societies: Archaeological Approaches to Evolution and Transformation,* edited by P. Kirch, pp. 1–5. Cambridge University Press, New York.

Kirch, P. V. (editor)
1986 *Island Societies: Archaeological Approaches to Evolution and Transformation.* Cambridge University Press, New York.

Kirkby, A. V.
1973 *The Use of Land and Water Resources in the Past and Present Valley of Oaxaca, Mexico.* Memoirs of the Museum of Anthropology, No. 5. University of Michigan, Ann Arbor.

Kolb, C. C.
1985 Demographic Estimates in Archaeology: Contributions from Ethnoarchaeology on Mesoamerican Peasants. *Current Anthropology* 26:581–599.

Konigsberg, L. W., J. E. Buikstra, and J. Bullington
1989 Paleodemographic Correlates of Fertility: A Reply to Corruccini, Brandon, and Handler and to Holland. *American Antiquity* 54:626–636.

Konigsberg, L. W., and S. R. Frankenberg
   2002   Deconstructing Death in Paleodemography. *American Journal of Physical Anthropology* 117:297–309.

Konigsberg, L. W., S. R. Frankenberg, and R. B. Walker
   1997   Regress What on What? Paleodemographic Age Estimation as a Calibration Problem. In *Integrating Archaeological Demography: Multidisciplinary Approaches to Prehistoric Population,* edited by R. R. Paine, pp. 64–88. Center for Archaeological Investigations, Occasional Paper No. 24. Southern Illinois University, Carbondale.

Kowalewski, S. A.
   1980   Population-Resource Balances in Period I of Oaxaca, Mexico. *American Antiquity* 45:151–165
   1982   Population and Agricultural Potential: Early I through V. In *Monte Alban's Hinterland, Part I: The Prehispanic Settlement Patterns of the Central and Southern Parts of the Valley of Oaxaca, Mexico,* edited by R. E. Blanton, S. Kowalewski, G. Feinman, and J. Appel. Memoirs of the Museum of Anthropology, No. 7. University of Michigan, Ann Arbor.

La Rosa Corzo, G., and R. Robaina
   1994   *Infanticidio y costumbres funerarias en aborígenes de Cuba.* Multigraf, Havana.
   1995   *Costumbres funerarias de los aborígenes de Cuba.* Editorial Academia, Havana.

Larsen, C. S.
   2002   Bioarchaeology: The Lives and Lifestyles of Past People. *Journal of Archaeological Research* 10:119–166.

Las Casas, B.
   1967   *Apologética historia sumaria.* Universidad Autónoma de México, Mexico City.

Lathrap, D. W.
   1970   *The Upper Amazon.* Praeger, New York.

Lewarch, D. E., and M. J. O'Brien
   1981   The Expanding Role of Surface Assemblages in Archaeological Research. In *Advances in Archaeological Method and Theory,* Vol. 4., edited by M. B. Schiffer, pp. 297–342. Academic Press, New York.

López Sotomayor, D.
   1975   *Vieques: Un momento en su historia.* Unpublished master's thesis, Escuela Nacional de Antropología e Historia, Mexico City.

Lovejoy, C. O., R. S. Meindl, T. R. Pryzbeck, T. J. Barton, K. G. Heiple, and D. Kotting
   1977   Paleodemography of the Libben Site, Ottawa County, Ohio. *Science* 198:291–293.

Lovejoy, C. O., R. S. Meindl, R. G. Tague, and B. Latimer
  1997   The Comparative Senescent Biology of the Hominoid Pelvis and Its Implications for the Use of Age-at-Death Indicators in the Human Skeleton. In *Integrating Archaeological Demography: Multidisciplinary Approaches to Prehistoric Population,* edited by R. R. Paine, pp. 43–63. Center for Archaeological Investigations, Occasional Paper No. 24. Southern Illinois University, Carbondale.

Lovén, S.
  1935   *Origins of the Taínan Culture, West Indies.* Elanders Boktryckeri Aktiebolag, Göteborg, Sweden.

Lundberg, E. R.
  1985   Settlement Pattern Analysis for South-Central Puerto Rico. In *Archaeological Data Recovery at El Bronce, Puerto Rico, Final Report, Phase 2,* Appendix L, edited by L. S. Robinson, E. R. Lundberg, and J. B. Walker, pp. L1–L32. Submitted to the United States Army Corps of Engineers, Jacksonville.
  1991   Interrelationships among Preceramic Complexes of Puerto Rico and the Virgin Islands. In *Proceedings of the Thirteenth International Congress for Caribbean Archaeology,* edited by E. N. Ayubi and J. B. Haviser, pp. 73–85. Reports of the Archaeological-Anthropological Institute of the Netherlands Antilles, Curaçao.

Lundberg, E., E. C. Righter, and M. D. Caesar
  1992   The Late Ceramic Age in the Northern Virgin Islands. Paper presented at the 57th Annual Meeting of the Society for American Archaeology, Pittsburgh.

MacArthur R. H., and E. O. Wilson
  1967   *The Theory of Island Biogeography.* Princeton University Press, Princeton.

Maíz López, E. J.
  1996   La fauna ornitológica de la familia columbidae en el sitio arqueológico Hernández Colón de Puerto Rico. In *Ponencias del primer seminario de arqueología del Caribe,* edited by M. Veloz Maggiolo and A. Caba Fuentes, pp. 90–99. Museo Arqueológico Regional Altos de Chavón, Dominican Republic.
  2002   *El sitio arqueológico Hernández Colón: Actividades subsistenciales de los antiguos habitantes del Valle del Río Cerrillos-Bucaná, Ponce, Puerto Rico.* Unpublished master's thesis, Centro de Estudios Avanzados de Puerto Rico y el Caribe, San Juan.

Maíz López, E. J., and E. Questell Rodríguez
  1984   *Reconocimiento arqueológico preliminar de la cuenca hidrográfica del Río Yauco.* Centro de Investigaciones Folklóricas de Puerto Rico, Inc., Programa de Investigaciones Sociales, Sección Arqueología, Ponce, Puerto Rico. Submitted to the State Historic Preservation Office, San Juan.

1990   Reconocimiento arqueológico preliminar de la cuenca hidrográfica del Río Yauco. In *Proceedings of the Eleventh Congress of the International Association for Caribbean Archaeology,* edited by G. Pantel Tekakis, I. Vargas Arenas, and M. Sanoja Obediente, pp. 311–327. Fundación Arqueológica, Antropológica, e Histórica de Puerto Rico, San Juan.

Marcus, J.
1982   The Plant World of the Sixteenth- and Seventeenth-Century Lowland Maya. In *Maya Subsistence,* edited by K. V. Flannery, pp. 239–273. Academic Press, New York.

Márquez Morfín, L., and J. Gómez de León (editors)
1998   *Perfiles demográficos de poblaciones antiguas de México.* Instituto Nacional de Antropología e Historia, Mexico City.

Martínez Gabino, A., E. Vento, and C. Roque
1993   *Historia aborígen de Matanzas.* Ediciones Matanzas, Matanzas, Cuba.

McGinnis, S. A. M.
1997   *Ideographic Expression in the Precolumbian Caribbean.* Unpublished Ph.D. dissertation, Department of Anthropology, University of Texas, Austin.

2001   Patterns, Variations, and Anomalies in Ideographic Expression in the Precolumbian Caribbean. In *Proceedings of the Eighteenth International Congress for Caribbean Archaeology,* Vol. 2, edited by G. Richard, pp. 99–114. International Association for Caribbean Archaeology, Guadeloupe.

McGuire, R. H., and D. J. Saitta
1996   Although They Have Petty Captains, They Obey Them Badly: The Dialectics of Prehispanic Western Pueblo Social Organization. *American Antiquity* 61:197–216.

Meggers, B. J.
1954   Environmental Limitation on the Development of Culture. *American Anthropologist* 56:801–824.

1992   Prehistoric Population Density in the Amazon Basin. In *Disease and Demography in the Americas,* edited by J. W. Verano and D. H. Ubelaker, pp. 197–205. Smithsonian Institution Press, Washington, D.C.

Meggers, B. J. and C. Evans Jr.
1957   *Archaeological Investigations at the Mouth of the Amazon.* Bureau of American Ethnology, 67. Smithsonian Institution, Washington, D.C.

Meindl, R. S., and K. F. Russell
1998   Recent Advances in Method and Theory in Paleodemography. *Annual Review of Anthropology* 27:375–399.

Mercado, M. C.
1990   Estrategias de pesca de las poblaciones indígenas Antillanas en relación a la ecología del manatí. In *Proceedings of the Eleventh International Congress for Caribbean Archaeology,* edited by A. G. Pantel Tekakis, I. Vargas Arenas, and

M. Sanoja Obediente, pp. 438–441. La Fundación Arqueológica, Antropológica, e Histórica de Puerto Rico, San Juan.

Milner, G. R., D. A. Humpf, and H. C. Harpending
1989 Pattern Matching of Age-at-Death Distributions in Paleodemographic Analysis. *American Journal of Physical Anthropology* 80:49–58.

Milner, G. R., J. W. Wood, and J. L. Boldsen
2000 Paleodemography. In *Biological Anthropology of the Human Skeleton,* edited by M. A. Katzenberg and S. R. Saunders, pp. 467–497. Wiley, New York.

Moore, J. H.
2001 Evaluating Five Models of Human Colonization. *American Anthropologist* 103(2):395–408.

Morse, B. G.
1992 Late Ceramic Age Manifestations in St. Croix, Virgin Islands. Paper presented at the 57th Annual Meeting of the Society for American Archaeology, Pittsburgh.

Moscoso, F.
1986 *Tribu y clases en el Caribe antiguo.* Universidad Central del Este, San Pedro de Macorís, Dominican Republic.
1999 *Arcaicos de Angostura, pasado remoto de Puerto Rico: Diálogo de Francisco Moscoso, historiador, con Carlos M. Ayes Suárez y Ovidio Dávila, Arqueólogos.* Sociedad de Investigaciones Arqueológicas e Históricas Seboruco, Vega Baja, Puerto Rico.

Narganes Storde, Y.
1985 Restos faunísticos vertebrados de Sorcé, Vieques, Puerto Rico. In *Proceedings of the Tenth International Congress for the Study of the Pre-Columbian Cultures of the Lesser Antilles,* edited by L. Allaire, pp. 251–264. Centre de Reserches Caraïbes, Université de Montréal, Montreal.
1993 *Fauna y cultura indígena de Puerto Rico.* Museo de Historia, Antropología y Arte, Centro de Investigaciones Arqueológicas, Universidad de Puerto Rico, Río Piedras, Puerto Rico.
1995 La lapidaria de la Hueca, Vieques, Puerto Rico. In *Proceedings of the Fifteenth International Congress for Caribbean Archaeology,* edited by R. E. Alegría and M. Rodríguez, pp. 141–154. Centro de Estudios Avanzados de Puerto Rico y el Caribe, San Juan.

Navarro, J.
1847 *Descripción topográfica del pueblo de Maunabo.* Fondo de Obras Públicas, Serie Obras Municipales, Legajo 45, Exp. 7, Caja 270, Archivo General de Puerto Rico, San Juan.

Nelson, M. C., and G. Schachner
2002 Understanding Abandonment in the North American Southwest. *Journal of Archaeological Research* 10:167–241.

Newsom, L. A.
1993 *Native West Indian Plant Use.* Unpublished Ph.D. dissertation, Department of Anthropology, University of Florida, Gainesville.

Newsom, L. A., and K. A. Deagan
1994 Zea mays in the West Indies: The Archaeological and Early Historic Record. In *Corn and Culture in the Prehistoric New World,* edited by S. Johannessen. and C. A. Hastorf, pp. 203–218. Westview Press, Boulder, Colorado.

Noble, G. K.
1955 *Proto-Arawakan and Its Descendants.* Indiana University Publications in Anthropology and Linguistics, No. 38. Indiana University, Bloomington.

Noli, D., and G. Avery
1988 Protein Poisoning and Coastal Subsistence. *Journal of Archaeological Science* 15:395–401.

Oliver, J. R.
1998 *El centro ceremonial de Caguana, Puerto Rico: Simbolismo iconográfico, cosmovisión y el poderío caciquil Taíno de Borínquen.* BAR International Series, No. 727, Oxford.
1999 The "La Hueca Problem" in Puerto Rico and the Caribbean: Old Problems, New Perspectives, Possible Solutions. In *Archaeological Investigations on St. Martin (Lesser Antilles),* edited by C. L. Hofman and M. L. P. Hoogland, pp. 253–297. Faculty of Archaeology, Leiden University, Netherlands.
2000 Gold Symbolism among Caribbean Chiefdoms: Of Feathers, Cibas, and Guanín Power among Taíno Elites. In *Precolumbian Gold: Technology, Style, and Iconography,* edited by C. McEwan, pp. 196–219. British Museum Press, London.

Ortega, E. J., and G. Atiles
2003 *Manantial de la Aleta y la arqueología en el Parque Nacional del Este.* Academia de Ciencias de la República Dominicana, Santo Domingo, Dominican Republic.

Ortiz Aguilú, J. J., J. Rivera Meléndez, A. Príncipe Jácome, M. Meléndez Maiz, and M. Lavergne Colberg
1993 Intensive Agriculture in Pre-Columbian West Indies: The Case for Terraces. In *Proceedings of the Fourteenth International Congress for Caribbean Archaeology,* edited by A. Cummins and P. King, pp. 278–285. International Association for Caribbean Archaeology, Barbados.

Paddock, J.
1983 The Oaxaca Barrio at Teotihuacan. In *The Cloud People: Divergent Evolution of the Zapotec and Mixtec Civilizations,* edited by K. V. Flannery and J. Marcus, pp. 170–175. Academic Press, New York.

Paine, R. R.
1997a The Need for a Multidisciplinary Approach to Prehistoric Demography. In

Integrating Archaeological Demography: Multidisciplinary Approaches to Prehistoric Population, edited by R. R. Paine, pp. 1–18. Center for Archaeological Investigations, Occasional Paper No. 24. Southern Illinois University, Carbondale.

1997b Uniformitarian Models in Osteological Paleodemography. In *Integrating Archaeological Demography: Multidisciplinary Approaches to Prehistoric Population,* edited by R. R. Paine, pp. 191–204. Center for Archaeological Investigations, Occasional Paper No. 24. Southern Illinois University, Carbondale.

2000 If a Population Crashes in Prehistory, and There Is No Paleodemographer There to Hear It, Does It Make a Sound? *American Journal of Physical Anthropology* 112:181–190.

Paine, R. R., and H. C. Harpending

1996 Assessing the Reliability of Paleodemographic Fertility Estimators Using Simulated Skeletal Distributions. *American Journal of Physical Anthropology* 101:151–159.

1998 Effect of Sample Bias on Paleodemographic Fertility Estimates. *American Journal of Physical Anthropology* 105:231–240.

Pantel, A. G.

1988 *Precolumbian Flaked Stone Assemblages in the West Indies.* Ph.D. dissertation, University of Tennessee, Knoxville. University Microfilms International, Ann Arbor.

1996 Nuestra percepción de los grupos preagrícolas en el Caribe. *El Caribe arqueológico* 1:8–11.

Paquette, R., and S. Engerman (editors)

1996 *The Lesser Antilles in the Age of European Expansion.* University Press of Florida, Gainesville.

Pendergast, D. M.

1997 Up from the Shallows. *Rotunda* 30:28–31.

1998 The House in the Water. *Rotunda* 31:26–31.

Petersen, W.

1975 A Demographer's View of Prehistoric Demography. *Current Anthropology* 16:227–245.

Picó, R.

1974 *Geography of Puerto Rico.* Aldine, Chicago.

Pino, M., and N. Castellanos

1985 *Acerca de la asociación de perezosos cubanos extinguidos con evidencias culturales de aborígenes cubanos.* Reporte de Investigación del Instituto de Ciencias Sociales, No. 4. Academia de Ciencias de Cuba, Havana.

Ponce de León y Troche, J., and J. y A. de Santa Clara

1582 (1914) Memorias de Melgarejo. In *Boletín histórico de Puerto Rico,* edited by C. Coll y Toste, Vol. I, pp. 75–91, San Juan, Puerto Rico.

Rainbird, P.
    1999   Islands Out of Time: Towards a Critique of Island Archaeology. *Journal of Mediterranean Archaeology* 12:216–234.
Rainey, F. G.
    1940   Porto Rican Archaeology. In *Scientific Survey of Porto Rico and the Virgin Islands,* Vol. 18, pt. 1, New York Academy of Science, New York.
Rappaport, R. A.
    1968   *Pigs for the Ancestors: Ritual in the Ecology of a New Guinea People.* Yale University Press, New Haven.
Rattray, E. C.
    1987   Los barrios foráneos de Teotihuacan. In *Nuevos datos, nuevas síntesis, nuevos problemas,* edited by E. McClung de Tapia and E. C. Rattray, pp. 243–273. Instituto de Investigaciones Antroplógicas, Serie Antropológica. Universidad Autónoma de México, Mexico City.
Renfrew, C.
    1986   Introduction: Peer Polity Interaction and Socio-Political Change. In *Peer-Polity Interaction and Socio-Political Change,* edited by C. Renfrew and J. F. Cherry, pp. 1–18. University of Cambridge Press, Cambridge.
Righter, E.
    2003   *Tutu Archaeological Village Site: A Case Study in Human Adaptation.* Routledge, New York.
Rivera, V., and M. Rodríguez
    1991   The Playa Blanca 5 Site: A Late Prehistoric Ceramic Site in Eastern Puerto Rico (A Preliminary Report). In *Proceedings of the Thirteenth International Congress for Caribbean Archaeology,* edited by E. N. Ayubi and J. B. Haviser, pp. 541–558. Reports of the Archaeological-Anthropological Institute of the Netherlands Antilles, No. 9, Curaçao.
Rivera Fontán, J. A., and D. Silva Pagán
    1997   Proyecto arqueológico barrio Quemado, Mayagüez (Batey Delfín del Yagüez). In *Segundo encuentro de investigadores: Ocho trabajos de investigación arqueológica en Puerto Rico,* edited by J. A. Rivera Fontán, pp. 53–64. Instituto de Cultura Puertorriqueña, San Juan.
    2002   Batey del Delfín: Un asentamiento taíno en el cauce medio del río Yaguez. *Cuarto encuentro de investigadores: Trabajos de investigación arqueológica,* edited by C. A. Pérez Merced and J. A. Rivera Fontán, pp. 69–84. Instituto de Cultura Puertorriqueña, San Juan.
Rivero de la Calle, M.
    1990   *Los esqueletos aborígenes de la Cueva de los Indios, Hoyo de Padilla, Cumanayagua, Cienfuego.* Universidad de la Habana, Havana.
Rockman, M., and J. Steele (editors)
    2003   *Colonization of Unfamiliar Landscapes: The Archaeology of Adaptation.* Routledge, New York.

Rodman, M. C.
 1985   Moving Houses: Residential Mobility of Residences in Longana, Vanuatu. *American Anthropologist* 87:56–72.

Rodríguez, M. A.
 1983   *Prehistoria de Collores.* Unpublished master's thesis, Centro de Estudios Avanzados de Puerto Rico y el Caribe. San Juan.
 1984   *Estudio arqueológico del Valle del Río Caguitas, Caguas, Puerto Rico.* Museo de la Universidad del Turabo, Caguas, Puerto Rico.
 1985   *Cultural Resources Survey at Camp Santiago, Salinas, Puerto Rico.* Museo de la Universidad del Turabo, Caguas, Puerto Rico.
 1986   *La Arboleda: Un proyecto de rescate arqueológico en la costa sur de Puerto Rico.* Museo Universidad del Turabo, Serie Arqueológica No. 3. Universidad del Turabo, Caguas, Puerto Rico.
 1989a The Zoned Incised Crosshatch (ZIC) Ware of Early Precolumbian Ceramic Age Sites in Puerto Rico and Vieques Island. In *Early Ceramic Population Lifeways and Adaptive Strategies in the Caribbean,* edited by P. E. Siegel, pp. 249–266. BAR International Series 506, Oxford.
 1989b La Colección Arqueológica de Puerto Rico en el Museo Peabody de la Universidad de Yale. *Revista del Centro de Estudios Avanzados de Puerto Rico y el Caribe* 8:27–41.
 1990   Arqueología del Río Loíza. In *Proceedings of the Eleventh International Congress for Caribbean Archaeology,* edited by A. G. Pantel Tekakis, I. Vargas Arenas, M. Sanoja Obediente, pp. 287–294. La Fundación Arqueológica, Antropológica, e Histórica de Puerto Rico, San Juan.
 1991   Arqueología de Punta Candelero. In *Proceedings of the Thirteenth International Congress for Caribbean Archaeology,* edited by E. N. Ayubi and J. B. Haviser, pp. 605–627. Reports of the Archaeological-Anthropological Institute of the Netherlands Antilles, No. 9. Curaçao.
 1992   Diversidad cultural en la tardía prehistoria del este de Puerto Rico. *Revista del Centro de Estudios Avanzados de Puerto Rico y el Caribe* 15:58–74.
 1997   Maruca, Ponce. In *Ocho trabajos de investigación arqueológica en Puerto Rico: Segundo encuentro de investigadores,* edited by J. A. Rivera Fontán, pp. 17–30. Instituto de Cultura Puertorriqueña, San Juan.
 1999   Excavations at Maruca, a Preceramic Site in Southern Puerto Rico. In *Proceedings of the Seventeenth Congress of the International Association for Caribbean Archaeology,* edited by J. H. Winter, pp. 166–180. Molloy College, Rockville Centre, New York.

Rodríguez, M. A., and V. Rivera
 1983   Sitio "El Destino," Vieques, Puerto Rico: Informe preliminar. In *Proceedings of the Ninth International Congress for the Study of the Pre-Columbian Cultures of the Lesser Antilles,* edited by L. Allaire and C. M. Mayer, pp. 163–172. Centre de Reserches Caraïbes, Université de Montréal, Montreal.

Rodríguez Ramos, R.
- 2001a *Lithic Reduction Trajectories at La Hueca and Punta Candelero Sites, Puerto Rico.* Unpublished master's thesis, Department of Anthropology, Texas A&M University.
- 2001b Lithic Reduction Trajectories at La Hueca and Punta Candelero Sites (Puerto Rico). In *Proceedings of the Eighteenth International Congress for Caribbean Archaeology,* Vol. 1, edited by G. Richard, pp. 251–261. International Association for Caribbean Archaeology, Guadeloupe.
- 2002a Dinámicas de intercambio en el Puerto Rico prehispánico. *El Caribe arqueológico* 6:16–22.
- 2002b Una perspectiva diacrónica de la explotación del pedernal en Puerto Rico. *Boletín del Museo del Hombre Dominicano* 32:167–192.

Roe, P. G.
- 1989 A Grammatical Analysis of Cedrosan Saladoid Vessel Form Categories and Surface Decoration: Aesthetic and Technical Styles in Early Antillean Ceramics. In *Early Ceramic Population Lifeways and Adaptive Strategies in the Caribbean,* edited by P. E. Siegel, pp. 267–382. BAR International Series 506, Oxford.
- 1995 Eternal Companions: Amerindian Dogs from Tierra Firme to the Antilles. In *Proceedings of the Fifteenth International Congress for Caribbean Archaeology,* edited by R. E. Alegría and M. Rodríguez, pp. 155–172. Centro de Estudios Avanzados de Puerto Rico y el Caribe, San Juan, Puerto Rico.

Roper, D. C.
- 1976 Lateral Displacement of Artifacts Due to Plowing. *American Antiquity* 41:372–374.

Roosevelt, A. C.
- 1980 *Parmana: Prehistoric Maize and Manioc Subsistence along the Amazon and Orinoco.* Academic Press, New York.
- 1991 *Moundbuilders of the Amazon: Geophysical Archaeology on Marajo Island, Brazil.* Academic Press, New York.

Rouse, I.
- 1939 *Prehistory in Haiti: A Study in Method.* Yale University Publications in Anthropology, No. 21, New Haven.
- 1951 Areas and Periods of Culture in the Greater Antilles. *Southwestern Journal of Anthropology* 7:248–265.
- 1952 Porto Rican Prehistory. In *Scientific Survey of Porto Rico and the Virgin Islands,* Vol. 18, pts. 3–4. New York Academy of Science, New York.
- 1956 Settlement Patterns in the Caribbean Area. In *Prehistoric Settlement Patterns in the New World,* edited by G. R. Willey, pp. 165–172. Viking Fund, Publications in Anthropology, No. 23, Washington, D.C.
- 1964a Prehistory of the West Indies. *Science* 144:499–513.

1964b   *Prehistory in Haiti: A Study in Method.* Yale University Publications in Anthropology, No. 21. New Haven.

1982   Ceramic and Religious Development in the Greater Antilles. *Journal of New World Archaeology* 5:45–55.

1986   *Migrations in Prehistory: Inferring Population Movement from Cultural Remains.* Yale University Press, New Haven.

1989   Peoples and Cultures of the Saladoid Frontier in the Greater Antilles. In *Early Ceramic Population Lifeways and Adaptive Strategies in the Caribbean,* edited by P. E. Siegel, pp. 383–403. BAR International Series 506, Oxford.

1992   *The Taínos: Rise and Decline of the People Who Greeted Columbus.* Yale University Press, New Haven.

Rouse, I., and Alegría, R. E.

1990   *Excavations at María de la Cruz Cave and Hacienda Grande Village Site, Loíza, Puerto Rico.* Yale University Publications in Anthropology, No. 80. New Haven.

Rouse, I., and L. Allaire

1978   Caribbean. In *Chronologies in New World Archaeology,* edited by C. Meighan and R. Taylor, pp. 431–481. Academic Press, New York.

Rouse, I., and J. Cruxent

1963   *Venezuelan Archaeology.* Yale University Press, New Haven.

Sahlins, M. D.

1958   *Social Stratification in Polynesia.* University of Washington Press, Seattle.

Saitta, D. J.

1997   Power, Labor, and the Dynamics of Change in Chacoan Political Economy. *American Antiquity* 62:7–26.

Sanders, W. T.

1976   The Agricultural History of the Basin of Mexico. In *The Valley of Mexico,* edited by E. R. Wolf, pp. 101–159. University of New Mexico Press, Albuquerque.

Sanoja, M.

1981   *Los hombres de la yuca y el maíz.* Monte Avila Editores, Caracas.

1989   Los orígenes del cultivo en el noroeste de Venezuela. In *Homenaje a José Luis Lorenzo,* edited by L. Mirambell, pp. 365–379. Colección Científica, Instituto Nacional de Antropología e Historia, Mexico City.

Sanoja, M., and I. Vargas

1974   *Antiguas formaciones y modos de producción venezonlanos.* Monte Avila Editores, Caracas, Venezuela.

Sattenspiel, L., and H. Harpending

1983   Stable Populations and Skeletal Age. *American Antiquity* 48:489–498.

Saunders, N. J., and D. Gray

1996   Zemís, Trees, and Symbolic Landscape: Three Taíno Carvings from Jamaica. *Antiquity* 70:801–812.

Schacht, R. M.
- 1981 Estimating Past Population Trends. *Annual Review of Anthropology* 10:119–140.

Schreiber, K. J., and K. W. Kintigh
- 1996 A Test of the Relationship between Site Size and Population. *American Antiquity* 61:573–580.

Service, E. R.
- 1962 *Primitive Social Organization: An Evolutionary Perspective.* Random House, New York.

Siegel, P. E.
- 1989 Site Structure, Demography, and Social Complexity in the Early Ceramic Age of the Caribbean. In *Early Ceramic Population, Lifeways, and Adaptive Strategies in the Caribbean,* edited by P. E. Siegel, pp. 193–245. British Archaeological Reports, Oxford.
- 1991a Migration Research in Saladoid Archaeology: A Review. *The Florida Anthropologist* 44:79–91.
- 1991b Political Evolution in the Caribbean. In *Proceedings of the Thirteenth International Congress for Caribbean Archaeology,* edited by N. E. Ayubi and J. B. Haviser, pp. 232–250. Reports of the Archaeological-Anthropological Institute of the Netherlands Antilles, Curaçao.
- 1992 *Ideology, Power, and Social Complexity in Prehistoric Puerto Rico.* Ph.D. dissertation, Department of Anthropology, State University of New York, Binghamton. University Microfilms International, Ann Arbor.
- 1993 Saladoid Survival Strategies: Evidence from Site Locations. In *Proceedings of the Fourteenth International Congress for Caribbean Archaeology,* edited by A. Cummins and P. King, pp. 315–337. International Association for Caribbean Archaeology, Barbados.
- 1996a Ideology and Culture Change in Prehistoric Puerto Rico: A View from the Community. *Journal of Field Archaeology* 23:313–333.
- 1996b An Interview with Irving Rouse. *Current Anthropology* 37:671–689.
- 1999 Contested Places and Places of Contest: The Evolution of Social Power and Ceremonial Space in Prehistoric Puerto Rico. *Latin American Antiquity* 10:209–238.

Smith, A.
- 1995 The Need for Lapita: Explaining Change in the Late Holocene Pacific Archaeological Record. *World Archaeology* 26:366–379.

Smole, W. J.
- 1976 *The Yanoama Indians: A Cultural Geography.* University of Texas Press, Austin.

Spence, M. W.
- 1976 Human Skeletal Material from the Oaxaca Barrio in Teotihuacan, Mexico. In *Archaeological Frontiers: Papers on New World High Culture in Honor of*

J. Charles Kelley, edited by R. Pickering, pp. 129–148. University Museum Studies, No. 4. Southern Illinois University, Carbondale.

Spencer, C. S.
- 1993 Human Agency, Biased Transmission, and the Cultural Evolution of Chiefly Authority. *Journal of Anthropological Archaeology* 12:41–74.

Spielmann, K. A.
- 1991a Interactions among Nonhierarchical Societies. In *Farmers, Hunters, and Colonists: Interactions between the Southwest and the Southern Plains,* edited by K. A. Spielmann, pp. 1–17. University of Arizona Press, Tucson.
- 1991b Coercion or Cooperation? Plains and Pueblo Interaction in the Prehistoric Period. In *Farmers, Hunters, and Colonists: Interactions between the Southwest and the Southern Plains,* edited by K. A. Spielmann, pp. 36–50. University of Arizona Press, Tucson.

Spielmann, K. A. (editor)
- 1991 *Farmers, Hunters, and Colonists: Interactions between the Southwest and the Southern Plains.* University of Arizona Press, Tucson.
- 1998 *Migration and Reorganization: In the Pueblo IV Period in the American Southwest.* Anthropological Research Papers, No. 51. Arizona State University, Tempe.

Steward, J. H.
- 1948 Cultural Areas of the Tropical Forests. In *Handbook of South American Indians, Vol. 3, The Circum-Caribbean Tribes,* edited by J. H. Steward, pp. 883–889. Bureau of American Ethnology, Bulletin 143. Smithsonian Institution, Washington, D.C.

Stokes, A. V.
- 1998 *A Biogeographic Survey of Prehistoric Human Diet in the West Indies Using Stable Isotopes.* Ph.D. dissertation, Department of Anthropology, University of Florida, Gainesville. University International Microfilms, Ann Arbor.

Storey, R., and K. Hirth
- 1997 Archaeological and Paleodemographic Analyses of the El Cajón Skeletal Population. In *Integrating Archaeological Demography: Multidisciplinary Approaches to Prehistoric Population,* edited by R. R. Paine, pp. 101–130. Center for Archaeological Investigations, Occasional Paper No. 24. Southern Illinois University, Carbondale.

Sturtevant, W.
- 1961 Taíno Agriculture. In *The Evolution of Horticultural Systems in Native South America: Causes and Consequences, a Symposium,* edited by J. Wilbert, pp. 69–82. Sociedad de Ciencias Naturales La Salle, Caracas.
- 1969 History and Ethnography of Some West Indian Starches. In *The Domestication and Exploitation of Plants and Animals,* edited by P. J. Ucko and G. W. Dimbleby, pp. 19–42. Aldine, Chicago.

Sullivan, S. D.
1981 *Prehistoric Patterns of Exploitation and Colonization in the Turks and Caicos Islands.* Ph.D. dissertation, University of California, Los Angeles. University Microfilms International, Ann Arbor.

Sumner, W. M.
1989 Population and Settlement Area: An Example from Iran. *American Anthropologist* 91:631–641.

Tabío, E. E.
1988 *Introducción a la arqueología de las Antillas.* Editorial de Ciencias Sociales, Havana.

Tavares María, G.
1996 Límites territoriales de los aborígenes de la isla de Haití a la llegada de los españoles. In *Ponencias del primer seminario de arqueología del Caribe,* edited by M. Veloz Maggiolo and A. Caba Fuentes, pp. 34–47. Museo Arqueológico Regional Altos de Chavón, Dominican Republic.

Terrell, J. E.
1986 *Prehistory in the Pacific Islands.* Cambridge University Press, Cambridge.
1999 Comment on Paul Rainbird, "Islands Out of Time: Towards a Critique of Island Archaeology." *Journal of Mediterranean Archaeology* 12:240–245.
2001 The Uncommon Sense of Race, Language, and Culture. *In Archaeology, Language, and History: Essays on Culture and Ethnicity,* edited by J. E. Terrell, pp. 11–30. Bergin and Garvey, Westport, Connecticut.

Terrell, J. E. (editor)
2001 *Archaeology, Language, and History: Essays on Culture and Ethnicity.* Bergin and Garvey, Westport, Connecticut.

Terrell, J. E., J. P. Hart, S. Barut, N. Cellinese, A. Curet, T. Denham, C. M. Kusimba, K. Latinis, R. Oka, J. Palka, M. E. D. Pohl, K. O. Pope, P. R. Williams, H. Haines, and J. E. Staller
2003 Domesticated Landscapes: The Subsistence Ecology of Plant and Animal Domestication. *Journal of Archaeological Method and Theory* 10(4):323–368.

Tolstoy, P.
1982 Advances in the Valley of Oaxaca, Part 1. *Quarterly Review of Archaeology* 3:1, 8–11.

Torres, J. M.
2001 *Settlement Patterns and Political Geography of the Saladoid and Ostionoid Peoples of South Central Puerto Rico: An Exploration of Prehistoric Social Complexity at a Regional Level.* Unpublished master's thesis, Department of Anthropology, University of Colorado, Denver.

Trigger, B. G.
1989 *A History of Archaeological Thought.* Cambridge University Press, Cambridge.

Tronolone, C. A., M. A. Cinquino, and C. E. Vandrei
- 1984 *Cultural Resource Reconnaissance Survey for the Vieques Naval Reservation,* 5 Vols. Submitted to the Department of the Navy, Norfolk.
- 1990 A Discussion of Prehistoric Resources on the Vieques Naval Reservation in Relation to Prehistorical Settlement Pattern of Vieques Island, Puerto Rico. In *Proceedings of the Eleventh Congress of the International Association for Caribbean Archaeology,* edited by G. Pantel Tekakis, I. Vargas Arenas, and M. Sanoja Obediente, pp. 459–471. Fundación Arqueológica, Antropológica, e Histórica de Puerto Rico, San Juan.

Turnbull, C.
- 1962 *The Forest People.* Doubleday, Garden City, New York.

Ulloa Hung, J.
- 1999 Aproximación a la cerámica temprana del Caribe. *El Caribe arqueológico* 3:28–42.

Ulloa Hung, J., and R. Valcárcel Rojas
- 2002 *Cerámica temprana en el centro del oriente de Cuba.* View Graph Impresos, Santo Domingo, Dominican Republic.

Valcárcel Rojas, R.
- 1999 Banes precolombino: Jerarquía y sociedad. *El Caribe arqueológico* 3:84–89.
- 2002 *Banes precolombino: La ocupación agricultora.* Ediciones Holguín, Holguín, Cuba.

Vega, B.
- 1980 Herencia taína: Nuestros corrales de pesca. *Boletín del Museo del Hombre Dominicano* 13:315–320.
- 1996 Frutas en la dieta precolombina en la isla Española. In *Ponencias del primer seminario de arqueología del Caribe,* edited by M. Veloz Maggiolo and A. Caba Fuentes, pp. 48–85. Museo Arqueológico Regional Altos de Chavón, Dominican Republic.

Veloz Maggiolo, M.
- 1972 *Arqueología prehistórica de Santo Domingo.* McGraw-Hill, New York.
- 1977– *Medioambiente y adaptación humana en la prehistoria de Santo Domingo,*
- 1978 2 Vols., Editora de la Universidad Autónoma de Santo Domingo, Santo Domingo, Dominican Republic.
- 1987 Distribución de espacios en los asentamientos pre-urbanos en las Antillas precolombinas. In *Actas del tercer simposio de la Fundación Arqueológica del Caribe: Relaciones entre la sociedad y el ambiente,* edited by Mario Sanoja, pp. 78–85. La Fundación, Washington, D.C.
- 1989 Para una definición de la cultura taína. In *La cultura taína,* pp. 15–23. Sociedad Estatal Quinto Centenario, Turner Libros, Madrid.
- 1991 *Panorama histórico del Caribe precolombino.* Banco Central de la República Dominicana, Santo Domingo, Dominican Republic.

1993 *La isla de Santo Domingo antes de Colón.* Banco Central de la República Dominicana, Santo Domingo, Dominican Republic.

Veloz Maggiolo, M., J. González, E. Maíz, and E. Questell
1975 *Cayo Cofresí, un sitio precerámico de Puerto Rico.* Ediciones de Taller, Santo Domingo, Dominican Republic.

Veloz Maggiolo, M., and E. J. Ortega
1986 *Arqueología y patrón de vida en el poblado circular de Juan Pedro, República Dominicana.* Museo del Hombre Dominicano, Santo Domingo, Dominican Republic.
1996 Punta Cana y el orígen de la agricultura en la isla de Santo Domingo. In *Ponencias del primer seminario de arqueología del Caribe,* edited by M. Veloz Maggiolo and A. Caba Fuentes, pp. 5–11. Museo Arqueológico Regional Altos de Chavón, Dominican Republic.

Veloz Maggiolo, M., E. Ortega, and F. Luna
1993 Los ocupantes tempranos de Punta Cana, República Dominicana. In *Proceedings of the Fourteenth International Congress for Caribbean Archaeology,* edited by A. Cummins and P. King, pp. 315–337. International Association for Caribbean Archaeology, Barbados.

Veloz Maggiolo, M., I. Vargas, M. Sanoja O., and F. Luna Calderón
1976 *Arqueología de Yuma: República Dominicana.* Taller, Santo Domingo, Dominican Republic.

Veloz Maggiolo, M., and B. Vega
1982 The Antillean Preceramic: A New Approximation. *Journal of New World Archaeology* 5:33–44.

Versteeg, A. H., J. Tacoma, and S. Rostain
1997 Burials and the Culture of Death at Tanki Flip. In *The Archaeology of Aruba: The Tanki Flip Site,* edited by A. H. Versteeg and S. Rostain, pp. 315–330. Publications of the Archaeological Museum Aruba 8, Publications of the Foundation for Scientific Research in the Caribbean Region 141, Aruba and Amsterdam.

Versteeg, A. H., J. Tacoma, and P. Van de Velde
1990 *Archaeological Investigations on Aruba: The Malmok Cemetery.* Publications of the Archaeological Museum Aruba 2, Publications of the Foundation for Scientific Research in the Caribbean Region 126, Aruba and Amsterdam.

Versteeg, A. H., and K. Schinkel (editors)
1992 *The Archaeology of St. Eustatius: The Golden Rock Site.* St. Eustatius Historical Foundation, St. Eustatius.

Vescelius, G. S.
n.d. Isla Chiva—National Register of Historic Places Inventory—Nomination Form. Ms. prepared under contract by Ecology and Environment, Inc.,

Buffalo, for the Department of the Navy, Atlantic Division, Puerto Rico Branch.

Voorhies, B.
1978 Previous Research on Nearshore Coastal Adaptation in Middle America. In *Prehistoric Coastal Adaptations: The Economy and Ecology of Maritime Middle America,* edited by B. L. Stark and B. Voorhies, pp. 5–22. Academic Press, New York.

Walker, J. B.
1980 A Preliminary Report on the Lithics and Osteological Remains from the 1980, 1981, and 1982 Field Seasons at Hacienda Grande (12PSj7-5). In *Proceedings of the Tenth International Congress for the Study of the Precolumbian Cultures of the Lesser Antilles, Fort-de-France,* edited by L. Allaire and F. M. Mayer, pp. 181–224. Centre de Recherches Caraibes, Université de Montréal, Montreal.
1993 *Stone Collars, Elbow Stones, and Three-Pointers, and the Nature of Taíno Ritual and Myth.* Ph.D. dissertation, University of Oregon, Eugene. University Microfilms International, Ann Arbor.

Watters, D. R., and J. B. Petersen
1999 Is the Hueca Style Pottery Present at Trants? In *Archaeological Investigations on St. Martin (Lesser Antilles),* edited by C. L. Hofman and M. L. P. Hoogland, pp. 299–301. Faculty of Archaeology, Leiden University, Netherlands.

Weiss, K. M.
1973 *Demographic Models for Anthropology.* Memoirs of the Society for American Archaeology, American Antiquity 38, Number 2, Part 2. Washington, D.C.

Whitehead, N. L. (editor)
1995 *Wolves from the Sea: Readings in the Anthropology of the Native Caribbean.* KITLV Press, Leiden, Netherlands.

Willey, G. R., C. C. DiPeso, W. A. Ritchie, I. Rouse, J. H. Rowe, and D. Lathrap
1956 An Archaeological Classification of Culture Contact Situations. In *Seminars in Archaeology: 1955,* edited By R. Wauchope, pp. 1–30. Memoirs of the Society for American Archaeology, No. 11, Salt Lake City.

Wilson, S. M.
1990 *Hispaniola.* University of Alabama Press, Tuscaloosa.
2001a Cultural Pluralism and the Emergence of Complex Society in the Greater Antilles. In *Proceedings of the Eighteenth International Congress for Caribbean Archaeology,* Vol. 2, edited by G. Richard, pp. 7–12. International Association for Caribbean Archaeology, Guadeloupe.
2001b The Prehistory and Early History of the Caribbean. In *Biography of the West Indies: Patterns and Perspectives,* edited by C. A. Woods and F. E. Sergile, pp. 519–527. CRC Press, Boca Raton.

Wilson, S. E. (editor)
 1997 *The Indigenous People of the Caribbean.* University Press of Florida, Gainesville.
Wilson, S. E., H. B. Iceland, and T. R. Hester
 1998 Preceramic Connections between Yucatán and the Caribbean. *Latin American Antiquity* 9:342–352.
Wing, E. S.
 1989a Human Exploitation of Animal Resources in the Caribbean. In *Biogeography of the West Indies,* edited by C. A. Woods, pp. 137–152. Sandhill Crane Press, Gainesville.
 1989b La adaptación humana a los medioambientes de las Antillas. In *La cultura taína,* pp. 93–101. Sociedad Estatal Quinto Centenario, Turner Libros, Madrid.
 2001a The Sustainability of Resources Used by Native Americans on Four Caribbean Islands. *International Journal of Osteoarchaeology* 11:112–126.
 2001b Native American Use of Animals in the Caribbean. In *Biogeography of the West Indies: Patterns and Perspectives,* edited by C. A. Woods and F. E. Sergile, pp. 481–518. CRC Press, Boca Raton.
 2001c Patterns of Resource Use in the Prehistoric Caribbean. In *Proceedings of the Eighteenth International Congress for Caribbean Archaeology,* Vol. 2, edited by G. Richard, pp. 78–86. International Association for Caribbean Archaeology, Guadeloupe.
Wing, E. S., and E. J. Reitz
 1982 Prehistoric Fishing Economies of the Caribbean. *Journal of New World Archaeology* 5:13–32.
Wing, E. S., and S. R. Wing.
 1995 Prehistoric Ceramic Age Adaptation to Varying Diversity of Animal Resources along the West Indian Archipelago. *Journal of Ethnobiology* 15:119–148.
Wittfogel, K.
 1957 *Oriental Despotism.* Yale University Press, New Haven.
Wood, J. W.
 1998 A Theory of Preindustrial Population Dynamics: Demography, Economy, and Well-Being in Malthusian Systems. *Current Anthropology* 39:99–135.
Wood, J. W., G. R. Milner, H. C. Harpending, and K. M. Weiss
 1992 The Osteological Paradox: Problems of Inferring Prehistoric Health from Skeletal Samples. *Current Anthropology* 33:343–370.
Wright, L. E., and C. J. Yoder
 2003 Recent Progress in Bioarchaeology: Approaches to the Osteological Paradox. *Journal of Archaeological Research* 11:43–70.
Yaukey, D.
 1990 *Demography: The Study of Human Population.* Waveland Press, Prospect Heights, Illinois.

Zuazo, A. de
- 1518 (1971) Carta que escribió el Lic. Alonso de Zuazo enviado con poderes amplios a la isla de Santo Domingo por el Cardenal Cisnero, al Ministro Flamenco Xevres en 22 de enero de 1518, sobre los excesos cometidos en aquella isla contra los indios, y su remedio. In *Los dominicos y las encomiendas de indios en la isla Española,* edited by R. Demorizi, pp. 249–269. Academia Dominicana de la Historia, Santo Domingo, Dominican Republic.

Zubrow, E. B. W.
- 1971 Carrying Capacity and Dynamic Equilibrium in the Prehistoric Southwest. *American Antiquity* 36:127–138.
- 1975 *Prehistoric Carrying Capacity: A Model.* Cummings, Menlo Park, California.

Index

Age-at-death, 190, 194–196; distribution, 197, 198, 213–216; Paso del Indio, 209, 211; Punta Candelero, 200, 202; Tibes, 204, 205, 207, 208
Arawak language, 78–79
Archaic, 7, 15–16, 18, 20, 61–65, 178; in Ostionoid expansion, 76–91, 93–94, 225; interaction with Saladoid groups, 66–75, 92–93, 132, 225

Bahamas. *See* Bahamian Archipelago
Bahamian Archipelago, colonization of, 29, 62, 76, 83, 89
Ball courts, 22, 23, 25, 90, 141–143; in the Loíza River Basin, 102, 104, 130; in the Salinas River Basin, 117, 120–121, 133; in Tibes, 203
Barrancoid series, 66

Caguana, 137
Canoes, 39
Capá style, 24
Carrying capacity, 145, 150, 153–154, 183–184; based on maize production, 170–173; based on manioc production, 164–170; definition, 155–159; of the Valley of Maunabo, 160–173, 176–178, 180–181
Cassava. *See* manioc
Cedrosan subseries, 16, 129, 134, 136; in Salinas River Basin, 117, 118; in Vieques Island, 136; in Yauco River Basin, 123–124, 128
Ceramic Age, 5, 27, 63, 66, 100, 107, 160, 181
Chanlatte Baik, Luis, 16–18, 20, 77, 80–81, 89, 93, 94, 127, 151, 226
Chican subseries, 23–26, 129–131, 136–138, 153; in Loíza River Basin, 100; in Paso del Indio site, 209; in Salinas River Basin, 117, 121; in Valley of Maunabo, 179; in Vieques island, 108; in Yauco River Basin, 123, 126, 128
Chiefdoms, 9, 23, 90, 94, 139, 145, 154, 180–182; demographic models, 145–152
Colonization, 41–43, 45, 52, 53, 56, 58; models, 47–52
Complex, ceramic or cultural, 12. *See also* style
Corn. *See* maize
Corosan subseries, 15
Coroso people/culture, 15–16
Cuba, 24, 82, 83, 86, 87, 93

Cueva María de la Cruz, 16, 70
Cuevas people/culture/style, 16, 19, 113, 131; in Loíza River Basin, 100; in Vieques island, 108, 112

Demography, 3, 5, 10, 30, 34, 44, 188, 189, 221, 232, 233

Elenan subseries, 20–23, 25, 77, 80, 81, 83, 90, 94, 108, 128, 129–132, 134, 140–143, 151, 153; in Loíza River Basin, 101; in Maunabo, 179; in Salinas River Basin, 116, 118, 120, 123; in Tibes site, 203–204
Esperanza style/people/culture, 24, 129, 130, 133, 138, 139, 141; in Loíza River Basin, 100, 101, 103, 104; in Maunabo Valley, 177–180; in Salinas River Basin, 117, 118; in Vieques island, 108, 112–114

Fertility, 194, 197; rate, 194, 196–198, 202, 215–217; in Paso del Indio site, 211; in Punta Candelero site, 202–203; in Tibes site, 208
Formative: level of cultural development, 23

Guayanilla River, 121–123; bay, 121, 125

Hacienda Grande: in the Loíza River Basin, 100; in Maunabo Valley, 179; in the Salinas River Basin, 120; site, 70, 71, 129, 133, 136, 141; in Tibes site, 204; in Vieques island, 113–114; style/people/culture, 16–18, 71, 73
Hispaniola, 19, 21, 22, 24, 25, 69, 71–72, 76–78, 82–90, 92, 93
Huecan subseries, 17
Huecoid series, 18

Jamaica, 76, 77, 78, 81–86

Keegan, William, 29, 66, 82–83, 89, 93, 94, 158–159, 163–164, 172, 183–184, 226

La Hueca: in Ostionoid expansion, 77, 80, 81, 87–90; migration, 62, 63–76; style/people/culture/complex, 17–19, 92, 83, 94
La Hueca site, 18
Language, 78–80
Life expectancy, 195–197
Life tables, 195–197; in Tibes site, 205
Loíza River Basin, 99–104, 129–143

Maize, 158, 170; carrying capacity in Maunabo Valley, 170–173
Manioc, 164–165; carrying capacity in Maunabo Valley, 164–170
Maunabo, Valley of, 160; carrying capacity, 160–173; population estimates, 173–176
Meillacan subseries, 82, 89, 93
Migration: in the Caribbean, 28–30, 62–94; consequences of, 52–56; decision to, 38–42; definition, 33; models on, 47–52; Ostionoid expansion, 76–91; reasons for, 34–38; Saladoid-La Hueca, 63–76; size and structure of migrant population, 43–47
Modified Ostiones: style/people/culture, 21–22
Mona Passage, 21, 22, 24
Montones, 147, 149
Mortality rates, 196–198

Osteological Paradox, 191
Ostionan subseries, 20–23; in the Yauco River Basin, 123, 125–128
Ostionoid series, 20–26

Paleodemography, 188
Paso del Indio, 208–212
Population: estimates for Maunabo Valley, 173–176; growth rates, 176, 177–178, 196; stable, 190; stationary, 190
Punta Candelero, 199–203
Pure Ostiones: style/people/culture, 20–21

Rouse, Irving, 65–66, 67–68, 71, 73, 77–78

Saladoid Series, 16–20; migration, 62–76
Salinas River Region, 114–121
Sample bias, in paleodemographic studies, 192–194
Series, concept of, 13
Sex distribution, 190, 191, 197, 213–214, 217, 218; in Paso del Indio, 211; in Punta Candelero, 200, 202
Site abandonment, 138–141

Style, concept of 13
Subseries, concept of 13

Tibes site, 203–208
Transculturation, 65, 77, 79–81, 83, 87–89, 91

Uniformitarian principle, 189–192

Vieques, Island of, 104, 114
Vieques Sound, 18, 21, 22, 24

Yauco River Basin, 121–128